The World's Worst Records: Volume Two

another arcade of audio atrocity

Darryl W Bullock

Contents

Introduction

Hello, and welcome to Volume Two of The World's Worst Records; another catalogue of crap, if you will.

As I wrote in the introduction to the first book, I've been fascinated with bad music for decades, eschewing novelty records to concentrate on those recordings that are simply 'wrong'. Records made by people who were serious about what they did: they might have been talentless and terrible, but they cared about what they were doing.

Very few people are so utterly hopeless as to be able to make a really bad record. In my eyes a great bad record has to be the product of someone (the song's writer, the performer, the producer or the label which puts the damn thing out) who genuinely believes that the end result would interest people enough for them to go out and buy it. But it was only when I started writing The World's Worst Records blog (www.worldsworstrecords.co.uk) back in 2007 that I realised that there were hundreds of people out there who thought the same as me.

A great many of these awful records were collected in the first book (it's still in print, folks, and available from all the usual outlets!) I was so proud of the first volume - until I read it though again that is and realised how much I had missed out. How could I have failed to introduce you to the delights of *Lord Sutch and Heavy Friends*, or to the stellar careers or Paul Vance and Major Bill Smith? How could I have let William Shatner get away with barely a passing reference?

Well, they're all here. And a great many more too.

One of the comments that kept coming back to me from people who had bought the first volume was that many of the artists I had included were rather obscure. Sure, with the omnipresent YouTube you can find most of them if you want to go off and do some research of your own, but this time around I thought I'd have a pot at some better-known artists as well as try and introduce you to some that you may not already know. Not one for believing in sanctity or sacred cows, in this volume of The World's Worst Records you'll discover the horrors lurking in the back catalogues of Frank Sinatra, the Four Seasons, Duran Duran, Jim Reeves, and such superstars as Elton John, Bette Midler, Robin Thicke, Bob Dylan and the hateful Coldplay.

And no, in case you're wondering, I have no plans for a Volume Three – at least not for a good long while. I think I've pretty much mined the seam clean of classic bad records and so much of what is released these days is so dreadful that it really is like shooting misogynistic rap artists in a barrel. I won't say that it won't happen, but I think I'll need to get my ears tested or my head examined before I subject myself to as many audio atrocities as I have included in these two books.

Enjoy!

Frank Sinatra
Mama Will Bark (1951)

Frank Sinatra: the voice. The Chairman of the Board; Old Blue Eyes. Eulogised and mythologised more than any other singer - with the possible exceptions of Bob Dylan and Elvis Presley – his personal life may be forever tainted by bad marriages, mob connections and that hideous toupee but the one thing that the critics all agree on is that when he was at the top of his game, no-one could touch Frankie. The melancholic voice that made bobbysoxers melt, the quality of the Capitol sides, his on-screen presence and brooding good looks add up to one hell of a bundle. Chuck in an arrest, a brace of failed suicide attempts, his involvement in the Kennedy election and a kidnapping and you've got all the elements of a modern-day fable.

In a recording career that stretched some 55 years, Hoboken-born Sinatra performed many of the greatest songs of the 20th Century and scored some of the biggest and most-loved hits of our time. His work with the Nelson Riddle Orchestra and Billy May at Capitol in the 50s – captured forever on brilliant albums including *In the Wee Small Hours* and *Frank Sinatra Sings for Only the Lonely* – is exemplary. However, shortly before he joined Capitol Sinatra recorded a song that can only be described as a dog: **Mama Will Bark**.

Dismissed by *Billboard* as *'an experimental effort to bring TV to wax'* and *'a silly novelty piece'* this humiliating speck of nonsense is the result of the difficult relationship between Sinatra and musician/arranger/producer Mitch Miller. Miller, as musician, had played on Frankie's first album (*The Voice of Frank Sinatra*) in 1946 but had recently taken over as head of A&R at Columbia, Frank's record label. Miller, who would go on to spectacular success with his sing along TV shows and albums in the 60s, was known for two things – favouring novelty songs and interfering in recording sessions – two things that Sinatra would not tolerate. Sinatra famously ordered Miller out of one of his recording sessions when he discovered him tweaking the knobs of the control panel: Miller has been accused of forcing Sinatra to record **Mama Will Bark**, a duet with TV personality Dagmar, in retribution.

Almost forgotten now, Dagmar was – for a brief period - a major television star. The small screen version of Jayne Mansfield, the buxom bombshell was born Virginia Ruth Egnor but originally took on the stage name Jenny Lewis when she moved to New York to work as a model. She was given the name Dagmar when she appeared on *Broadway Open House*, an early forerunner of *The Tonight Show*, which began its run on NBC in 1950. Although she was billed as a singer, Dagmar seldom sang, instead she would simply recite poems and lyrics deadpan.

The archetypal dumb blonde, she became so famous so quickly - receiving more than 8,000 fan letters a month - that the way she dressed was debated on the floor of the House of Representatives and, when her salary rose to a then-astronomical $3,250 a week, the outcry was so great that the government's Wage Stabilization Board got involved. *Life* magazine took notice, featuring her on the cover and following her (and her family) for a week around her home town.

In April 1951 Dagmar and Sinatra appeared together on TV for the first time. Miller was immediately struck by what he saw as an onscreen chemistry between the two of them. Sinatra's career was in the doldrums at the time – it had been months since he last had any chart success and his popularity with the bobbysoxers was rapidly declining – and, when offered a song by writer Dick Manning, Miller sniffed a hit. Alarm bells should have rung: Manning had a proven track record for hits and would go on to co-write **Takes Two To Tango**, **Fascination** and **Papa Loves Mambo**, but he had previously written the equally hideous **The Pussy Cat Song (Nyow! Nyot Nyow!)**, recorded by Patty Andrews and Bob Crosby in 1949.

Mama Will Bark is a dog turd of a song. Inane lyrics performed by Sinatra with deadpan interjections from Dagmar, accompanied by *'imitations by Donald Bain'*. You can almost understand Miller's reasoning; novelty was – and would continue to be – big business, Guy Mitchell, Rosemary Clooney, Patti Page, Frankie Laine and dozens of others were scoring massive hits with novelty songs in the twilight world of the pre-rock 'n' roll hit parade, but **Mama Will Bark** is such a desultory example of the form that any one of the stars of the day would have struggled to make something worthwhile of it.

My feet were killing me, my dogs were barkin'
I must have fallen asleep where I was parkin'
And then I dreamed two dogs were talkin', take my word
It was the doggone-est thing you ever heard

(*Mama Will Bark*, written by Dick Manning. Recorded by Frank Sinatra and Dagmar on Columbia Records. © 1951, Universal Music Publishing)

Honestly – a song about singing feet! It's shockingly bad: Frank tosses off the vocal with all the panache of a bored teenager, and don't get me started on the bizarre imagery the line *'Papa will spank'* conjures up in my head every time I hear it. There are other horrors in the Sinatra canon: **Chattanoogie Shoe Shine Boy**, **Castle Rock** (which band leader Harry James called "the worst thing that either of us has ever recorded"), his abominable disco

version of **Night And Day**, the idiotic **Bim Bam Baby** (*take a mip map mop and a brim bram broom and clim clam clean up the rim ram room...*) and the miserable **One Finger Melody** all deserve mention, but **Mama Will Bark** marks the absolute nadir. It's not all Frank's fault, as *Billboard* pointed out on its release: *'the disk only proves that Dagmar is better seen than heard'*.

Unsurprisingly, Sinatra hated the song ("The only good it did me was with dogs," he told his son Frank Junior dismissively) but he went through with the session anyway. "Nobody brings Sinatra in to the studio (to do something) that he doesn't want to do," Miller has often been quoted as saying. "He had the right to okay its release." That's certainly true: according to James Kaplan's book *Frank: the Making of a Legend*, a year prior to the recording of **Mama Will Bark** Sinatra had stormed out of a Miller-led session refusing to record two songs and telling the producer "I'm not recording this f***ing shit. You get yourself some other boy – I'm not doing this in a million years." The two songs in question – **My Heart Cries For You** and **The Roving Kind** - were recorded by Guy Mitchell and went to number two and four respectively on the *Billboard* charts.

"He could have bombed it," Miller added, "But with novelties you never know. We made this record as a shot in the dark."

"You cannot force anyone to do a song," the producer told Will Friedwald when interviewed for his book *Sinatra! The Song is You*. "Sinatra said I brought him all these shit songs; I forced him to do shit songs."

Mama Will Bark achieved a modicum of success, scraping in at 21; the flip side, the Sinatra co-write **I'm A Fool To Want You**, charted a little better at 14. Frankie followed with the terrible **Tennessee Newsboy** (co-written by Manning), but it was all over for Frank and Mitch and shortly after its release Sinatra was dropped by Columbia. Depressed over his downward-spiralling career and the endless fights with then-wife Ava Gardner, Frankie tried to kill himself by shoving his head in a gas oven. Luckily for us the owner of the apartment that he tried this ludicrous stunt in returned in time and foiled his attempt.

A year later a revitalised Sinatra moved to Capitol, scored a hit role on-screen (and won an Oscar for Best Supporting Actor) as Maggio in *From Here to Eternity* and began a whole new phase in his career, but he never forgave Miller for this canine catastrophe. Years later, passing each other in a Las Vegas hotel lobby, Miller extended his hand to Sinatra: "F*** You," Frankie is reputed to have snarled. "Keep walking".

The Russian-born Dick Manning died in April 1991. Francis Albert Sinatra left the stage for the last time in May 1998, aged 82. His health had been deteriorating since suffering a blow to the head during a concert in Richmond, Virginia four years earlier. His last words, whispered to his fourth wife, Barbara, were "I'm losing". Daughter Nancy was not at her father's side: she later admitted that she was at home watching the final episode of *Seinfeld.* Mitch Miller – who went on to record even more dreck under his own name (and with Mitch Miller and his Gang) including a horrible, sanitised version of **Give Peace A Chance** on his 1970 album *Peace Sing-Along* - joined them in April 2010, just four weeks after his 99th birthday. Dagmar - who had long since retired from showbiz - died in 2011, aged 79, at her home in Ceredo, West Virginia.

I guess you could say that all four of the perpetrators of this hideous crime have finally gone to the dogs.

Singing Animals

The fad for recordings by talking and singing animals is as old as the history of recorded music itself. The German-born pioneer of recorded sound, Emile Berliner, issued what was probably the first example: a single-sided five-inch disc of barnyard noises (**Voix d'Animaux/Farmyard**, in May 1888, but it would take another fifty-plus years before the genre would reach its apotheosis.

The 50s were a boon time for animal recordings. First came the more obvious examples – talking budgies, mynah birds, twittering canaries and all sorts of songbirds. As early as 1937 the American Radio Warblers (a collection of between 10 and 17 song canaries) could be heard live on your wireless set, broadcast by the Mutual Broadcasting Company (the same station that gave airtime to Orson Welles as both The Shadow and as the leader of the Mercury Theatre). Those birds, known as 'the original feathered stars of the air' were kept in cages placed next to an organ (played by Preston Sellers) and could be heard singing as Sellers played. Each of the birds was given a name: some (such as Bing, Rudy, Duke and Eddie) were named after popular entertainers of the day; others included Sandy, Tuppy, Morrie and Ernie. They went on tour, promoting a line of bird seed from American Bird Products, and could be heard on record too: recordings of the canaries 'singing' popular classics – including Offenbach's **Barcarolle** and Strauss's **Blue Danube** – were produced by Arthur C. Barnett and proved surprisingly popular. The original 10" discs were reissued in the early 1950s on 7".

Hot on their heels (or should that be talons?) came the Hartz Mountain Master Radio Canaries, another set of singing birds with their own radio show, which again was primarily used by its' sponsor - Hartz Mountain Products - to promote their line of pet products. This time accompanied by organ, violin and xylophone, the birds released a single - a red vinyl 10" featuring the tracks **Come Back To Sorrento** and **Moonlight Madonna** - and a 10" (later reissued on 7" EP) called *The Canary Training Record* on the Hartz Mountain Products label. Around the same time (1948) another canary training record was issued by Herman Osman in California. Started by German émigrés Max and Gustav Stern in 1926, Hartz would go on to become the number one brand of pet products in America before the parent company sold off its pet division. Today Hartz Mountain Industries and the Stern family – which at one point also owned the alternative New York newspaper *The Village Voice* - earns its money through real estate.

Major companies, including Decca (Provol's Golden Birds) and RCA (*Teach Your Parakeet to Talk*), were eager to get in on the singing/talking bird act and the idea even crossed the pond: around June 1954 Decca in the UK issued the double A-side 10" **Sandy Paul – The Talking Budgerigar** backed with **Beauty Metcalfe – Talking**  **Budgerigar.** However in Britain it would have been far too common and coarse to have these wretched animals actually sing; instead the two birds – of equally limited talent – squawked a few barely-recognisable words and phrases with oddly clipped, BBC accents. It was only a matter of time before other, less obviously 'vocal', animals were let loose in the recording studio and, within 12 months of Sandy Paul and Beauty Metcalfe doing their rather pathetic thing a disc by The Singing Dogs appeared in Britain.

The daddy of all doggie acts, this canine quintet scored two hit 45s, issued an album and have also made countless appearances on compilations. Their biggest hit, **Jingle Bells**, has been reissued on more than one occasion in the States – becoming a hit for the second time in 1971 and selling at least as many copies as it did first time around.

The idea behind the Singing Dogs came from Carl Weismann, a record producer and self-taught ornithologist working in Copenhagen, Denmark. Legend has it that the bird watcher – who also owned his own record company, specialising in the sounds of nature - was often chased away from the fields by farm dogs, and that his recordings of birdsong were regularly ruined by their barking. For fun, when editing out the noise of the dogs from his field recordings, he gathered the discarded yelps together and, in 1949, assembled them to form a collection of traditional Danish songs apparently sung by dogs for a children's TV programme.

Playing with different editing techniques, and realising that he could alter the pitch of the individual notes by speeding up or slowing down his tapes, Weismann made further recordings of neighbourhood dogs barking, spliced them together and arranged the 'notes' into recognisable tunes. Teaming up with a music producer by the name of Don Charles* (with an agreement that the duo would split any income from Weismann's Singing Dog records straight down the middle), Weismann produced a version of the Stephen Foster standard **Oh! Susanna** which was issued by Metronome Records in his native Denmark before being picked up by Pye/Nixa in the UK and then by RCA Victor in America. Credited as *Don Charles presents The Singing Dogs, conducted by Carl Weismann*, the record became a hit, reaching number 22 on the *Billboard* Pop Singles chart and selling over half a million copies.

With a hit single on his hands demands started coming in for personal appearances from the Singing Dogs. But, of course, they didn't exist… well, not as such. *Life* magazine called Weismann, insisting on a story: there had been complaints in the US press about the act and how the originator of the recording must have been cruel to his dogs to make them 'sing'. The editors at *Life* wanted to disprove this. A photographer was dispatched, leaving Weismann with no option but to quickly pull together five dogs (with the assistance of friends and even the local police, who provided the two German Shepherds for the photoshoot) to help hoodwink the man from the magazine.

In December 1955 *Life* printed their article (*The Carolling Dogs of Copenhagen*) which later appeared, in full, on the reverse of the LP *Singing Dogs*: '*Armed with his portable tape recorder, he wandered around town taping the best barks by two shepherds, a poodle, a terrier and a pinscher he called Caesar, King, Pearl, Dolly and Pussy. Back in his studio Weismann snipped and spliced taped barks so that the pinscher would tweet the one high note, the shepherds would woof the low ones. The poodle and terrier, both two-noted barkers, did the mezzo work in between,*' it claimed. With America successfully hoodwinked, RCA issued a second 45, **Hot Dog Rock 'n' Roll** backed with **Hot Dog Boogie**.

It wasn't a hit, and Weismann quietly went back to producing records of bird calls. He passed away in 1999, at the grand old age of 92.

It would be almost a quarter of a century before a 'singing' animal would trouble the charts again, and **Sausages**, by Prince the Wonder Dog, is probably the nearest that a real live dog has come to having an actual hit single as a named performer.

Those of you who are either under 40 or didn't live in the UK during the 70s and 80s may not know of the TV phenomenon that was *That's Life*, a Sunday night magazine programme which mixed humorous stories with crusading campaigns (such as establishing the Childline charity), light entertainment, a witty song and a handful of rude-looking vegetables. For 20 years presenter Esther Rantzen, her jolly band of male sidekicks and an ever-changing musical guest (which, at various times included Pam Ayres, Jake Thackeray, Victoria Wood, Richard Stilgoe and Doc Cox, aka Ivor Biggun of **The Winker's Song (Misprint)** fame) fronted one of British TV's highest-rated shows – vilified by the upcoming wave of 'alternative' comedians but absolutely adored by the great British public.

Talented pets were a *That's Life* staple: often, after a hard-hitting exposé of some dodgy bloke and his Page Three girlfriend knocking out fake slimming tea, a cute puppy, cat, ferret or other cuddly critter would be dragged on by its owner to the 'oohs' and 'aahs' of the adoring studio audience. Each of these animals we were told would possess a aptitude for something bizarre – playing a musical instrument, for example – but when forced to perform under the sweltering lights of a TV studio could usually to do little more than urinate over Esther's ghastly frocks or chase Cyril Fletcher (famously portrayed as "a camp old twat" by Griff Rhys-Jones in a hysterical *Not the Nine O'clock News* sketch) around the set.

Not so Prince or, as he's credited on his one and only single, Prince the Wonder Dog; a small, scruffy terrier whose owner insisted he could talk. Only he couldn't. Basically he'd make a growling noise (pretty much like every other dog on the planet) and his owner, Paul Allen, would manipulate his throat and lower jaw to make 'words'. He had a small repertoire, principally the words 'hello', 'Esther' and 'sausages'.

Put simply the pair were the world's worst ventriloquist act, but the public lapped it up; Prince and Paul became, for a very short time, Leeds' biggest stars (this was a good few years before the birth of the brilliant Wedding Present) and, obviously, the next thing for them to do after finding a huge audience of pensioners with nothing to spend their money on but gin and endless rounds of bingo was to release a record.

Enter Columbia who, in 1979, brought Paul and Prince into the studio to record a version of the Joe Loss 1961 hit **Wheels Cha Cha**, renamed **Sausages** (naturally) for the occasion and given a set of Prince-specific lyrics. The result was – unsurprisingly – awful, but not as bad as the B-side, Paul's own winsome composition **We've Got A Dog**. Unfortunately, according to Paul's nephew Antony (writing on *www.sheffieldforum. co.uk*): "Prince died by accidentally falling down a hole dug during house renovations. The resulting injuries claimed his life. A shame; as a child I loved to play with him."

A shame indeed - and a loss to the family and Prince's many fans. Luckily we still have his one solitary single to remember him by.

It would be Carl Weismann's Singing Dogs, rather than Prince and his jaw-manipulating sidekick, that would provide the inspiration for the next batch of canines to attempt a pop career – and the first out of the traps would present a future music mogul with his first real taste of success. Oh yes: Simon Cowell, world-famous star maker and head of a multi-billion dollar business which includes the *X Factor* and *Britain's Got Talent* TV shows, got his first big break in show business in 1982, when he appeared on a handful of UK TV shows dressed as a six-foot tall blue dog, miming to a throwaway novelty called **Ruff Mix**.

In his early days as a record plugger Cowell heard a track by German producer Harald 'Harry' Thumann, who had put together a song that was built around the sampled sounds of dogs barking. As we've already seen, Thumann wasn't the first producer to do this, but technology had come on a long way since the days of Carl Weismann, and no fiddly tape splicing was necessary for Thumann (who died in 2001) to piece together **Ruff Mix**. Cowell, who was a partner in E&S Music with Ellis Rich (his former boss when Cowell worked at EMI), acquired rights to the song and began promoting it, crediting it to the entirely fictitious Wonder Dog. It was Simon who drew the short straw, dressing up as the big blue dog to promote the song, which peaked at number 31 in the UK Singles Chart. The follow up **A Christmas Tail** (confusingly titled **Christmas Tails** on the sleeve) was issued a few months later by ERC records but failed to chart. Fittingly E&S traded from offices in a converted gent's toilet in a car park on Brewer Street in London's Soho.

The following year assistants in record shops in Australia and America were being send barking mad by the release of *Beatle Barkers*, a collection of 12 of the Beatles' best known songs played by a reasonably competent covers band, but with the 'vocals' performed by cats, sheep, birds and – obviously – dogs. Credited to *The Woofers and Tweeters Ensemble*, the project sprang from a mad idea that former musician Gene Pierson had one drunken evening. Pierson had seen some chart success in Australia in the late 60s and early 70s, usually with covers of au courant UK and US pop hits – including a Brian Auger-influenced take on the Four Tops brilliant **Reach Out (I'll Be There)** – before moving into artist management and promotion: he was involved in the careers of AC/DC and INXS amongst many others. He also launched his own label, Laser Records.

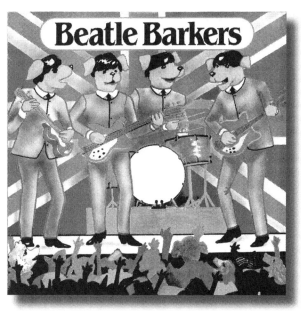

Pierson went to visit the Sydney studio of his mate Roy Nicolson, a British-born but Australia-based musician (and co-author of the Toto Coelo hit **I Eat Cannibals**). Pierson and Nicholson had often worked on demos together, and on this particular visit Roy showed Gene his new toy, an Emulator 1 sampler that could imitate a wide range of different sounds - including the kinds of noises that animals make. Nicholson agreed to put an album's worth of material together for Pierson on the strict understanding that his name would stay off the sleeve. Pierson provided the music – backing tracks he bought from a company in Germany – and Nicholson got to work assembling his chorus of critters. The album went on to sell over 850,000 copies in Australasia alone.

Pierson and Nicholson missed a joke: they should have called their act The Beagles.

Of course neither *Beatle Barkers* nor **Ruff Mix** featured an actual singing dog, and Prince didn't really sing (well, certainly not of his own accord), but since then we've had sampled sheep (Virgin main man Richard

Branson – as Jeff Mutton - sat in the producer's chair for the one and only time to oversee the 1982 Christmas single from The Singing Sheep - **Baa Baa Black Sheep/Flock Around The Clock)****, cats (producer Mike Spalla's Jingle Cats: the same man is also responsible for the utterly hateful Jingle Babies) and a myriad of other non-performing 'performing' animals. With easy access to autotune, editing software and video upload sites any idiot can make almost anything from a fish to a fox, a tortoise to a turkey 'sing' these days. I've no doubt that a true pioneer like Carl Weismann would be turning in his grave.

***

* *This particular Don Charles is not the same one who recorded for Joe Meek and went on to become a record producer in his own right.*

Three years prior to Branson's Singing Sheep debacle, Virgin Records had issued* **The Lost Sheep, a mediocre slice of sub-classical dullness which features a lamb bleating whilst a small orchestra – replete with bassist and drummer - play the most maudlin music you're ever likely to hear. Credited to* Adrian Munsey, his Sheep, Wind, and Orchestra, *the composer even performed this peculiar piece 'live' on television, accompanied by a lamb, its mother and an eight-piece ensemble. As the lamb was struck with stagefright, Munsey stood at the microphone, straight-faced and cradled the poor animal while he performed the recalcitrant beast's part himself.*

You Ought To Be In Pictures:
Singing Actors Revisited

In *The World's Worst Records Volume One* we took a look at how TV actors (and actresses) have been responsible for some of the most heinous crimes ever committed to vinyl – but how could I have possibly known that when I was penning that particular chapter I was merely scratching the surface of a deep, rich vein of calamitous crap?

TV is to blame for a slew of terrible music, but it all started much, much earlier, before television and even before the advent of talking pictures. Although the stars of what we now think of as the Golden Age of Hollywood were probably less than happy at being dragged in front of an orchestra and told to flex their pipes many of them did exactly that: Valentino, Gable, Crawford, Bette Davis, even the great Garbo were 'persuaded' by their bosses to issue recordings for their adoring public. A number of these discs were issued, principally for radio broadcast, but many others were made available commercially. In the UK the Decca Record Company issued a 4-disc series entitled *Voice Of The Stars* between 1934 and 1937, although these discs – released to raise funds for charity – mostly contained the artists (including Gable, Crawford, Shirley Temple, Myrna Loy and countless others) offering a short greeting to their fans

rather than a full-on performance; most of these performers would have their voices dubbed by professional singers in their movies – but that was not always the case on disc.

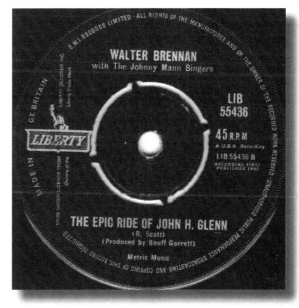

Fans of old movies, and anyone who's ever watched a western on a wet Saturday afternoon, will have fond memories of the actor

Walter Brennan. Forever the amiable, often irascible, sidekick (as he was to John Wayne in the classic *Rio Bravo*), Brennan is the only actor ever to win three Best Supporting Actor Oscars – and one of only three actors to win three Oscars throughout their careers (the other two being Jack Nicholson and Daniel Day Lewis, fact fans).

Born in 1894, Brennan began acting in vaudeville at the age of 15, but it wasn't until the late 20s that he started getting bit parts in the movies: apparently he was forced back into acting after losing the fortune he had made in real estate during the stock market crash. He appears, uncredited, in *Horse Feathers* (the Marx Brothers), *The Invisible Man* and *Bride of Frankenstein* amongst countless others, but it was his role in the Howard Hawks/William Wyler drama *Come and Get It* (1936) which first brought him to prominence, and won him the inaugural Academy Award for Best Supporting Actor. In a career that spanned almost 50 years, his 'grumpy old man with a heart of gold' shtick added colour to many a movie and, from the 1950s, he was a popular star of American TV, with the lead role in early sit-com *The Real McCoys*.

But we're not interested in his acting prowess: oh no! For Walter Brennan also released more than a dozen (honestly! A dozen!) albums. After narrating an album of Mark Twain tales in 1956 and continuing with the obscure *By The Fireside*, his recording career got off to a real start with the 1960 single release **Dutchman's Gold**. Many of these records – with their painful, homespun, spoken word performances – sold by the bucket load and even garnered him a couple of hit singles, the biggest of which, **Old Rivers** (the tale of a young boy's friendship with an older man and his mule), made the US Top Five! The B-side of that single, **The Epic Ride Of John H Glenn**, charts the career of the first American to orbit the earth. The cosmos was big in Brennan's life: he had previously scored a hit with the blatant Chipmunks rip-off **Space Mice**.

Many a non-singing artist has released a spoken word performance but I can't think of one who has released quite as many and with so much commercial success. However by the dawn of the 1970s Brennan's recording career had dried up: one of his last albums (apart from compilations and film soundtracks) was the bizarre, right wing political polemic *He's Your Uncle – Not Your Dad* which tore strips off the LBJ administration.

His last foray into the studio produced his final album, 1970's *Yesterday When I Was Young*, which features his horrific version of the Mel Tills/

PRESIDENT RECORDS LTD.

Kassner House,
1 Westbourne Gardens,
Porchester Road,
London W2 5NR.
Tel: 01 - 229 3411.

JACK WARNER

"YOU'VE GOT THE GEAR / SOMEBODY ASKED ME"   *PT 360*

Released: **November 1971**

JACK WARNER's favorite slogan is: "What can I do that I've never done before?"...
Having had such a distinguished career in Music Hall, Drama, Radio, Films and Television
(he is now notching up seventeen years as "DIXON OF DOCK GREEN" on BBC
Television) — one of the things JACK has never done is make a hit record !!

A similar thought occurred to well-known bandleader FRANK WEIR when he wrote
"YOU'VE GOT THE GEAR" — a beautiful melodic number which successfully bridges
the generation gap when a son takes problems about his love-life to his father; and the
father gives out with some great advice in the chat that the boy understands.

FRANK WEIR asked JACK WARNER to record the song. . . JACK agreed. . . . And
we, at PRESIDENT RECORDS, are very proud to announce the release of "YOU'VE
GOT THE GEAR" by JACK WARNER on PT360.

Outstanding among the many things for which this great entertainer is so well known, is
his brilliant impersonation of MAURICE CHEVALIER. . . . . JACK receives hundreds of
letters from people asking him to sing a CHEVALIER song in "DIXON OF DOCK GREEN".
Therefore, the obvious choice for the flip-side is JACK WARNER in the style of
MAURICE CHEVALIER singing "SOMEBODY ASKED ME". . . . . This charming story
about marriage was composed by JACK himself several years ago, and he describes it as
"an Anglo-French song". . . . . We think you'll like it.

There are lots of guest appearances lined up on Radio and Television to promote
"YOU'VE GOT THE GEAR" / "SOMEBODY ASKED ME" — and we all hope that JACK
WARNER will have a smash hit record!

FOR FU...   MADELEINE KASKET
                                             Press Officer.

Kenny Rogers classic **Ruby, Don't Take Your Love To Town** (also covered by Leonard Nimoy – but we'll save that for another chapter!)

Just as one veteran actor was bidding farewell to his recording career another, in the shape of British TV legend Jack Warner, was attempting to reinvigorate his by releasing the 1971 single **You Have Got The Gear/ Somebody Asked Me**. Despite what the title might suggest, this isn't a song about intergenerational drug dealing, rather the A-side features the star of *Dixon of Dock Green* intoning what the President record company called *'a beautiful, melodic number which successfully bridges the generation gap when a son takes problems about his love-life to his father'*.

You Have Got The Gear was written, produced and orchestrated by Frank Weir (who scored hits on his own, and with Vera Lynn, in the 1950s), with the B-side penned by Warner himself. According to a contemporary press release Warner's faux-French accent on the flip was inspired by the *'hundreds of letters from people asking him to sing a* (Maurice) *Chevalier song'*. There's no accounting for taste: both songs are just awful. His album of comic songs from the music halls has been reissued several times under different names, but I sincerely doubt anyone in their right mind would want to reissue **You Have Got The Gear**.

Born Horace Waters in 1895 (his sisters were well-known music hall act Elsie and Doris Waters) Warner made a name for himself on the stage and on radio before appearing in a number of classics from the famed Ealing studios, including *Hue and Cry* and *The Ladykillers*. In 1949 he first played the role for which he will forever be remembered – that of policeman George Dixon in the movie *The Blue Lamp*. Warner reprised the role in 1955 for the TV series *Dixon Of Dock Green*, which ran for 21 years – a hugely successful but baffling piece of casting, as Dixon had been killed off in the movie. He released a number of recordings during his long career, the last of which, **Your Silly Bird's A Liar** (which is not quite as sexist as it sounds) was issued in 1975, six years before Jack hung up his uniform for the last time.

Back in the 60s, when TV was king and pre-teens around the UK were being scared into sticking to the straight and narrow by a weekly visit from George Dixon, just about every primetime TV star was hauled into the recording studio to make a record. Some cut a few campy sides (pretty much the entire casts of Batman, Bonanza and Star Trek are guilty here); others made a half decent stab at pop balladry and quickly scuttled back to their respective soundstages. Others still, as we saw in *The World's Worst Records Volume One* with Peter Wyngarde, were offered the freedom to do pretty much whatever they wanted – with shocking results.

David McCallum, now aged 81, was one of the brightest stars of 60s TV. As Illya Kuryakin, a Russian-born secret agent, he co-starred in the hit series The Man from U.N.C.L.E. before going on to appear in *Colditz, Kidnapped*, late 70s science-fiction series *Sapphire & Steel, The Invisible Man* and, more recently *NCIS*. He's also a classically-trained musician with an impeccable heritage: his father, David Senior, was leader of the Royal Philharmonic Orchestra, the London Philharmonic Orchestra and the Scottish National Orchestra, gave Jimmy Page the idea of playing guitar with a cello bow and played on The Beatles' crowning achievement **A Day In The Life**. For a full decade he led Mantovani's orchestra. Phew!

When the younger McCallum was offered the chance to record an album he, very wisely, chose not to sing but to arrange and conduct light orchestral versions of au courant hits. Capitol teamed him up with producer and arranger David Axelrod, who employed his crack team of session musicians to record four albums of jazz-

tinged covers, all of which are pretty decent; unquestionably a cut above anything else put out by a TV star that you're likely to hear. The first two volumes *Music...A Part Of Me* and *Music...A Bit More Of Me* sold reasonably well and one particular track, **The Edge** has become one of the most sampled pieces in Hip-Hop, used by artists including Dr. Dre, Missin' Linx and Masta Ace.

But what Capitol didn't have was a hit single. So, despite his best intentions, McCallum recorded four vocal cuts for potential release. Working with songwriter H B Barnum (who had written a song called **The Man From U.N.C.L.E.** for Capitol act the Gallants and who would go on to write Northern Soul classic **What** – recorded by Judy Street and, later, Soft Cell) he came up with his first 45 – **Communication/My Carousel**.

This coupling must have frightened the life out of people when they dropped the needle on the record. Certainly, if they were expecting more of the same light jazz that his albums had offered they were in for a big surprise. On the B-side especially McCallum sounds like a man possessed. I do love the harmonica and the bass (if you think you recognise that bass sound you're right: that's ace bassist Carol Kaye, famous for her sessions with Phil Spector and Brian Wilson), but the vocal performance is demented. The A-side (compiled on the must-have CD *Music For Mentalists*) is just rubbish: the arrangement is awesome, especially the last few seconds which sound exactly like Brigitte Bardot's brilliant **Harley Davidson**, but the lyrics and vocals are ridiculous. What a great record!

Despite his worldwide fame, the single failed to resonate with the kids and was a massive flop. He followed this up with one further 45, I**n The Garden – Under The Tree/The House On Breckenridge Lane** which again, unsurprisingly, failed to chart.

The same fate would befall the single by former Jesus (and Jasper Carrot sidekick), Robert Powell, and his single **Once Upon A Time**.

A treatise on the subject of creation - how ironic that it would be delivered sonorously by a man who will forever be identified with the part of Jesus of Nazareth - It should come as no surprise that the man behind this pretentious prattle is one Richard Hewson. Outside of his 70s hits as the RAH Band, Hewson is best known for his work as an arranger, having scored strings for The Beatles (he worked with Phil Spector on the orchestrations for the *Let It Be* album) Paul McCartney, Rod Stewart, Cliff Richard and many, many more.

For some odd reason this wasn't a hit. Issued by Logo Records (an RCA imprint) in 1978 - that same year that Powell took the leading role of Richard Hannay in the third film version of John Buchan's *The Thirty Nine Steps* - The track turned up recently on the catch-all compilation *You Are Awful... But We Like You*. Its' B-side, the ridiculously-titled **Laudate**, is exactly the same track as **Once Upon A Time** but with Bob's vocal performance wiped.

Probably best remembered these days for her cameo as the Fairy Godmother in the Adam and the Ants video **Prince Charming**, the British actress Diana Dors appeared with Powell in the influential UK drama series *Thriller.* Born Diana Fluck in Swindon in 1931, Dors was once one of the most famous and recognisable women in Britain, at one point feted as Britain's answer to Marilyn Monroe. Marilyn died young and became an icon: unfortunately for Diana her early promise as an actress will forever be overshadowed by lurid tales of abortions, miscarriages, relationships with criminals, battles with her weight, and by her reputation as an orgy-throwing, drunken pill popper.

At 16 she was signed to the Rank Organisation: in her early films her chest was often strapped down, and her hair was its natural shade of brown. She made a bunch of unsuccessful films, but her stage appearances led to her winning *Theatre World* magazine's Actress of the Year Award.

In 1951 Diana met Dennis Hamilton Gittins (usually known as Dennis Hamilton), marrying him only five weeks later. There was little that the unscrupulous Hamilton would not do to further her career or to increase the income he derived from it. Her appearance became markedly similar to Marilyn's; she took on roles comparable to hers and quickly became known as 'the English Marilyn Monroe'. Hamilton made sure that her name, and stories of her lavish lifestyle, were seldom out of the tabloids. It's even been suggested that Hamilton would pimp Diana out to influential actors and producers.

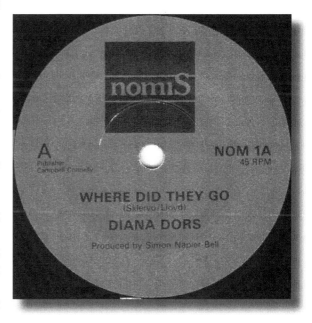

Chances to star in several US-made movies were ruined by Hamilton: once when she refused to divorce him and move to the States and later when Hamilton turned down parts without bothering to tell her. The result was that her early promising career was restricted from this point forward to mainly British films. When she did finally make it across the pond Hamilton again ruined her chances by punching out a photographer at a party where celebrities including Doris Day, Eddie Fisher, Zsa Zsa Gabor, Liberace, Lana Turner, Ginger Rogers and John Wayne were invited. The following day's headline in the *National Enquirer* read '*Miss Dors Go Home – And Take Mr Dors With You'*. Despite that, Dors managed to squeeze in an affair with Rod Steiger whilst the pair were filming *The Unholy Wife*.

She managed to get shot of Hamilton, shortly before his death in 1958 but not after he virtually bankrupted her, forcing her to take on a cabaret tour to pay her bills. After a string of affairs she married comedian Richard 'Dicky' Dawson, but the pair divorced in 1966. Two years later, and with her two sons Mark and Gary thousands of miles away in America with their father (who would go on to be a major star on US TV), she met and married the actor Alan Lake. Their relationship was stormy, not helped by Lake's heavy drinking and stint in prison for his part in a pub brawl, but it lasted right through until her death, from cancer, in 1984. Five months after she died a distraught Lake took his own life in the bedroom of the home they shared.

But back to the music. Diana's single **Where Did They Go** was issued as the first release (Nom 1) on manager and producer Simon Napier-Bell's own Nomis Records. Napier-Bell's own illustrious career includes managing the Yardbirds, John's Children (featuring a teenage Mark Feld aka Marc Bolan), Japan, Ultravox and Wham! He's also co-author of the English lyrics to the Dusty Springfield hit **You Don't Have To Say You Love Me** as well as of several books about his long career in showbiz. Diana had made a stab at recording several times: first way back in 1951 with the single **I Feel So Mmmm**, which she followed with her one and only album, *Swinging Dors*, in 1960.

This miserable offering was issued in 1982 and it's shocking: she sounds like a third-rate drag artist looking back over an all-too short life and wishing he'd drunk more booze and shagged more men. It's little more than a poor **Those Were The Days** ripoff – albeit 14 years too late - and everyone involved in this should be thoroughly ashamed of themselves. Knowing that Dors was battling cancer at the time - and would succumb to the disease less than two years later - might add a patina of poignancy but it's still horrible. The arrangement is poor, the musicianship workmanlike and dull and the disc's label incorrectly credits co-writer Gloria Sklerov as Sklervo: it's all a bit ham-fisted. The track was originally performed by Peggy Lee on her 1971 album of the same name, and had previously been covered by Sandie Shaw.

The B-side is no better: **It's You Again** is a dull-as-ditchwater duet with her son (now a TV producer) Gary Dawson, here billing himself as Gary Dors; his paper-thin voice no match for her weather beaten, booze-and-fags weariness. Worryingly, the pair are singing a love song to each other, but it's not a song about maternal love...
There's a statue of Diana outside Swindon's Shaw Ridge Leisure Complex. Sadly, the end-of-terrace mural of her and other local notables – including all five members of XTC – that once dominated a Swindon street is no longer extant.

In 1973 Dors starred in *Craze*, one of the many low-budget horror movie appearances she made once her career as a sexpot was over. Her co-star in that film was American hardman actor Jack Palance, here portraying a camp, bisexual antiques dealer and cult leader. A badly produced, sub-Hammer exploitation piece, *Craze* is a real horror – but no more horrific than Jack's 1970 country-western album *Palance*.

With three tracks written by Jack the Lad himself, *Palance* is pretty much exactly what you would expect: low-key country often spoken rather than sung by the man whose early success in movies quickly dissipated: he was Oscar nominated twice, for his roles in the 1952 movie *Sudden Fear* and for his portrayal of the villain in the 1953 classic *Shane*, but he spent most of his career fronting third rate TV fare or appearing in cruddy movies like *Craze*, *The Torture Garden* or the risible *Che!* until he was rediscovered by audiences in the 1990s thanks to his scene-stealing performance in *City Slickers* - the film for which he received his third (and first successful) Oscar nomination.

Ernie Winfrey, the engineer on *Palance*, says that working with Jack was "a real pleasure. I remember being very nervous about working with such a famous person but he immediately put me at my ease. He was such a nice guy: a gentleman."

A couple of decades earlier (in 1953, to be precise), Jack Palance had played opposite Robert Mitchum in the early 3-D thriller *Second Chance*... you can already see where this is going, can't you? Mitchum issued two albums during his lifetime, his 1957 collection *Calypso Is Like So* and 1967's *That Man, Robert Mitchum, Sings*. He also scored three hit singles. In all fairness the Mitchum albums aren't that bad: the most infamous

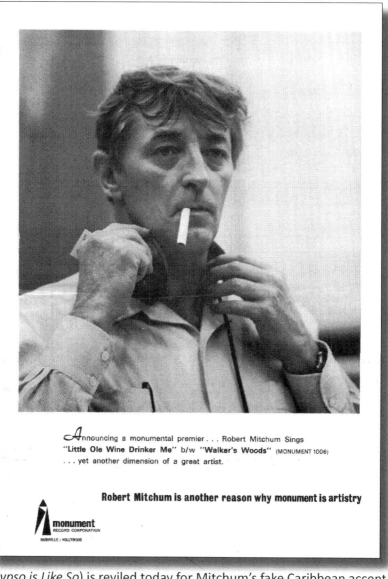

$\mathcal{A}$nnouncing a monumental premier . . . Robert Mitchum Sings
"**Little Ole Wine Drinker Me**" b/w "**Walker's Woods**" (MONUMENT 1006)
. . . yet another dimension of a great artist.

Robert Mitchum is another reason why monument is artistry

monument
RECORD CORPORATION
NASHVILLE / HOLLYWOOD

(*Calypso is Like So*) is reviled today for Mitchum's fake Caribbean accent, but – as Mike Read might say – you can't sing calypso with a Connecticut accent.

It's about time we visited the Richard Harris section of our museum of oddities – chiefly his 'seduction special', *The Richard Harris Love Album*. Some people actually like this kind of thing: no doubt the same people who like early Al Stewart and drink Mateus Rose.
Consisting primarily of tracks from his first three (yes, I know, there were

Richard Harris albums before, and after, this horror) plus both sides of his latest single - taken from the recent musical remake of *Goodbye Mr Chips* - *The Richard Harris Love Album* is basically a 'best of' the Irish-born actor's early recordings although, confusingly, one or two tracks have been renamed and could easily confuse the casual buyer into thinking he or she were getting new product for their pounds.

At the tail end of the 60s Harris's recorded work garnered much praise, although in all fairness most of that praise was aimed at the song writing and arrangement prowess of his co-conspirator Jimmy Webb rather than Harris's own vocal dexterity: "I admire Jimmy," says the great Burt Bacharach in Bill DeMain's book *In Their Own Words*. "I thought the album he did with Richard Harris was one of the great, great albums. I think the songs are just unbelievable on it". Yet to me he fails miserably to reach the heights of the only truly great singing actor, Peter Wyngarde. Webb, who also wrote Glen Campbell's smash hits **By The Time I Get To Phoenix**, **Wichita Lineman** and **Galveston**, had met Harris at an anti-war rally in Los Angeles and to this day won't hear a word against his friend. "If he missed a note or he didn't carry it off particularly well as a singer, he had the actor's ability to step his way through the lyric and to speak some of the lines and basically to carry it off...it's a little insulting to say that he couldn't perform, or that he couldn't sing," he told *songfacts. com*

Listen to **One Of The Nicer Things**, and make up your own mind. It's understandable that Webb would want to support his mate's performance, especially as Harris is no longer here to answer for himself: the Oscar- and Golden Raspberry-nominated actor passed away in 2002. He's probably best remembered

these days for having played Albus Dumbledore in the first two Harry Potter movies but his filmmaking career spanned more than 40 years. Still, I'm pretty sure you'll agree that his voice is awful: a thin, reedy wail that often misses its mark. Webb and Harris, of course, collaborated on the overblown horror that is **MacArthur Park** – and Webb's own story of how that particular track was recorded makes for enlightening and entertaining reading.

"Richard and I started hanging out after rehearsals and drinking Black Velvets: 50% Guinness, 50% champagne," he told *The Guardian* in 2013. "One night after a few, I said: 'We ought to make a record.' He'd starred in the movie *Camelot* and sang every song in it beautifully. A few weeks later, I received a telegram: 'Dear Jimmy Webb. Come to London. Make this record. Love, Richard'.

"Over the course of two days we tore through 30 or 40 of my songs. I was playing the piano and singing. He was standing there in his kaftan, waving his arms and expressing excitement at some songs, not so crazy about others. The best went into his debut album, *A Tramp Shining*. **MacArthur Park** was at the bottom of my pile. By the time I played it, we had moved on to straight brandy, but Richard slapped the piano. '*Oh Jimmy Webb. I love that! I'll make a hit out of that, I will'.*

"I recorded the basic track back in Hollywood, with myself on harpsichord accompanied by session musicians the Wrecking Crew. When Richard did the vocals at a London studio, he had a pitcher of Pimm's by the microphone. We knew the session was over when the Pimm's was gone.

"We had doubts about releasing it as a single, but when radio stations began playing it I was asked to do a shorter version as a single. I refused, so eventually they put out the full seven minutes 20 seconds. George Martin once told me the Beatles let **Hey Jude** run to over seven minutes because of **MacArthur Park**." Incidentally, Harris was not the first choice to record MacArthur Park: the song had originally been offered to Californian pop band The Association (who scored a huge hit with **Windy**), who turned it down.

Also included on *The Richard Harris Love Album* is a song called **First Hymn From Grand Terrace** which, on the disc's label is listed as **The First Hymn From Grand Terrace (Part 2)**, but was originally part of a suite of songs that appeared on the second Webb/Harris album *The Yard Went On Forever* entitled **The Hymns From The Grand Terrace**. If the arsing around with the title doesn't annoy you, the performance will. Harris's forced vibrato is uncomfortable to listen to, and the strain in his voice when he hits the key change will hurt all but the most insensitive ears. Coming out of a Dansette, in a bedsit full of scatter cushions and thick with marijuana smoke this probably sounded brilliant...I can see how a young lady would be wooed by Jimmy's seductive lyrics and lush arrangements, but today it's a kitsch reminder that, back in the 60s, people would buy any old nonsense. Although Harris would release several albums of new material after he and Webb parted company, he would never again reach the heights he once did.

Jim Reeves & Eddy Arnold

James Travis Reeves is rightly revered as one of the all-time greats of country music. A pioneer of the Nashville sound (the country-pop crossover popularised by Reeves, Eddy Arnold and Patsy Cline), Gentleman Jim scored his debut hit in 1953 and managed more than 30 chart singles in the United States – including the standards **He'll Have To Go** and **Welcome To My World** - before tragedy struck a little over a decade later.

The life of this colossus of country ended ridiculously early – three weeks before his 41st birthday in July 1964 – when the plane he was piloting (and which also carried his manager Dean Manuel) was caught in a violent thunderstorm. The single-engine plane stalled, went into a tailspin and crashed, killing both occupants. There's a lesson here: pop stars should not fly. Buddy Holly, Ritchie Valens, the Big Bopper, John Denver, Aaliyah, Randy Rhodes, Otis Redding, Ricky Nelson, Jim Croce, Stevie Ray Vaughn and several members of Lynyrd Skynyrd would no doubt (posthumously) agree.

But death was not the end of Reeves' career (nor would it be for pretty much everyone mentioned above): he left a massive backlog of unreleased music – from rough demos to finished sessions and, between 1965 and 1984, he landed even more chart smashes than he had during his life. His posthumous UK number one **Distant Drums** became not only his biggest international hit but also the biggest selling single of his pre- and post-mortem career.

The unfortunate thing for Reeves is that he was signed to RCA, a company who have never let the death of an act bother them too much. Thanks to them – and to his widow Mary (to whom, apparently, Jim was less than faithful) – many of his recordings have been slathered with new instrumentation and some have even been artificially turned into duets with the equally dead Patsy Cline, who also met her untimely end in a plane crash. I think it's incredible that no-one at RCA or MCA (who owned Cline's back catalogue) thought that issuing a fake duet of the song **I Fall To Pieces** was in poor taste for two people whose own lives had ended with various parts of their bodies strewn across the countryside. But before RCA paired Jim's ghost with Patsy's they issued a few other howlers, including **Old Tige**, the B-side to **Distant Drums**, and a dead dog of a song about – fittingly - a dead dog. **Old Tige** is beyond horrible; a ridiculously sentimental piece of claptrap with a denouement that is as obvious as it is distasteful. This risible tale of a soldier saved from an early grave by the appearance of his ghostly mutt originally appeared on Gentleman Jim's 1961 album *Talkin' to Your Heart*, but it was its posthumous re-release (and its inclusion on countless compilations) that brought it to international attention.

Three years later RCA again plundered the vaults and exhumed the vile **But You Love Me Daddy**, issued in the UK as an A-side (believe it or not) in 1969. The song had been recorded 10 years earlier but Reeves wisely decided that it should not be released – something he couldn't prevent once he'd snuffed it. Incidentally the whiney child heard on the track – and credited as Steve Moore – is better known these days as the incredibly prolific low-fi legend R Stevie Moore. Moore's appearance on the 1959 recording marks his debut studio session. The song, which was written by Kathryn Twitty (a radio script writer and *Billboard* magazine correspondant who passed away in 1972; she was a distant relation to the singer Conway Twitty) who also wrote **Teach Me How To Pray** recorded and released in 1959 by Reeves, was later covered by wife-swapping Scots entertainers The Krankies.

RCA were more than happy to rob the graves of their deceased artists; the company was also desperate to make as much money as possible out of their living acts, 'encouraging' rock'n'rollers to cut country tunes, country stars to take a bash at the teenybop audience and even persuading opera singers – vis Mario Lanza – to stray into the calypso market the company had already all but sewed up with Harry Belafonte.

Born on May 15, 1918, Reeves' stablemate Richard Edward 'Eddy' Arnold was one of country music's most popular performers, with a career that spanned six decades, 147 hits on the *Billboard* Country Music charts and sales in excess of 85 million records. He was ranked 22nd on Country Music Television's list of *The 40 Greatest Men of Country Music* in 2003; Jim Reves didn't even make the list.

Nicknamed the Tennessee Plowboy (because he grew up on a farm and started his performing career while still working there, often turning up for gigs atop a mule with a guitar slung over his back), he was signed by Colonel Tom Parker more than a decade before the Colonel would get his claws into Elvis Presley, and cut his first disc – a schmaltzy piece of hillbilly music called **Mommy Please Stay Home With Me** - in 1944. That flopped, but the follow up (**Each Minute Seems A Million Years**) was a top five hit on the country charts and began an unprecedented run of 57 Top 10 successes. His early sides are rather good – if you ignore 1958's ridiculous rockabilly novelty **The Rockin' Mockin' Bird** that is; it was only when RCA tried to turn him into another Perry Como that things started to go pear-shaped. Unperturbed, Arnold re-recorded his old material in an orchestral pop style and stuck doggedly to his new Nashville crooner image, even going so far as to actively dismiss the first decade and a half of his recording career.

His success as a hit maker petered out, although he continued to find success as an album act and on TV, yet in the middle of the 60s he had an unexpected resurgence, with two massive hits, **What's He Doing in My World?** and **Make The World Go Away**. "I've never thought of myself as a country-and-western singer," he told a reporter from *The Charlotte Observer* in 1968. "I'm really a pop music artist. I want my songs to be accepted by everyone." By 1969 however those pop hits he so craved had completely dried up, although he continued to score on the country charts until 1983.

In 1971 he released what was easily the most misguided song of his career, a woeful piece of right wing propaganda entitled **A Part Of America Died**. Arnold, known for his smooth vocal style, felt that this particular portentous piece of crap needed something different and decided to recite the song's scaremongering lyrics whilst a choir hammered home the message by mumbling a hymn in the background.

According to Michael Streissguth (in his book *Eddy Arnold: Pioneer of the Nashville Sound*), with **A Part Of America Died** '*Eddy took a turn toward topical material, addressing Middle America's growing concern* *with crime, an issue brought to the fore by President Richard M. Nixon's rhetoric.* **A Part Of America Died** (was) *penned by Harry Koch – a policeman – and lashed out at the overemphasis on criminals' rights... Eddy condemns a policeman's murder while a disembodied chorus singing* **The Old Rugged Cross** *hovers behind him. "I think it's timely," Eddy said.'*

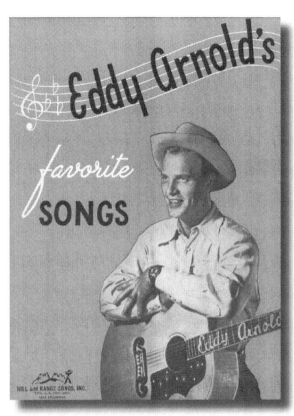

A stalwart Nixon supporter, Arnold was so convinced his record would sell to the moral majority that he regularly called RCA sales reps around the country to check on its progress. The lyrics to this awful dirge were even mentioned in the United States Congress when Mario Biaggi, the representative for New York's 24th District and a former policeman himself, rose to his feet and quoted parts of the song to the rest of the House of Representatives.

Despite that, and in spite of a *Billboard* review which claimed that *'this potent message could easily prove an important pop item'* the single struggled to gain a footing in the country charts – peaking at a miserable 41 - and failed to provide him with a much-wanted crossover hit. "I've always picked good song," he told Michael Streissguth. "I always picked a good lyric, and that gave me a wider audience than just the country buyers. I did that on purpose. I never was political about songwriters." Boy, did he pick a wrong 'un this time. Disappointed by the lack of mainstream success, he followed it up with a cover of Reeves' classic **Welcome To My World**, which limped into the country charts at 34.

Arnold died, in a care facility near Nashville, on May 8, 2008, just two weeks before his 90th birthday. Just three weeks later RCA issued **To Life,** a cut from Eddy's final album (recorded and released in 1996). The song debuted at 49 on the Country charts, setting the record for the longest span between a first chart single and a last: 62 years and 11 months, and extending Eddy's career chart history to seven decades.

The Wonder Who?
On The Good Ship Lollipop (1965)

Throughout the history of recorded music artists have occasionally resorted to the use of pseudonyms. Paul McCartney has done it time and time again (The Country Hams, Thrillington, The Fireman and so on), and each of his most famous co-conspirators have, on occasion, done the same thing: stand up and take a bow the Reverend Fred Gherkin, L'Angelo Mysterio and Ognir Rrats respectively. Then there's Prince, who for various reasons - some due to his dispute with his on/off record company - decided to rename himself Joey Coco, Alexander Nevermind and to use a completely unpronounceable squiggle that resulted in his being known as TAFKAP: The Artist Formerly Known as Prince.

The Wonder Who? was an alias utilised by 60s chart toppers The 4 Seasons, who released a cover of the Bob Dylan song **Don't Think Twice** (truncating the correct title of the song) under that name in 1965. An outtake from their *Sing Hits By Bacharach, David And Dylan* album, the story has it that lead Season Frankie Valli was not happy with his vocals during the recording of a 'straight' version of **Don't Think Twice, It's All Right** and he decided to record the song with a 'joke' falsetto vocal to ease the tension in the studio.

As the group were still riding high in the charts (**Let's Hang On** had been a Top Three hit recently and their next single, **Working My Way Back To You** would go Top 10) to save damaging the group's career it was decided to issue the track with the Wonder Who? nom-de-plume. Confusingly this would lead to the group scoring three hits under different names - as The 4 Seasons Featuring The 'Sound' Of Frankie Valli, as The Wonder Who? and as Frankie Valli solo (although his original version of **The Sun Ain't Gonna Shine Anymore** - later a hit for the Walker Bothers - was actually recorded at a 4 Seasons session) that year. No other group has ever matched this peculiar feat.

Everyone involved was surprised when the helium-fuelled **Don't Think Twice** became a major hit, peaking on the *Billboard* charts at number 12. Called *'about the most camp cover of a Dylan tune that could be imagined'* by music writer Richie Unterberger on *allmusic.com*, lead singer Frankie Valli adopts his best castrato voice for the performance and, bizarrely, decides to blow falsetto raspberries throughout the recording. Valli made this rather peculiar sound (which, to be perfectly honest, I first assumed was a flaw in the mastering) in imitation of the famous 40s singer Rose Murphy, who used the brrp, brrp sound of a telephone ringing on her hit **Busy Line** and became known as the chee-chee girl.

"We had an album, six Bacharach-David songs on one side and six Dylan songs on the other," Valli told *Billboard* magazine in 2013. "In the studio, I started to clown around with **Don't Think Twice**. In reality, it was an impression of a very famous black singer, Rose Murphy. She did **I Can't Give You Anything But Love**. We played it for a disc jockey in Atlantic City and he said, *'Please give it to me. I just want to play it. I won't tell anybody who it is. I'll run a contest.'* When the record company found out, they were really pissed. They said, *'Now we have to put it out. But we already have a 4 Seasons song out, and this will kill it. So we'll say it's the Wonder Who?'"*

Not ones to look a gift horse in the mouth, the 4 Seasons and Philips kept the joke going a little longer. The 4 Seasons were still doing very well, thank you - which makes you wonder why they would resurrect the Wonder Who? for their dismal and, frankly, ridiculous cover of the Shirley Temple classic **On The Good Ship Lollipop**, backed with an equally awful reworking of the old chestnut **You're Nobody Till Somebody Loves You** - with both songs again featuring Frankie doing his best (or worst) impersonation of a Trimphone.

Although the release did nothing to demonstrate the group's creativity or musical direction, expensive, full page adverts heralded a Top Five smash; *Billboard's* own reviewer (*'two exciting sides from this 'Mystery' group. Shirley Temple's classic gets a humorous dance beat revival'*) deemed it worthy of a Top 20 placing, yet both sides barely managed to scrape into the *Billboard Hot 100*, with **On The Good Ship Lollipop** (which had first appeared in little Shirley's 1934 film *Bright Eyes*) peaking at 87 during its' three-week run and **You're Nobody Till Somebody Loves You** reaching the giddy heights of 96. Both sides would later resurface on the 1990 compilation album *Rarities Volume One*.

Their third outing as the Wonder Who?, 1967's **Lonesome Road**, peaked at 89 – in the same week that Valli scored a 'solo' Top Three hit with **Can't Take My Eyes Off You**. A fourth Wonder Who single (sans the question mark) was simply a reissue of an old 4 Seasons recording, **Peanuts**, issued as a cash-in by the group's former label Vee-Jay. **On The Good Ship Lollipop** would later be covered, and issued as a single, by perennial pop outsider Tiny Tim in 1969.

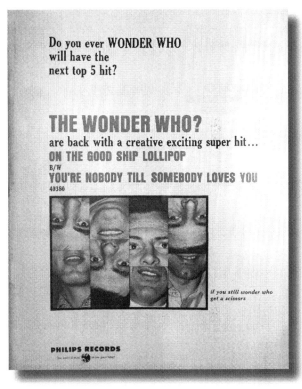

Do you ever WONDER WHO will have the next top 5 hit?

THE WONDER WHO?
are back with a creative exciting super hit...
ON THE GOOD SHIP LOLLIPOP
B/W
YOU'RE NOBODY TILL SOMEBODY LOVES YOU
40380

if you still wonder who get a scissors

PHILIPS RECORDS

One of the most successful groups of all time, with sales in excess of 100 million, eight UK and 19 US Top Ten hits, the Four Seasons* have had a colourful and complicated career, issuing 23 singles before their first hit, Sherry, in 1962. Throughout their now 60-plus year history the various line-ups of the group (since 1960 always lead by Valli and Bob Gaudio, who each own a 50 percent stake in the Four Seasons Partnership) have performed and/or issued tracks under a variety of names, 18 (including The Four Lovers and Frankie Valle and the Romans) before their first major chart success. To add to the confusion Frankie Valli solo releases have turned up on Four Seasons albums and vice versa.

As the new millennium arrived the hit musical Jersey Boys reignited interest in their career once again, Valli appeared in a number of episodes of the hit TV series *The Sopranos* and, in 2007, a remix of their 40-year old single **Beggin'** saw the act return to the UK charts a full 45 years after **Sherry** gave them their first British chart entry. Valli – who suffered a debilitating deafness for almost two decades before having it corrected by surgery – is still touring today, fronting a new version of the Four Seasons as he enters his 80s: not bad going for a man who issued his first recordings (as Frankie Valley) in 1953.

***

* What's in a name? Although the band issued their first single as The Four Seasons *in 1961 (***Bermuda***, backed with* **Spanish Lace***, on Gone Records), they scored their first chart successes as* The 4 Seasons *whilst signed to VeeJay Records, changing the name of the act to* The 4 Seasons Featuring the "Sound" of Frankie Valli *when they moved to Philips in 1964. In the 1970s, when the band moved first to Warners, then to Motown imprint Mowest and back to Warners again they officially changed their name to* Frankie Valli and the Four Seasons *but, when illness forced Valli to take a backseat, they became simply* The Four Seasons. *Since 1980 the band has been officially known as* Frankie Valli & The Four Seasons.

The Curse Of The Singing DJ

Jimmy Savile's reputation is in tatters. The former (arguably the world's first: Savile began spinning discs in 1943) DJ and TV presenter was once seen as a harmless eccentric or, at worse, a long-haired weirdo; his death, in October 2011, was quickly followed by the revelation that he was a sexual predator, a paedophile and, quite possibly, a necrophiliac. It is impossible to look at his four-decade long broadcasting career without thinking of the 450-plus complaints against him made to the police and the millions of pounds paid out by his estate in compensation to those whose lives he tarnished. So complete is his downfall that I'm loath to mention the disgusting pervert here at all, but it would be remiss – in a chapter about singing DJs - not to make at least a passing reference to his three UK 45s, **Madison Time** (1960, with the Vernons Girls), **Ahab The Arab** (1962, a cover of Ray Stevens' US novelty hit) and **The Bossa Nova** (1963). Each is horrible, and each would deserve your condemnation even without what we now know about the perpetrator.

Operation Yewtree, the police investigation instigated by the revelations about Savile's heinous crimes, and other ongoing investigations into sexual misconduct have forever blotted the copybooks of many well-known names. Dave Lee Travis, Radio 1's beloved Hairy Cornflake – who, with fellow DJ Paul Burnett issued a brace of singles under the pseudonym Laurie Lingo and the Dipsticks including the massive novelty hit **Convoy GB** and the Christmas-themed **Live at the Blue Boar** - was arrested in November 2012 on suspicion of historic sexual offences. In February 2014, he was found not guilty on 12 of the counts, with the jury unable to reach a decision on a further two. At a retrial that September he was found guilty of one count of indecent assault and was given a three-month prison sentence, suspended for two years.

Former Radio 1 DJ Chris Denning was jailed for 13 years in December 2014 for 40 offences against 24 boys aged nine to 16 in a three-decade long reign of terror, and other TV and radio personalities including Paul Gambaccini, Jimmy Tarbuck, Jim Davidson, Freddie Starr (all, thankfully, now exonerated) and – inevitably – Gary Glitter have been investigated. In February 2015 Glitter was found guilty of historical sex abuse against three young girls. The 70-year-old singer - real name Paul Gadd - was convicted of attempted rape, four counts of indecent assault and one of having sex with a girl under the age of 13 and was sent down for 16 years. Rolf Harris, the Antipodean entertainer who had hosted kids TV shows, painted the Queen and scored a number one hit with the frightful **Two Little Boys** is currently serving time at Her Majesty's Pleasure after being found guilty of 12 charges of indecent assault on four victims – one aged only eight.

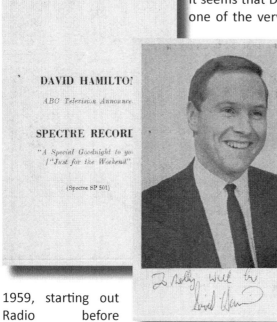

DAVID HAMILTO?

ABC Television Announce

SPECTRE RECORE

"A Special Goodnight to yo
["Just for the Weekend"

(Spectre SP 501)

It seems that David 'Diddy' Hamilton is one of the very few stars of Radio 1's 70s line up who has not had his name dragged through the mud in the wake of the Savile scandal.

David has been broadcasting now for 55 years. Born in Manchester in 1938 he began his career in 1959, starting out with Forces Radio before becoming an on-screen announcer for ABC-TV. In 1962 he began his long association with BBC radio, starting out with *The Beat Show* for the Light Programme and moving on to present *Family Choice* on the fledgling Radio 1 in 1967.

It was while he was appearing on the ABC-TV show *Doddy's Music Box* that Liverpudlian comedian Ken Dodd gave the height-challenged Hamilton the 'Diddy' nickname, which has stuck ever since. Hamilton was a regular foil to Dodd on the show, which featured many of the biggest pop acts of the day plugging their latest releases. Sandie Shaw, Tom Jones, Peter and Gordon and the Scaffold were among the dozens of acts who appeared on the programme, which ran for just 18 episodes, broadcast in two series January-March 1967 and January–March 1968.

Since then he has had regular shows on national and local radio in the UK and is still a regular face on TV, with recent appearances on *Pointless*

Celebrities, Cash in the Celebrity Attic, Sport Relief, Loose Women, The One Show and many others. He's also one of the few presenters of vintage episodes of Top of the Pops that the BBC can still broadcast without fear of giving airtime to a sex offender. David made two singles, the first - **A Special Goodnight To You** and its B-side **Just For The Weekend** – whilst acting as stooge to Dodd.

"The record came about like this," he told me. "I was appearing with Ken Dodd on the series *Doddy`s Music Box* on ABC-TV. On one show I sang a few bars of a song and girls ran on and screamed and pulled at my clothing. I hasten to add that they were not fans, but extras! Some people based in Liverpool suggested I make a record which they thought might sell on the popularity of the TV series. I think the year was 1968."

"Two songs were hastily written by Ricky Woodruff, the pianist with the ABC orchestra and Fred Lloyd who produced the record," David adds. "**A Special Goodnight To You** (was) based on the phrase I used as an announcer to close down the station at night; **Just For The Weekend** was the time that ABC was on air in the North and Midlands. It was the first – and possibly only – release on Spectre Records.

"At their suggestion, we promoted it hard, visiting record shops and bingo halls where it sold very well. Sadly, being an independent record company, Spectre had poor distribution and this success was not repeated in other record shops around the country. Although I sold a lot of records across the counter, I didn`t receive a penny in royalties." David recalls that the tracks were recorded at the fabled Abbey Road studios which, at the time, were home to the Beatles, Pink Floyd and countless other major acts. "It just shows that not everything that came out of Abbey Road was a smash," he laughs.

David Hamilton had no shame when it came to flexing his tonsils in the recording studio. In 1973 he released his second 45 - **Just Like That** - on the short-lived Dart label, written and produced by Harold Spiro, who had previously worked with Herman's Hermits, the Yardbirds, Olivia Newton John, Cliff Richard and many others. Spiro also co-wrote the dreadful football anthem **Nice One Cyril**.

This particular audio turd seems to have been purpose built to be a bad record, with its dreadful, out of tune kiddy choir, stupid lyrics (which give Hamilton plenty of opportunity to showcase his terrible Tommy Cooper impersonation) and an accompaniment built around a goddamn banjo and a euphonium! It's vile. The B-Side, **Have You Heard The News**, is a stupid anti-nuclear song framed as a news report. And it's almost as bad: the kids are still there (damn them!) and Hamilton's plaintive, off-key vocal makes me want to retch. Just the thing to ruin your weekend.

Fellow Radio 1 DJ Dave Cash was born in Chelsea in 1942, although his family moved to Canada by the time he was seven. While working as a copywriter for a Vancouver-based menswear shop, Dave was offered the chance to record a radio voice-over when the original actor assigned to the job became ill. Cash was a smash and he was quickly signed up for more commercial work and the occasional presenting stint.

The burgeoning pirate radio scene brought Dave back to Blighty in the early 1960s, and he soon came to the attention of Radio London, where he teamed up with the late, great Kenny Everett for *The Kenny And Cash Show*, which became enormously popular and influential. The pair issued a 45, with the A-side confusingly titled **The B-Side**, on Decca in 1965. Dave left Radio London to join the even more influential Radio Luxembourg before, in 1967 becoming one of the first DJs heard on Radio 1. And it was here that Cash perpetrated the audio crime that is **Groovy Baby**.

Radio DJs in those days had an endless stream of regular jingles and fictional characters which they used to fill airtime or simply to give them space to think whilst reaching for the next piece of vinyl to whack on the deck. Who can forget Tony Blackburn's Arnold, Jimmy Young's Raymondo and the endless cast of crazies which spewed out of Kenny Everett's fertile mind? Amongst Cash's repertoire was a winsome toddler known as Microbe. The voice of Microbe was Ian Doody, the son of Radio 1 newsreader Pat Doody. A huge hit on the show, his catch phrases (the 'Knock Knock' joke about Doctor Who and his signature 'Groovy Baby') are still known today by a generation (people of my age) who grew up next to the radio.

But Cash and Doody weren't satisfied with radio stardom for Microbe – they wanted something bigger so, in 1969, the three year old Ian was dragged off into a recording studio – along with backing singers Madeline Bell, Leslie Duncan and (allegedly) Dusty Springfield (although this seems highly unlikely as her career had recently been revitalised and she was making it big in the States at the time) to record **Groovy Baby**. Issued by CBS in the UK, by May of that year the single had reached the heady heights of number 29 in the charts. The song's B-side **Your Turn Now** was credited to the Microbop Ensemble and featured Cash himself offering listeners the chance to imitate Microbe for their own amusement.

Cash left the BBC for Independent Local radio (ILR) in 1973, first at Capital where, with Everett, he relaunched *The Kenny And Cash Show*, before resigning in 1994 to spend more time writing and to develop his other interests. After six years he rejoined the BBC, presenting programmes for Radio Kent, Radio Cambridgeshire, and Radio Essex.

Cash's one-time consort, Kenny Everett, issued several singles during his tragically-short career (he died, aged 50, from an AIDS-related illness in 1995) as well as fronting essential compilation *The World's Worst Record Show* which – in a roundabout way - gave birth to this very book you're now perusing. Most of Cuddly Ken's discs were novelty records (the aforementioned **The B-Side** and its B-side **Knees**, the various Captain Kremmen and Sid Snot 45s) but two of his earliest, the 1968 coupling of two Nilsson covers **It's Been So Long/Without Her** and the following year's **Nice Time/And Now For A Little Train Number** were fairly 'straight', psychedelic pop releases – albeit sung by a man who should have stuck to spinning records, not performing on them.

Canadian-born DJ Duncan Johnson is responsible for one of the most awful singles ever released: a disc which made number 19 in Kenny Everett's first *Bottom 30*, broadcast in 1977.

After a string of radio jobs in Canada, the US and Bermuda Johnson moved to Britain in search of work. He eventually landed a job with Radio London before going on to join the embryonic Radio 1 line up, hosting one of the station's earliest shows, *Midday Spin*. However he was axed from the show after a few weeks, Johnson's sonorous style at odds with the bright, upbeat approach that Radio 1 was trying to cultivate. Even so, he was still hauled in to the recording studio in 1968 by Spark Records to lay down his take on the pompous reinterpretation of the biblical story of creation that is **The Big Architect**. This overblown piece of hokum eventually reappeared on the Everett-compiled *The World's Worst Record Show* album.

After a couple of years working for various pirate radio stations – and as a presenter for Radio London - Johnson joined EMI as a label manager. His one claim to fame while at EMI was championing the release of **Eye Level**, the theme to the TV detective show *Van der Valk*, which went to number one in the UK singles chart in September 1973.

Another singing DJ with an Everett connection is Dan Hoffman, known throughout the 1960s to listeners of Nashville's biggest Top 40 station WKDL simply as 'DJ Dan'. In 1975, a few years after he left WKDL, he recorded an appalling piece of God-bothering garbage called **Revelation**, which would appear at number 25 in

Cuddly Ken's first *Bottom 30* selection. Released under the name Daniel, this impossibly awful piece of dreck comes with an impeccable heritage.

It was written by Bobby Braddock, a member of the Country Music Hall of Fame and composer of upteen hits over his 40-plus year career, and produced by Hoffman – who had gone into A&R after his stint behind the microphone. Both men had worked with many big-name Nashville stars, including Tammy Wynette, and DJ managed several local bands, including the Nashville Shadows and the Anglo Saxons, and helped promote other local acts including the Counts of No Where.

Revelation was originally written in 1971 and was recorded in the same year by Waylon Jennings: Waylon's 'traditional' (i.e. sung rather than narrated) version of the song appeared on his 1972 album *Ladies Love Outlaws*. It's been recorded by a number of different artists since then, all wisely eschewing Daniel's unique, portentous style. With his sonorous vocal performance - not a million miles away from the spoken word horrors of Eamonn Andrews or Red Sovine - he sounds like Tim Lovejoy's boring brother delivering a slice of Christian country balladry.

Although the majority of copies that turn up for sale are mono/stereo promos (as is my own), this appalling single did actually receive a limited commercial release in the States, backed with a track titled **Gone Are The Days**, co-written by Hoffman himself. Thankfully it failed to chart and Daniel does not appear to have recorded a follow up, although as Daniel D Hoffman he had previously issued a 45 - **String (a Tribute)** - on Cherish records in 1974, a saccharine homage to the murdered Grand Ole Opry star David 'Stringbean' Akeman who, along with his wife Estelle, was shot dead by robbers at his cabin the previous year. Akeman was known to keep a lot of cash at his home and the robbers - cousins John and Doug Brown - had been looking for it when the couple returned home unexpectedly. Sentenced to 198 years in prison, John Brown was paroled after serving 40 years in October 2014. Cousin Doug died in prison in 2003.

Late night Radio 1 Rock Show host Richard Anthony Crispian Francis Prew Hope-Weston, or Tommy Vance to you and me, issued a handful of mediocre singles in the 60s, including covers of the Jagger/Richards compositions **You Must Be The One** and **Off The Hook** for Columbia in 1966. It's perfectly possible that he may have recorded more than a dozen cuts, released under various pseudonyms. So embarrassed was he by his early forays into the world of pop that he refused to talk about them or even acknowledge his embryonic chart career.

Other 'wonderful' Radio 1 DJs have issued records with varying degrees of success: Alan Freeman provided the voice over for the quasi-instrumental non-hit **Madison Time** in 1962 (the very same song that Jimmy Savile had issued two years previously), and both Jimmy Young and Tony Blackburn had moderately successful recording careers. Actually, you can hardly call Jimmy Young's career 'moderately successful': the doyenne of British radio scored two successive number ones with his versions of **Unchained Melody** and **The Man From Laramie** as well as three further Top 10 smashes in a decade-long chart career that saw him score a dozen hits all told. Professional Cliff Richard wannabe Mike Read has issued a whole pile of crap, but you'll need to go and read the chapter on *Music and Politics* to discover just how much.

These days the owner of two gospel music radio stations in Arkansas (KMTL and KWXT), George Virgil Domerese – known professionally as Little George Domerese - has been broadcasting for more than half a century. He's also made a name for himself by promoting country music shows on stage, performed as part of a duo with mandolin player Carl Blankenship, fronted a country music hour on KFDF Van Buren for more than 30 years and - at some point in the mid 60s - recorded a diabolically-awful self-composed 45, issued on the tiny Power record label, of Jonesboro, Arkansas.

And what a shocker it is. On **Daddy, Dear Daddy I'll Pray For You** George pretends to be a small child praying for his father, who is fighting in Vietnam. At the end of the first side of this manipulative piece of trash we find George's Mom crying after receiving a letter, as the badly-plucked notes of the Last Post ring from George's guitar. By the time you flip the record over for **A Message From Daddy In Heaven**, George's papa has become another casualty of the conflict. Yet even though he's gone, he wants to reassure his scion that his prayers did not go unanswered.

Even if 'daddy' had gone to war at the outset of the conflict in 1956, George Domerese would have been 29 – hardly 'just a little boy'. However both sides of the disc refer to the prohibiting of state sponsored prayers in US schools, which became law in 1963. That means that Little George had to have been at least 36 when he recorded this calculated slice of Christian propaganda.

Dozens of other US radio DJs would commit heinous audio crimes: we met several of them, including Shad O'Shea and Scott Muni (perpetrator of the vile **Letter To An Unborn Child**) in the first volume of *The World's Worst Records*. There simply isn't the room here to go in to all of them, but if you have a spare few hours its worth Googling the discographies of Rosko (not Emperor Rosko, but the New York based DJ of similar appellation) and his beyond bizarre B-Side **Where Are You Mama**, Wolfman Jack and Murray the K amongst many, many more.

The Real Don Steele, who was one of the most popular disc jockeys in the United States from the early 60s right up until his death ion 1997, issued a brace of 45s, 1966's dreadful, r'n'b-influenced **Hole In My Soul** (which, judging by the lyrics, should correctly be titled **Hole In My Sole**) backed with **Tina Delgado Is Alive**, a 90-second quasi-instrumental based on a nicked Rolling Stones riff whose 'lyrics' consist of Steele shouting the title twice. Steele also had a nice sideline in the movies, appearing in around half a dozen including personal favourites *Eating Raoul* and *Gremlins*.

In 1963 Dick Whittinghill, a former member of The Pied Pipers (a vocal group which sang with Tommy Dorsey's big band) and, since 1950, the popular morning disc jockey at KMPC in Los Angeles, issued **Apology At Bedtime**, the sad tale of a father's regrets with Whittinghill - over a deathly instrumental backing - listing the many, many occasions on which he lost his temper and humiliated his young son, usually without reason. I know that not everyone will agree with me, but I think that it's a nasty record: a feeble act of contrition from a bully of a father masquerading as a sweet tale of paternal love and forgiveness.

It wasn't that I didn't love you
It was that I was expecting too much of youth
I was measuring you by the yardstick of my own age
And son, I am sorry

(*Apology at Bedtime*, written by Gleason/Miller/Larned. Recorded by Dick Whittinghill on Dot Records. © 1963, Song Smiths Inc., ASCAP)

In 1965 Whittinghill (born in Montana in 1913) issued the album *The Square*, which included **Apology At Bedtime** as well as the 45s B-side **Musings Of A Father**, the saccharine saga of life in a typical 60s American home and a bunch of other winsome, treacle-y tracks. The title track of his one and only album was also issued as a single and scraped in to the *Record World* top 200 charts at number 144. The actor Jackie

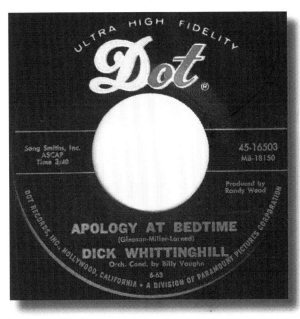

Gleason had previously recorded a version of **Apology At Bedtime** (and issued it as a killer twofer, backed with **To A Sleeping Princess**) on Capitol.

Whittinghill's discs were issued by Dot, home – of course – of our old friend Pat Boone.

For a truly wretched end to our look at record releasing DJs we need to stay in America and take a look at the career of Casey Kasem, known world over as the original voice of Shaggy in the cartoon series *Scooby Doo* and as the presenter of the video clip show *America's Top 10*. He also narrated the ridiculous album *Astrology For Young Lovers: Horoscope For The NOW Generation* ('*I do know it's happening and NOW! Keep your feet on the ground and let's start reaching for the stars!*') and issued two singles, the mushy, **Letter From Elaina** (1964), purporting to be a letter from a Beatles fan about the night she got to touch George Harrison (and, because it is set to the tune of **And I Love Her**, 'written' by John Lennon and Paul McCartney) and 1970's **No Blade Of Grass**, a view of life in a dystopian world which came from the soundtrack to the apocalyptic thriller of the same name, which *Billboard* called *'a poignant and moving narrative that offers much in programming and sales'*. Incidentally, the theme to *No Blade Of Grass* had originally been performed by Roger Whittaker; we'll cross paths with him again soon!

Kasem's death - from Lewy body dementia - in July 2014 was overshadowed by an unholy row between the members of his surviving family over his final wishes (did he or did he not wish to be kept alive using artificial means), access to him during his final months (the children from his first marriage were barred from his house and, later, care facility, by his second wife Jean, who then had their bedridden father moved out of state) and - naturally - his estate.

It was a sorry end for America's most beloved deejay. At least he's finally at rest now.

Ellen Marty
Bobby Died Today (1966)

One of the most wonderful things about immersing oneself in obscure and odd recordings is that occasionally you'll rediscover an artist who has been criminally ignored - one whose genius seriously deserves reappraisal. That's certainly true of the wonderful Ellen Marty, composer and chanteuse who released a series of what can only be

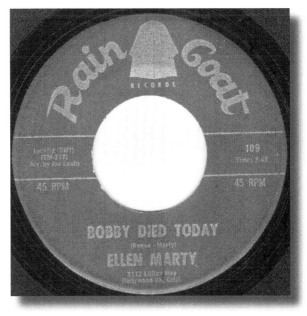

described as eccentric 45s in the 1960s. Since I first became aware of her work I've been doing my level best to find out as such as I can about her career. To be honest, it's not that much.

There's something wonderfully engaging about Ellen Marty: she doesn't have a great voice (well, not by what might be thought of as traditional standards), but personally I find it rather charming and naive. I'm loath to include her in a book about the World's Worst Records, but if I didn't how would you get to discover her charms for yourselves?

Of Swedish descent (although the liner notes on her one and only album attest she is actually half Norwegian and half Irish), Ellen Marty's real name was Mary Ellen Mart. Born in the American mid-west but schooled in New York, she appears to have started writing songs at an early age, copyrighting her first compositions in the late 1950s. Moving from New York to California - Ellen based her working life in Hollywood, keeping an office for her publishing company, Lycklig, at 1216 Cole Ave, Los Angeles - she initially tried to break into showbiz as an actress, appeared in at least two films, *Spring Affair* in 1960 and *House of Women* in 1962. Mary Ellen chose the name Lycklig for her publishing company as it's the Swedish word for 'happy': the company was still operational in 1980, although she seems to have been busy doing nothing during the majority of the 70s. An extensive search of the internet would suggest that – at the time of writing - she is still alive and is happily enjoying an anonymous retirement, having raised a family and worked for most of her married life outside of the music industry.

Ellen seems to have made most of her recordings pre-1966, releasing 45s under her own name and also as Buttons. Although she recorded several sides as Buttons there's no connection between her and the female vocal act The Buttons who recorded for Dot and Columbia around the same time, nor with the act of the same name who recorded for Arlen. A fourth act called The Buttons recorded for RCA later in the 1960s, but as they originated in Brazil I guess it's safe to assume that Ellen was not affiliated with them either.

There are at least three Buttons 45s on the Rain Coat label and several others under Ellen's own name on Raincoat, the interchangeable name of the record company owned by Joe Leahy, the bandleader, arranger, writer and producer who previously set up the Unique Records label (which would soon become RKO/Unique and issue Leona Anderson's collection *Music To Suffer By*).

At Unique he had discovered the 14 year-old Canadian singer Priscilla Wright and had a sizeable hit with her debut waxing **The Man In The Raincoat**: both Ellen Marty and Joe Leahy would later cover this song, and Joe was so attached to the song that its title would inspire the name of his own label. He left Unique a year or so after the RKO buyout to go to Dot (home, of course, to the doyenne of bad records Pat Boone). An odd coincidence - and a major point of confusion for Ellen Marty collectors - is that Joe was one of Dot's lead A&R men during The Buttons' time at the label. I wonder why he never told Ellen Marty that? Perhaps he did. There's a distinct possibility (in my mind at least, I'll be perfectly honest and admit that I have no evidence at all for this hypothesis) that Ellen may have recorded as Buttons in an effort to emulate some of the success of The Buttons. Or perhaps calling Ellen Marty Buttons was a simple joke: after all, raincoats usually do have buttons, don't they? Perhaps once they realised that there was already an act using that particular moniker the duo decided to revert to Mary Ellen's stage name. Your guess is as good as mine.

Ellen also recorded an album, *Mixing and Making*, for her own Marty Records, an album given three stars by *Billboard* magazine. That LP - on which Ellen was backed by a stellar line up of musicians including drummer Hal Blaine and guitarist Bud Coleman - included her cover of **The Man in the Raincoat** (retitled **Man In A Raincoat**), which was later issued as a 45 (catalogue 601) on both the Raincoat and Marty record labels under its correct title. Perplexed? She followed this up with the 45 **Bobby Died Today** which, despite rumours to the contrary, has nothing whatsoever to do with the death of Bobby Kennedy. There are no dates on any of these releases, but **Bobby Died Today** appears to have been issued in 1966, two years prior to Senator Kennedy's assassination.

Stay away from Bobby they all said
Stay away from Bobby 'cause he's bad
But loved him yeah, how I loved him – oh!
Bobby died today - hey hey! Hey hey! Hey hey!
Bobby died today - hey hey! Hey hey! Hey hey!
Now they're all sorry, they are oh so sorry
Too late! They're sorry, sorry, sorry!

(*Bobby Died Today*, written by Sammy Reese and Ellen Marty. Recorded by Ellen Marty on Raincoat Records. © Lycklig Music)

Bobby Died Today occasionally turns up on the kind of forum that people turn to to discuss their favourite bad records. But it's not a bad record *per se*: it's odd, certainly: the vocal performance is unusual, and the lyrics could have been written by a particularly bratty child, but unlike many of the discs featured on those Worst Records lists – and indeed in this very book – it has its own winsome appeal.

In fact all of Ellen Marty's recordings are a delight: her voice is unconventional to say the least, veering from a kittenish whisper (as on the 45 **Lovetime**) to that of a truculent teenager (vis **Bobby Died Today**) and she occasionally sounds as if she's about to slit her wrists. Her lyrics are distinctly odd (her single **The Barn Is So Far From The Steeple** starts off with the line *'On a day that was warm I decided to be born'*, for example), and her sense of scansion and timing is often at odds with what pop record buyers are used to - as in the odd, hiccoughing rhythm of **Give Me A Raincheck, Baby** which, when I first heard it, had me rushing to ensure that the needle of my tone arm was not skipping across the precious vinyl.

And yet the more of her work I discover, the more in love with her I am becoming. One of her earliest 45s – **A Petal A Day/Baby Blue Eyes** – is a fine example of her slightly off-kilter world. I love the B-side, with its wailing police sirens and jaunty tack piano accompaniment, and the little giggle in Ellen's voice towards the end is a real winner. It could easily be the soundtrack to a cartoon about a prohibition-era speakeasy. The more subdued plug side, **A Petal A Day**, is a miserable little ditty about unrequited love whose lyrics clash ridiculously with the jolly backing track: a suicide note sung to a fast food jingle. The one thing you can say about Ellen's material is that it genuinely deserves the epithet extraordinary.

Unfortunately Ellen Marty the recording artist, songwriter and erstwhile actress seems to have retired: my research has lead me down several dead ends, and the only person I can find still extant today is a 72 year-old housewife whose maiden name was also Mary Ellen Mart. Sadly the two email addresses I have managed to track down for this woman  are both no longer functioning. The former Lycklig offices – just a stone's throw away from Hollywood Boulevard - are now part of an apartment complex.

Perhaps I'll never know who the 'real' Ellen Marty is (or was). Maybe I don't need to. At least she has left me the key to her treasure chest of ever-so-slightly peculiar recordings. And for that I shall always be grateful.

Equipe 84
Auschwitz (1966)

Don't let the majority of the selections in this book kid you into thinking that bad records are the sole preserve of British or American artists: countries around the globe have turned out some spectacularly turgid examples over the years. Often responding to a perceived need for local tongue versions of international hits, there are endless bad covers of Beatles' songs in French, German and Italian (there's even a bizarre Brazilian version of **The Ballad Of John And Yoko** by Los Rockin' Devils) as well as a foreign language version of just about every 50s or 60s hit you can conjure up, ranging from the pedestrian (which covers just about everything ever recorded by French singing sensation Johnny Hallyday) to the downright perverse. Gastone Parigi's attempt at Chubby Checker's enormously popular **The Twist** illustrates the latter beautifully: trumpet player Parigi performs an adequate version of the song in a style that presages Herb Alpert and James Last by several years. It's all perfectly acceptable - until the wacky, unnamed, lead vocalist walks up to the microphone that is and, in his best Peter Lorre voice, adds an altogether bizarre dimension to the recording.

Parigi wasn't the only Italian doing odd things in the name of popular music in the 60s. Who in their right mind would have thought that, just two short decades after the liberation of Auschwitz, the world would have been ready for a pop song about the horrors encountered there? The mind fairly boggles. Perhaps it was an attempt at atonement for the country having chosen to throw their lot in with Mussolini and back the wrong side?

Whatever the reason Italian psychedelic pop act Equipe 84 clearly thought it was a good idea, issuing their song **Auschwitz** in their native country in 1966. The band appears to have been obsessed with violence: it was released as the flip side to their cover of the Cher's hit **Bang Bang** (Dischi Ricordi, 1966), a song which uses shooting guns as a metaphor for the end of a relationship.

I can't quite work out why it stiffed. Surely a song about life (and, consequently, death) in an infamous Nazi concentration camp should have been a hit? How could it fail to chart with lyrics like:

I died when I was a child
I died with hundreds of people
From a furnace through a chimney
And now I am cradled by the wind

(*Auschwitz*, written by Lunero, M Vandelli and T Scott. Recorded by Equipe 84 on Major Minor Records. © 1966, Tee Pee Music Ltd)

It absolutely beggars belief. This was issued in Britain and America in 1967! Peace and love! Hippies and flowers! Hitler and gas chambers! It is thought that around 1,300,000 people were murdered at Auschwitz, and this is the best you can do to honour their memory?

29th September, the B-side of the UK edition, is even better; histrionic caterwauling, dreadfully out of tune vocals and someone intoning the phrase *'29th of September'* (and, later, *'30th of September'*) over and over again. It makes a little more sense in its original language where the disembodied voice repeating the date endlessly is replaced by a radio announcer reading a news story; unfortunately you still get the same histrionic caterwauling, only this time in Italian.

Under its original title of **29 Settembre**, the track first appeared as the A-side of the follow up to **Auschwitz** in early 1967, and provided the group with a huge hit in their native country. Both tracks were re-recorded specifically for the English-speaking market, with English lyrics written by Tommy Scott (a minor 60s recording artist who also coined the English lyrics to the brilliant, Serge Gainsbourg-penned early Eurovision hit **Poupée De Cire, Poupée De Son**), and released as a single in the UK on Major Minor. Equipe 84 had been chosen to spearhead an assault on the British charts by artists from the Dischi Ricordi stable, along with male vocalist Bobby Solo and female singers Milva and Wilma Goich: none of these acts made even the slightest dent on the UK charts. Despite a three-day promotional trip by the group to London, **Auschwitz** really didn't stand a chance: high-profile DJs including David Jacobs and Simon Dee refused to play the record on the grounds of it being in appallingly bad taste.

With the sides flipped, the disc was issued in the USA by Imperial in October 1967. Surprisingly the record flopped there too, making it relatively hard to find these days and rather expensive when copies do turn up. So controversial would **Auschwitz** turn out to be that when Kenny Everett was compiling tracks for his second Bottom 30 (see appendix), although listeners chose the A-side Capital Radio refused to allow him to play it, reluctantly agreeing to air **29th September** instead.

Originally formed in Modena in 1963, Equipe (Italian for Team) 84 was one of Italy's most successful beat/psych bands, their chart career filled with covers of British and American hits such as **Blackberry Way** (as T*utta Mia la Citta*), **Papa Oom Mow Mow** (as *Papa e Mamma*), **Go Now** (*Ora Puoi Tornare*) and the aforementioned **Bang Bang** badly translated into Italian, plus their own highly derivative originals and some examples of leftfield madness like **Auschwitz** and **29th September**. The band released seven albums (and a whole bunch of live albums and compilations) and around 30 singles before splitting at the end of the 1970s: drummer Alfio Cantarella was forced out of the band for three years (1970-73) after he was arrested for possession of a small amount of marijuana (this act necessitated a short-term name change to Nuovo Equipe 84).

A new version of the band, fronted by original members Victor Sogliani and Franco Ceccarelli came together - appropriately enough - in 1984. That incarnation continued for a further decade, releasing one album of new material, before once again imploding. Singer and bass guitarist Sogliani formed a new band, Equipe Extra-D, in 1995, but sadly died of a brain aneurysm the same year. Co-founder Franco Ceccarelli, the group's lead singer and guitarist, who originally left in 1970 shortly after Cantarella was ousted from the band, continued to step out from time to time under the band's moniker until he passed away, at the age of 70, a few days before Christmas 2012.

Star Dreck

When, in 1964, scriptwriter Gene Roddenberry came up with the idea for a TV western set in outer space ("a Wagon Train to the stars", is how he pitched it to production company Desilu) he could have had no idea that *Star Trek* would grow into the behemoth it is today. Inspired by 30s cinema serials including *Buck Rogers* and *Flash Gordon*, the original three season run has spawned spin off after spin off, a massively successful film franchise, cartoons, books and collectables, all eagerly devoured by a legion of dedicated fans who immerse themselves in all things Trekkian - some going as far to have their own weddings conducted in Klingon. And, if you're looking for a Klingon-speaking spouse, there's even a *Star Trek* dating service – www.startrekdating.com. Roddenberry certainly could not have imagined, especially after his initial pilot (*The Cage*) was rejected, that his little show would grow and grow, outliving its' creator and continuing to be reinterpreted to this day. Five decades after it debuted, *Star Trek* is still huge: it's a genuine cultural phenomenon.

Of course, when a TV show is that big it's only a matter of time before someone involved realises that there are umpteen ways to make money out of its' fanatical following. First came the toys (including a board game and plastic replicas of the USS Enterprise), the children's annuals, the cereal packet giveaways and the comic books - although it wasn't until the show went in to syndication in the early 70s that the real drive to merchandise started. However with several larger than life characters appearing on American TV screens every week something else was needed to satiate the voracious desire of fans of the show for Trek-related material.

Desilu executive Herbert F Solow was the first to see the huge potential for merchandising . Approached by Dot Records (the home of Pat Boone) with the idea of a *Star Trek*-themed album, he sent a memo around the set telling his crew that *'I think we should push any record company that wants to do an 'outer space' or Vulcan or any other single record or album'.* Clearly quality was to be no hindrance to making a fast buck: as the memo made plain, that record could be *'straight dramatic music, weird music, Nichelle Nichols singing, Bill Shatner doing bird calls or even the sound of Gene Roddenberry polishing a semi-precious stone on his grinder'.*

Which is why, in December 1966, slap bang in the middle of the first season being aired, the breakout star of the show, Leonard Nimoy, was 'encouraged' to record and release his first album: *Mr Spock's Music From Outer Space*. Spock, the pointy-eared Vulcan, was the science officer and second-in-command of the Enterprise, and was the only character from the original pilot to appear in the series when it finally reached the screen. Nimoy himself, minus the weird ears, violently tweezed eyebrows and pudding basin haircut, was already a well-known face on US TV, with roles in *Bonanza, Rawhide, Perry Mason, The Outer Limits, The Virginian* and *Get Smart* among others. It seemed obvious then that Spock, the acceptable alien, was the perfect front man for an album of space age pop. Unfortunately on *Mr Spock's Music From Outer Space* Nimoy – who, according to the sleeve notes, had some experience of the musical stage – is little more than a guest star on his own record. The album features some retro cool lounge sounds and is a fun listen, although it's hardly a Leonard Nimoy 'solo' outing. He co-wrote the track **Twinkle, Twinkle Little Earth** with arranger and producer Charles Grean, and sings a wonderfully flat version of **Where Is Love** from the soundtrack of *Oliver!* but the album is a jumble of keyboard-based instrumentals with a couple of space-themed narrations and includes just three 'traditional' vocal performances.

"I had a great time doing it," he told Dave Itzkoff of the *New York Times* in 2009. "I never looked for a recording career. Somebody from the studio came to me one day and said, *'there's a gentleman in New York who's producing an album of music from* Star Trek. *Your picture as Spock is going to be on the cover. Would you like to be involved in the making of the album?'* I thought I should be. They had already recorded six of the 12 tracks, and in a very short period of time we recorded the other six tracks".

There are only 11 tracks on *Mr Spock's Music From Outer Space* but we'll forgive him this little error. After all, to argue with Spock would be highly illogical!

Fans of the truly awful would have to wait a few months for Nimoy to deliver on his promise. Over the next three years he would release four further albums; each took him further and further away from his Spock persona and each contained more than their fair share of truly dire performances. The standout track from his second album (*Two Sides Of Leonard Nimoy*) is probably the best known of all Trek-related music: the Charles Grean composition **The Ballad Of Bilbo Baggins**. "I was doing some recordings, and a producer sent me this song, which I thought was very charming. I was very interested in the Hobbit stories," Nimoy told Brazilian writer Salvador Nogueira in a 2003 interview. Issued as a single in July 1967, the infamy of this ridiculous romp through the Shire has grown and grown over the years, principally because there is also a film clip of Nimoy performing the song (from a long-forgotten US variety show), surrounded by a bunch of brazen beatnik girls in go-go pants and pointy ears.

Leonard's five albums include covers of some of the biggest hits of the time – **If I Were A Carpenter**, **I Walk The Line**, **Gentle On My Mind**, **Proud Mary**, **Love Of The Common People**, **Ruby Don't Take Your Love To Town** and **If I Had A Hammer** among them – all delivered in Len's flat-as-a-pancake, deadpan style. Many of his recordings have been compiled on CD, but fortunately for those of us with tender, non-Vulcan ears, he resolutely refused to enter a recording studio after 1970. Sadly, Leonard Nimoy passed away on February 27, 2015.

In early 1968, producer Don Ralke and William Shatner, whose chance to record an album of bird calls had been criminally overlooked two years earlier, entered the studio for a series of sessions that resulted in *The Transformed Man* – one of the most ridiculous (and ridiculed) records of all time. *'Until that moment my singing career had been limited to auditioning once for a Broadway musical and being told by the director to focus on acting,'* Bill wrote in his biography *Up Till Now*. *'But in 1968 Decca Records asked me if I was interested in doing an album. I hesitated, I wasn't a singer...'*

Perhaps the most famous (or infamous) Trek star turned musical performer, Shatner has claimed that he was inspired to make *The Transformed Man* after experiencing an epiphany in the desert following a motorcycle accident. Called 'a beautiful narrative offering that could easily be a winning sales item' by *Billboard, The Transformed Man* is an amazingly awful album, featuring Shatner reciting soliloquies from Shakespeare alongside bizarre renditions of acid-pop hits including **Lucy In The Sky With Diamonds** and **Mr Tambourine Man**. His interpretation of the Dylan classic has been lambasted for his idiosyncratic presentation: Bill has been quoted as saying he wanted his performance to mirror the anguish suffered by a drug addict going cold turkey. Well, it certainly is a turkey.

'The reviews were very mixed,' he wrote in *Up Till Now*. *'While some critics wrote that it was the worst album ever produced, others felt just as strongly that there had never been an album like it before. I didn't mind. I'd pushed the envelope, perhaps I'd pushed a little too far, but I'd tried. I'd taken a creative risk. I'd tried to do something unique.'*

'It all made perfect sense to me. But apparently it was a bit obtuse for some other people. All right, for most people.'

1967/8 was a tough year for Shatner – *Star Trek* was axed after its second season (only to be reprieved thanks to a massively successful letter writing campaign by fans of the show), his estranged father had died and his marriage had collapsed. Bill candidly admits that, during this time, he was "insane. I'd lost my family, I'd lost everything". Desperate, the star was reduced to living in a camper van as he toured the States looking for stage work. It was at this point that he had the accident that would change his life forever. Riding through the Mojave Desert with friends his bike hit a rock and he was thrown from his seat, knocking himself out. When he came to he swears that he was guided through the desert

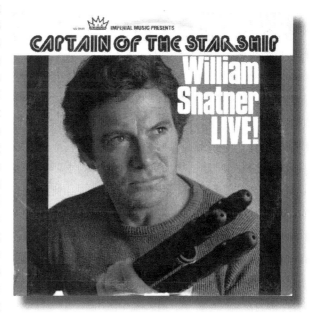

to safety by a dark presence and, along the way, encountered a UFO.

The full story on Shatner's near-death experience (overlooked completely in the original sleeve notes for *The Transformed Man)* has been examined in the book *The Emerald Tablet: Alchemy of Personal Transformation* by self-proclaimed modern-day alchemist Dennis William Hauck. Hauck is also the author of the scurrilous tome *Captain Quirk - the Unauthorized Biography of William Shatner*. A hatchet job if there ever was one, *Captain Quirk* paints Shatner as a UFO-obsessed, toupee-wearing tyrant. It would be 35 years before Shatner would dare enter a recording studio again when, under the auspices of Ben Folds, he would stun the world with the truly exceptional *Has Been*, featuring the talents of Henry Rollins, Joe Jackson and others, and its hit single **Common People**.

Since then he has released two further albums – *Seeking Major Tom* and *Ponder the Mystery* – both thick slices of overcooked but well-received ham performed in Bill's inimitable sing-speak style. I should also mention his 1977 release *William Shatner Live!*, a double album recorded when his career was in the doldrums – not for the material (basically Bill chatting to a rapt audience of Trek fans) but for its hideous cover, which featured Shatner in a cable-knit jumper, roughly the same colour as his *Star Trek* dress uniform, brandishing the base of a microphone stand as if it were some kind of intergalactic weapon. Unfortunately that particular slice of kitsch fell by the wayside when the album was reissued on CD.

In most examinations of Star Trek-related recordings Nichelle Nichols gets off rather easily. A genuine singer, the woman born Grace Nichols had performed with Lionel Hampton and Duke Ellington before she landed the role of Lieutenant Uhura on *Star Trek*, and it's often assumed that, as a singer, her albums are at least passable. Well, they're not. She may be famous for sharing TV's first interracial kiss with Bill Shatner (it wasn't, but it was the first between a Caucasian man and an African-American woman on prime time) but that does not excuse her from making some terrible records.

Down to Earth (1967), produced by the legendary Larry Williams (of **Dizzy Miss Lizzy** and **Slow Down** fame), highlights Nichelle's limitations: the opening track, a cover of the Nina Simone classic **Feelin' Good** would probably have been fine if arranger Gerald Wilson had given it a more obvious setting, but turning the song into a 60's discotheque stomper does Nichelle's voice no favours at all. Yes, she can sing, but she has a particular nightclub style that doesn't fit the lush orchestral arrangements, and her vocal swoops on **Tenderly** are, frankly, foolish.

At points – especially during **The More I See You** - it sounds as if the band and the artist are performing different songs. If Nichelle's voice had been given a more intimate backdrop – more smoky club than full-on Broadway review – I've no doubt that she would have fared far better. Still, it's nowhere near as bad as the offerings from Shatner or Nimoy. The shoddy CD reissue adds four extra tracks to the album's original 10 – misnaming two of them and including two that have no input from Nichelle at all: **Star Trek Theme** and **The Star Trek Philosophy**, the latter of which is 'performed' – or rather was culled from one of his many lecture tours - by head honcho Roddenberry, Nichelle's one-time lover. The track had originally appeared on the album *Inside Star Trek*, a mostly spoken word audio documentary about the making of the series, featuring Rodenberry, Shatner, Nichols, DeForest Kelley (Doctor Leonard 'Bones' McCoy) and sci-fi legend Isaac Asimov.

The album didn't do much business: just one year later, and while still a member of the *Star Trek* cast, Nichelle was forced to file for bankrupcy, telling a Los Angeles court that she was broke despite being paid $1,000 a week to appear on the show.

24 years later Nichelle would release her follow-up, *Out of This World* (she also issued a four track EP *The Dark Side Of the Moon* in 1974). This ghastly album includes two versions of **Gene**, a tribute to Roddenberry (*Gene, oh future visionary/ You gave me tears and laughter/you shined the starlight o'er my dreams, Gene*), a Eurodisco version of the **Theme From Star Trek** and **Beyond Antares** (which had

previously been issued as a single), a song which had been performed by Nichelle in character as Uhura in the first season episode *The Conscience Of The King* and which had appeared in instrumental form on *Mr Spock's Music From Outer Space. Out of This World* is not a good album: with her screeching and wailing vocals Nichelle often sounds like she's trying to imitate Yoko Ono. At other times she sounds like a goose trying to have sex with a car horn.

Nichelle's importance comes not from her role as Uhura, nor her singing, but for the amazing role model she has been for black women everywhere. A television trailblazer, she spearheaded a campaign to encourage women and people from minority ethnic backgrounds to apply to work for NASA, has worked for and set up charities to help the homeless and has tirelessly fought for the rights of the poor to a decent eduaction. She may not be the world's greatest singer, but she sure is one hell of a human being.

Even though he is virtually omnipresent these days, thanks to his Facebook, Twitter and his own website, it seems unlikely that we'll ever get the opportunity to purchase an album by George Takei, the show's Mr Sulu, however he did sing briefly on the US TV show *Secret Talents Of The Stars*. The late James Doohan (Scotty) sang in the *Star Trek* animated TV series – unfortunately though this was never committed to vinyl, and even Walter Koenig, the show's Mr Chekov, has been known to burst forth with a bar or two at fan conventions. However as far as I am aware, only one other member of the original *Star Trek* cast actually cut a record – and that was Grace Lee Whitney.

Whitney, who played Yeoman Janice Rand until she was axed halfway through the first season (she would rejoin the franchise in the 1970s after DeForest Kelley saw her in an unemployment line) sang with a number of orchestras and bands, and even opened for the legendary Billie Holliday. Plagued by a 20-year-old drinking problem — which was aggravated by the diet pills she took to fit into her Starfleet uniform and by a serious sexual assault that took place shortly before the role of Rand was cancelled, Whitney descended into a world of drink, drugs and promiscuity that, according to an interview she gave to *People* magazine in 1993, even led her to the brink of prostitution.

With her then-husband, Jack Dale, Grace wrote a number of *Star Trek*-related songs, issuing the 45 **Disco Trekkin'** backed with **Star Child** in 1976 (as Grace Lee Whitney and Star on her own GLW label), a miserable slice of sub-par disco with overwrought vocals that would make even Nichelle Nichols blush. Grace would go on to self-release a couple of cassette-only albums, *Light At The End Of The Tunnel* in 1996 and *Yeoman Rand Sings!* in 1999, produced for the Trek fan market. Unless you're a real Trek-head, or a

WILLIAM SHATNER, Decca artist and star of NBC-TV's "Star Trek," visits Joe Taras (right), Billboard's assistant director of reviews and charts, on behalf of the Decca LP, "The Transformed Man."

complete masochist, I wouldn't waste your time trying to track down either of them.

In September 1987 the *Star Trek* universe expanded with *Star Trek: The Next Generation* (or TNG, as it is known among fans) and since then a number of Trek actors have issued records. Brent Spiner, TNG's Commander Data has a brace of easy listening albums. His first, *Ol' Yellow Eyes Is Back* (1988), features backing vocals on one track from fellow TNG actors LeVar Burton, Michael Dorn, Jonathan Frakes and Patrick Stewart. Other Trek alumni to record include Nana Visitor (*Deep Space Nine*'s Kira Nerys), James Darren (the holographic lounge singer Vic Fontaine, also from DS9), Chase Masterson (Leeta) and Tim Russ, who portrayed different characters in TNG, DS9 and *Star Trek: Voyager*. Sadly for fans of the perverse none of them are as dreadful as their original series antecedents, so none of them really deserve more than a cursory mention here.

Dion
Purple Haze (1968)

You'll all remember Dion. You may well have cut a rug to his big hits: **Runaround Sue, A Teenager In Love** and **The Wanderer**. It's even possible that you know that he recorded the original version of the Marvin Gaye classic **Abraham, Martin And John**. However it's less likely that you'll know the follow up - the unmitigated flop (it barely scratched the charts, reaching a miserable number 63 in the States) that is his peculiar folkie version of the Jimi Hendrix classic **Purple Haze**.

Issued as a single in January 1969, although it debuted on Dion's self-titled comeback album the previous year, it really is a mess. But that's probably to be expected when you consider the absolute mess that Dion DiMucci's life had been in prior to recording this.

DiMucci grew up in the Bronx, a middle-class boy of Italian origin with a hard-nosed attitude. He also had quite a voice, and – as legend has it – he could often be found on street corners belting out traditional Italian songs and current hits. Along the way he also picked up a drug habit that would eventually lead him in to heroin addiction – something that would cause problems in his life for well over a decade. He released a few early cuts with a group called the Timberlanes, but by 1958 Dion had joined up with another Bronx-based group The Belmonts – so-called because the vocal quartet rehearsed in Belmont Avenue in the Bronx's Little Italy ghetto. Dion and The Belmonts were signed to Laurie records, recorded a song called **I Wonder Why** and scored the first of a string of doo-wop influenced hits.

A Teenager in Love followed, and in 1959 the group was booked on to a rock `n` roll tour, the Winter Dance Party, headlined by Buddy Holly but with a bill that also included Richie Valens and The Big Bopper. One night during the tour, fed up with motoring through the countryside on a bus with no heating, Holly decided to charter a single-engined Beechcraft Bonanza plane to fly the stars from Mason City, Iowa (not Clear Lake, as is usually reported: that was the venue for what turned out to be their last show), to Fargo, North Dakota for $36 apiece. Dion balked at the price - he could not justify spending what, he later wrote in his 1988 book *The Wanderer: Dion's Story* equalled the monthly rent his parents paid for his childhood apartment - and stayed with the bus.

Also on the bus was the young guitar player Waylon Jennings: when Holly learned that Jennings was not going to join him on the flight he is reputed to have joked: "Well, I hope your ol' bus freezes up". As Jennings wrote, in his own book *Waylon: An Autobiography*, he responded to Holly's joke with the line "Well, I hope your ol' plane crashes," a throwaway comment that would haunt Jennings until he himself passed away 43 years later. Holly, aged 22, JP "Big Bopper" Richardson (28) and Valens - who had not yet celebrated his 18th birthday - all perished when the tiny aircraft spun out of control during a snowstorm and crashed. The three rockers were thrown from the plane, dying instantly. Only the pilot, Roger Peterson, was still in the wreckage.

Dion left the Belmonts in 1960, enjoying a succession of solo hits including **Runaround Sue**, **The Wanderer** and **Ruby Baby**. But as tastes changed, and the British Invasion all but killed his career (a change of styles from doo-wop and rock'n'roll to pop and blues yielded zero hits and almost zero sales), his addiction to drugs – heroin and LSD – all but killed him: he attempted suicide. He checked into a hospital to try and beat his heroin addiction, only to become an alcoholic instead. He moved to Boca Raton, Florida with his wife and young daughter, kicked his alcoholism and took stock of where his life was at. Signing a new contract with his old label Laurie he recorded - at their behest - **Abraham, Martin And John**, which sold three million copies and reached number four. And then he released this clunker which, in an insult to end all insults, charted higher than the original.

I don't buy in to the idea that his unusual interpretation of **Purple Haze** was a brave move: it's a disaster. The radical arrangement, which buries Hendrix's wild, stomping original tune in a sub-Donovan acoustic hippy-dippy wash, is trying to be clever and hip but fails miserably. With its insipid *'fa-la-laa'* opening

Dion sounds like a bored club singer riffing along to the tune of **Puff, The Magic Dragon** to me. He's not the only artist to murder Purple Haze: in the same year that Dion recorded his version the now-beleaguered Bill Cosby stole the tune for his track **Hooray For The Salvation Army Band**, leaving Jimi uncredited and unpaid. In more recent years The Cure produced their own bizarre cover of the song for the album *Stone Free: A Tribute To Jimi Hendrix*.

Coming from a man who cheated death several times you'd expect something a bit more life affirming. And don't you think it a bit odd that a man who had recently beaten smack addiction should be singing a song which was widely believed to be about drug use? Perhaps the newly born-again Dion knew something that the rest of the world didn't: Hendrix himself would later state that **Purple Haze** was inspired by a dream he had in which he was walking under the sea with Jesus. The song's original title was Purple Haze – Jesus Saves. The B-side, a cover of the Fred Neil eco-awareness song **The Dolphins**, is just plain boring; a faux folkie snooze. The accompanying album, *Dion*, peaked at a pathetic 128; it would be his last album to chart any higher than 197 until his 1989 collection *Yo Frankie* launched the third stage in his career.

A born-again Christian who these days - at the age of 75 - gives ministry in prisons and uses his own dark experiences to inform his work with addicts, Dion is still recording and he's been nominated for a Grammy twice in recent years. Rightfully revered as one of the elder statesmen of Rock 'n' Roll – he was one of only two rock artists (along with Bob Dylan) to featured among the crowd on the Beatles' *Sgt. Pepper's Lonely Hearts Club Band* cover - let's just hope he never does anything this horrid again.

The Shaggs
Philosophy Of The World (1969)

'Betty, Helen and Dorothy Wiggin are the Shaggs. They are sisters and members of a large family where mutual respect and love for each other is at an unbelievable high. They study and practice together, encouraged and helped by those around them. They are happy people and love what they are doing' - From the original sleeve notes of *Philosophy of the World*.

No collection of bad records would be complete without a copy of *Philosophy of the World* by The Shaggs: the debut album by the group made up of three of the four daughters of the Wiggin family, of Fremont, New Hampshire. An uglier, more discordant mess would be hard to imagine; Frank Zappa rated it as his third favourite album of all time and thought that the Shaggs were, in his own words, 'better than the Beatles'.

The daughters of Austin Wiggin Jr. only issued one 45 and one album during their career, yet original copies are so hard to come by – and so prized by collectors – that on the rare occasion they do turn up for sale they command huge prices: an original Third World Recordings pressing of the album sold in March 2014 for $5,000, and you can expect to pay $500 or thereabouts for a copy of the Fleetwood Records 45 of **My Pal Foot Foot** backed with **Things I Wonder** (with the band's name misspelled as The Shags on the label).

An employee at the Exeter textile mill, legend has it that Austin's faith in the girls was inspired by a prophecy handed to him by his mother, an armchair psychic. She told her son that he would marry a strawberry blonde, that he would have two sons that she would not live to see, and that he would watch his daughters play in a band. The first two parts of her prediction came true, and Austin was determined that the third part would also come to pass, pulling the girls out of school and buying them instruments. Neither he nor his wife, Annie, were particularly musical (although Austin did play the Jew's Harp), and the girls showed little interest at first, although they were fans of many of the British invasion groups - particularly Herman's Hermits - and the US teen act Dino, Desi and Billy. "I don't think we would've thought about it if he didn't come up with the idea first," Dorothy 'Dot' Semprini (nee Wiggin) told Associated Press reporter Holly Ramer in 2000. "But we thought it was a good idea." The poor but superstitious Austin had the girls travel to Manchester each week, 20 miles away from their home, for music lessons, and each day they would practice their art in the basement of their house, leaving the concrete bunker only to eat, sleep and spend a couple of hours on lessons. Even though they were no longer in state school they kept up with their studies thanks to mail-order classes purchased by their parents from the Chicago-based American Home School.

Their first public performance was at a talent show in Exeter in 1968. The girls could barely play and didn't think they were ready, but naturally Austin knew better. The began their set with a cover of The String-A-Longs' instrumental hit **Wheels**, and were horrified when people in the audience jeered at their ineptitude and threw soda cans at them. Austin simply told his daughters that they needed to practice more. Shortly afterwards their father arranged for the basement band to play at dances held at the Fremont Town Hall every Saturday night: the girls performed almost exclusively there, and at a local nursing home, for the next five years. Their two brothers helped them by carrying and setting up their equipment, whilst the Shaggs (named by their father because of the girls' long, shaggy hairstyles) played cover songs and a handful of originals composed by Dot. A fourth sister, Rachel, would occasionally join the trio on bass, and Mom and Pop Wiggin ran the food and soft drinks concession. Most of the people who saw the sisters play would agree that they were terrible, but Austin Wiggin was convinced that his girls were going to be huge stars. "There were some kids who might poke fun or say mean things," Dot told Ramer. "But not a whole lot."

With plenty of practise and a few live gigs under their collective belts, Austin decided that it was time for his girls to do their thing for a wider audience. On March 9, 1969 he drove them 50 miles south, to Fleetwood Studios in Revere, Massachusetts (housed in a converted supermarket) so that the young women – by now aged between 18 and 22 – could record the tracks that would end up on their album. The Shaggs recorded all 12 tracks for *Philosophy Of The World* in one session. "I want to get them while they're hot," Austin is reputed to have told the recording engineer. "We didn't think we were ready to record anything," Betty later confided in Holly Ramer.

The sounds that the girls laid down in that recording studio are like nothing on earth: these recordings are not good, but they are great. Helen's drumming is woefully inept and the guitars are ridiculously out of tune. The Wiggin sisters display no sense of timing, either racing through their songs - all written by Dot and covering everything from family friction (**What Are Parents**), a two legged, missing cat (**My Pal Foot Foot**) and religion (**We Have A Savior**) to teenage angst (**Why Do I Feel?**) and holidays (**It's Halloween**) - or plodding through them in the vain hope that the hapless Helen might eventually catch up. As Susan Orlean wrote in *The New Yorker* magazine in 1999 *'Listening to the Shaggs' album will further confound. The music is winsome but raggedly discordant pop. Something is sort of wrong with the tempo, and the melodies are squashed and bent, nasal, deadpan. Are the Shaggs referencing the heptatonic, angular microtones of Chinese ya-yueh court music and the atonal note clusters of Ornette Coleman, or are they just a bunch of kids playing badly on cheap, out-of-tune guitars?'* Orlean also reveals that Austin had been intimate with at least one of his daughters (Helen) and that *'Austin's father and Annie's mother, after they were both widowed, became romantically involved and lived together in a small house on the Wiggin property'*. Talk about keeping it in the family.

Given a decent producer and a few days in the studio then it's vaguely possible that the Wiggin girls may have been able to come up with something salvageable. However, with Austin in the producer's chair and barely enough funds for one 12-hour session that was never going to happen. The embryonic record label Third World Recordings - set up by former Fleetwood staffers Charlie Dreyer and Bobby Herne - was charged with pressing and distributing 1,000 copies of *Philosophy Of The World* but, apparently, only 100 were ever circulated to the public. The remaining 900 were either taken by Dreyer and/or Herne, kept under lock and key by Austin (paranoid that other acts would copy The Shaggs' sound) or thrown out with the trash because the band, their father, or their record company could not give them away. According to Dot (in the liner notes to *The Shaggs*) *'the man who released Philosophy just disappeared. We were supposed to get a lot of albums for the price my father paid, and we only got one box. He just didn't keep his word...my father even got a lawyer after him to locate him and find out what the story was, and the lawyer couldn't find him'.*

The album's success was further hampered by the fact that there were at least two other acts called The Shaggs on the circuit at the same time as the Wiggin girls: a psych-garage band from Florida (who recorded for Power Records) and the Michigan rock 'n' roll revivalists who issued a cover of the Elvis hit **Mean Woman Blues** on Capitol. Austin managed to get a little local airplay for his daughters' album, and the girls even wrote and performed a jingle for Boston-based WBCN, but outside of that *Philosophy Of The World* received zero promotion.

The Town Hall performances stopped in 1973: alcohol and drugs had started to infiltrate the dances and, after several violent incidents Fremont town council decided enough was enough: *'it started getting rowdy and there were a few fights,'* Dot admitted, *'so they made us quit.'* The Wiggin family patriarch was furious; especially when he discovered that Helen - at that point still living under his roof - had secretly married her first and only boyfriend, Henry Bickford, a man that she had met at the very same weekly Town Hall hops. The band's drummer continued living at home for three months after her secret wedding, too terrified to tell her abusive father what she had done. When he finally found out he took a shotgun and went looking for his new son-in-law. Thankfully the police intervened before any blood was spilled. Helen was forced to choose between the two men in her life: she left with her husband, and it was months before Austin spoke to her again. Helen was 26 years old and summarily dismissed from her role behind the drum kit.

On Christmas Eve 1973 tracks from *Philosophy Of The World* were aired nationally for the first time, when Frank Zappa, acting as gust DJ on the syndicated Dr Demento radio show, played two songs by The Shaggs: **My Pal Foot Foot** and **It's Halloween**.

In 1975, after the family dramas died down and father and daughter were reconciled, Austin dragged the girls back into the studio to record a follow up to *Philosophy Of The World*, but the girls' sophomore effort failed to materialise. Austin died of a heart attack the same year. Several of the tracks from that aborted second album turned up on the posthumous release *The Shaggs' Own Thing* (which also featured contributions from Austin and the girls' youngest brother, Robert) in 1982.

And that should have been it. Well, it would have been if it were not for the sterling work of DJ, writer, and outsider music aficionado Irwin Chusid, and Terry Adams, the keyboard player with NRBQ, who championed the band and ensured that *Philosophy Of The World* was reissued (via NRBQ's own Red Rooster label). It's thanks to these two men that the Godmothers of Outsider Music are known to us at all.

Acting on the interest garnered by their interest in the Wiggin sisters, the album was reissued once again by Rounder Records, prompting *Rolling Stone* to pronounce the group the Comeback of the Year (even though the same magazine dismissed the girls as *'lobotomised Von Trapp Family Singers'*) and for one reviewer to call *Philosophy Of The World* *'the most stunningly awful wonderful record I've ever heard.'* The magazine would later rank *Philosophy Of The World* as one of the 100 Most Influential Alternative Releases of All Time. Legendary rock critic Lester Bangs declared it to be a *'landmark in rock 'n' roll history'* in *The Village Voice*, and Nirvana front man Kurt Cobain became a huge advocate the band, putting their album at number five in his all-time Top 50 and cementing their reputation among indie artists as pioneers of the DIY movement. To their puzzlement the three Wiggin girls – by now middle-aged, married and with children of their own – not only began to receive fan mail from all over the world but also saw their very first royalty cheques.

On Chusid's recommendation RCA decided to reissue *Philosophy Of The World* on CD, making their music available to an even wider audience. A CD-only compilation *The Shaggs* – collecting their entire recorded output

– appeared, and a stage musical based on the Shaggs' career – also called *Philosophy Of The World* – debuted in 2003; there are tentative plans in the pipeline for a movie version. There's even been a tribute album, its title inspired by Zappa: *Better Than The Beatles*.

"The really cool part, to me, is that it's thirty years later and we're still talking about it," Dot told Susan Orlean in 1999. "I never thought we'd really be famous. I never thought we'd even be as famous as we are. I met a girl at the Shop 'n Save the other day who used to come to the dances, and she said she wanted to go out now and buy the CD. And I saw a guy at a fair recently and talked to him for about half an hour about the Shaggs. And people call and ask if they can come up and meet us - that's amazing to me."

The girls have only played together once since their heyday, with Dot and Betty supporting their supporters NRBQ at a showcase event in 1999. Helen, after suffering from years of crippling depression, sadly passed away in 2006. She was just 59, yet spent her last days in the Glencliff Home for the Elderly, around 100 miles north of the family's Fremont home. More recently Dot has resumed a career in music, fronting her own Dot Wiggin Band and releasing her debut solo album *Ready! Get! Go!* - which featured the previously unrecorded Shaggs songs **Banana Bike** and **The Fella With A Happy Heart** - on Alternative Tentacles in October 2013.

Check it out: it's a fun album, and Dot has lost none of her charm. True, it's much more polished than anything put out by The Shaggs, but it still has a rough and ready appeal and Dot's earnest, naïve lyrics shine through.

Welcome home Dot: it's great to have you back.

Troy Hess
America's Singing Souvenir

Singer and songwriter Troy Hess is used to packing out halls. Performing all over his home state, Hess was born to sing: "I love it," he tells me. "It's in my blood." After years of fronting hardworking covers band Zebra Three and, more recently, the Texas Heartbreakers, he's still working on his own new material and hopes to release some of it soon.

Yes, Hess was born to sing: literally. The scion of country singer Bennie Hess, by the age of two he was appearing on stage; within 12 months he had released his first single and by the age of 10 he was being pilloried in the press - a has-been before he'd even entered his teenage years. Still plying his art, in his early 20s he had another stab at fame, only to have it cruelly snatched away from him. It's hardly surprising that it's taken him this long to dare to step into the recording studio again. Especially when he gets such a rough ride from critics for his early output: a collection of singles much-loved by aficionados of the obscure that he began at the age of three and which includes such classics as **Christmas On The Moon, Wild Hog Boogie, The Ballad Of Troy Hess** and **Please Don't Go Topless, Mother**.

Born in 1965, before he'd reached his fourth birthday Troy had released a brace of 45s and was being promoted variously as the *World's Youngest Recording Star* or as *America's Singing Souvenir*. Bennie – at 6'6" a veritable giant of the country scene - had been recording since the 1940s and had a colourful career of his own, founding

several record labels and associating with Elvis Presley: the King's early manager Biff Collie also promoted Bennie Hess, often on the same bill as the Tupelo Kid. Born Orville Hess in 1914, he was taught how to play guitar by the legendary white blues singer Jimmie Rodgers (Bennie's father Cap and Rodgers had worked on the railways together) and his own performing style was heavily influenced both by Rodgers and by country pioneer Ernest Tubb.

Bennie hero-worshipped Jimmie: it is claimed that Carrie Rodgers (Jimmie's widow) gave The Singing Brakeman's guitar to young Bennie – an instrument which, if the story is true (this is disputed by Rodgers' biographer Nolan Porterfield) was the first Martin guitar ever made and was worth a small fortune. Bennie was also reputed to be the keeper of several unreleased Rodgers acetates. Although prolific and well-connected, Bennie would never have a hit under his own name – and the effort he put into promoting Troy's career would lead many people to accuse him of fulfilling his dreams of fame vicariously through his son.

"It's been an up-hill battle since I was a child," Troy confides. "I made my first appearance on stage with Bob Wills & His Texas Playboys in my hometown of Caldwell, Texas; Bob was an old friend of my dad's. I was considered to be a novelty, and it afforded me the opportunity to play on stage with folks like Johnny Cash, Ernest Tubb, Porter Wagoner, Dolly Parton and George Jones - whom my dad actually had in his band back in the early 50s playing lead guitar." It was around this time – 1969 - that Troy released his first record, a cover of Jimmie Rodgers' **Blue Yodel Number 9**, backed with the three year-old's debut solo composition **The Ballad Of Troy Hess**. It's a ridiculous record: Troy sounds exactly like a three year-old should sound. The backing band is fine, but the child's vocal performance is a virtually unintelligible caterwaul: out of tune, out of time and as flat and raspy as a woodworking tool. It's a sound only a grandmother could love. He followed this up the following year with the equally unlistenable **Christmas On The Moon**, written for him by his father, which music blogger Steve Carey once described as *'Huckleberry Hound talking to you on a broken telephone, with a bad connection, in a big echo-y bathroom, standing ten feet away from the phone. Also he's wearing a mask and eating a banana.'*

Others have followed in his footsteps: in 1974 country music's golden couple – George Jones and Tammy Wynette – roped their eight-year-old daughter Tina in to record a horrid version of **No Charge** (backed with the dreadful **Telephone Call**); over in Oklahoma Little Kristy *'She's*

Only 6 Year's Old!' (sic) McIntire was gurgling the line *'You ain't woman enough to take my man and these boots'* on her Ranger Records 45 **I Want Someone Who Needs Me/Little Miss Dynamite**. Little Brad Williams was just five years old when he recorded and released his first album *Elvira*. Still performing today, as bass player with the group Southern Accent, according to the sleeve notes *'Brad performed his first song,* **Just A Little Talk With Jesus** *when he was 20 months old'*. "Being a novelty opened a lot of doors for me," Troy candidly admits, "But some remained closed. My parents were told that the music industry would never seriously consider me as an artist because I was just a child. There were stars like Donny Osmond and Michael Jackson, but the country music industry of the early 70s was much more conservative so I was never taken seriously. Still, it didn't stop me from performing."

Bennie, who had produced some of Kenny Rogers' earliest sides and was now running his own company Show Land Records, continued to issue Troy's 45s as well as discs by other local artists. And, at the ripe old age of seven, Troy would record a song for his dad's company for which he will forever be remembered. That song was called **Please Don't Go Topless, Mother**.

The story begins when nascent songwriter Ron Hellard brought Bennie and his second wife Dorothy (or Dot, as she was always known) a tune he had written specifically with Troy in mind. "Gary Paxton *(the songwriter famous for* **The Monster Mash** *and, as we saw in The World's Worst Records Volume One, the horrific anti-abortion classic* **The Big "A" = The Big "M"**) came into Buddy Lee Attractions in Nashville where my mom was working," says Troy. "He had Ron Hellard with him, and Gary introduced Ron to mom. Ron and Gary knew of me, and mom jokingly asked Ron to write me a song. The result was **Please Don't Go Topless Mother**, and mom was not impressed."

In fact, Troy's churchgoing parents were highly offended by the impious subject matter of this particular song but, as he tells me: "As word of the song got around - and with Paxton and other music people supporting it - mom and dad finally caved in and had me record it."

Oh, please don't go topless, Mother
I hate to be quite so blunt
The kids all laugh but I don't cry
You're not the only one who's putting up a front

(*Please Don't Go Topless, Mother*. Written by Ron Hellard; recorded by Troy Hess on Show Land Records. © 1972, Acoustic Music)

Troy regards the release as "a catastrophe! Radio station managers refused to play the song, even though I had received airplay before; I believe the only disc jockey who did play it was Ralph Emery on (Nashville-based AM station) WSM. But it was a disaster and, after mailing out a little over 1000, pressing was halted and the record shelved!" It has since been reissued – without licence - on Dutch Oven Records and turned up on the essential compilation of outsider country music *God Less America*.

"I sat down and wrote this extremely tongue in cheek crap in about five minutes," Ron Hellard told *boingboing.net* in 2005. "I slapped it on a cassette and gave it to her. The best thing you can say about the record was that it was round!" He agrees with Troy's own assessment: "Show Land Records probably pressed a thousand copies at most. I thought that would be the last I heard of this joke. But thirty years later it shows up on web sites and play lists here and across the pond. I am amazed.

"It took ten minutes out of my life and it was a joke. I am a professional writer with cuts by dozens of legitimate artists (he's had songs recorded by George Jones, Loretta Lynn, Jerry Lee Lewis, Tammy Wynette, Conway Twitty and others), but this thing sticks to me like glue. One reviewer assumed that **Topless** was an attempt to write a serious country song, and slammed the writer for it. That's what got to me: it was meant to be, and most certainly is, a parody of country music."

1973 was a big year for Troy: he reached his eighth birthday and released his eighth single; he became the youngest singer to appear on the *Dean Martin Summer Show* and he also appeared on TV in Atlanta on a fundraising telethon after spending two hours earlier the same day soliciting money for muscular dystrophy research from motorists passing the family's Nashville home. He also released a single featuring a brace of duets. Credited to Little Troy Hess and Little Angela Perry, the World's Youngest Recording Duet: the tracks on the 45 were **Little Sister** and **I'll Be All Smiles Tonight**.

Mum Dot, who looked after Bennie's business as well as the Hess home, also ran Troy's fan club, which still existed well into the 90s. The Hesses even appeared in the 1977 documentary series *All You Need is Love* where the 11 year-old boy performed an impromptu version of **Jambalaya** and his father proudly showed filmmaker Tony Palmer around a room full of Hess family memorabilia. People have been very unkind about Bennie and Dot, especially when discussing how the couple pushed their son into the spotlight, but Troy has nothing but praise for his parents. "My parents never forced me to do anything," he insists. "No one was holding a gun to my head saying, *'sing this song'*."

According to Nolan Porterfield's book *Jimmie Rodgers: The Life and Times of America's Blue Yodeler*, Bennie spent *'a lot of time and cash promoting Little Troy Hess. If he accomplished nothing else, he at least managed to get the tyke photographed with practically every big star in town, and has the pictures to prove it. Some people around Nashville thought Bennie was exploiting the youngster, but when Country Music said so in print, Bennie promptly sued the magazine for several million dollars.'*

The headline read *Troy Hess: A Child On The Streets of Nashville*. Bennie and Dot had given writer Mary Sue Price full access to their family, but were horrified when her article appeared in print. *'Tonight in Nashville little Troy Hess is going downtown to play for the drunks on Broadway,'* the piece began. *'He is going downtown in his red, white, and blue van seated between his father, a forgotten country music singer from the thirties, and his mother, a tiny woman with wide eyes and a sagging stomach.'*

The article presents Troy — as writer Joe Bonomo put it in his article *Mama Loved The Ways Of The World* (published in *The Normal School*, Spring 2013) — as *'used by his parents, overworked, already a has-been'*. It's a massively unfair assessment, and one that still upsets Troy. "It was filled with nasty lies," he tells me, "And just meant to help sell magazines. It stated my mom and dad prostituted me out to make their living, which was nothing but a lie! We sued the magazine for libel, but one after another of our attorneys got bought off by the magazine. Then came the David Allen Coe special on PBS where he repeated some of the same garbage that the magazine had previously stated. Again we sued PBS, but that was like trying to sue God! Finally my dad's health began to fail, so we moved back to our native Texas." Papa Hess eventually dropped the suit, and Troy – now in High School – decided to put his musical past behind him and get on with being a normal teenager.

Bennie passed away in November 1984. "It was only after the death of my dad that I really started growing an appreciation for what all I'd been involved in," Troy told Joe Bonomo. "**Please Don't Go Topless, Mother** was one of those songs that I would never have played, let anyone listen to. I've got several copies of the record, but I never would have tried to push it, let anyone hear it before it came out on *God Less America*. But it's one of those things where you go *'Hey, at least they spelled your name right'*."

In 1986, when he was still only 21, Troy formed his first band, Troy Hess and the Yellow Rose Express. "We played all over Texas," he says proudly. Two years later, he tells me: "Mom got in touch with one of her old bosses from Nashville, Rick Blackburn. Rick had been Vice President at Columbia Records and, after having me sign a record contract, I went to Nashville and recorded a four-song demo for Columbia at RCA's legendary Studio B; the producer was Blake Mevis, who had produced several George Strait albums.

"I thought at age 23, I had arrived! I had finally made it! But, once again, I had gotten the short end of stick, as my version of **Wild Horses** wound up on Garth Brooks' *No Fences* album. Apparently, according to Mevis, Blackburn had **Wild Horses** (not the Rolling Stones song which was later murdered by TV talent show runner up Susan Boyle) in his own publishing company, and convinced Columbia to pay for a demo on me as a prospective artist, but he used me to push his song to a major artist. The rest is history."

Some history! Blackburn was the man who, in 1986, decided not to renew Johnny Cash's contract with Columbia; when Sony bought Columbia/CBS Blackburn left the company and formed Venture Entertainment with Mevis.

Now fast approaching 50 and with a career that stretches 48 years Troy is still rocking, leading the Texas Heartbreakers at well-received gigs and still hoping for that big break. His audience is mostly unaware of the legacy of his prepubescent recordings, and he's happy for things to stay that way. Today's Troy Hess writes mature country songs about love and heartbreak, some coloured by his own, painful, divorce. "But life goes on," he cheerfully adds, "and it's given me some great material. Here's to making lemonade out of lemons!"

Attila
Attila (1970)

How do you fancy-some ear shattering, head banging heavy metal from the rock god that is Billy Joel?

Yes, you read that right: Billy Joel.

Before Mr Joel began his career as a simpering, piano playing songsmith, before he married a model, wrote an international smash about her and then divorced her, even before his attempted suicide by drinking Mr Sheen, an incident which provided the creative spark for the song **Tomorrow Is Today** on his first solo album ("I drank furniture polish. It looked tastier than bleach," he said) and long, long before his box office-busting tours with Elton John, Billy Joel was trying to earn a living as the poor man's Jon Lord in a heavy metal duo called Attila.

Formed from the ashes of his previous band The Hassles, Attila consisted of Joel on keyboards and vocals and drummer Jon Small. Small was Joel's best friend; it was he who rushed Joel to hospital after his attempted suicide, and he who was repaid when Joel ran off with Small's wife. Billy has since admitted that he drank the furniture polish in the first place because of the difficulties surrounding his relationship with Elizabeth Small. He and Jon seem to have patched things up though, and have collaborated on several projects since.

According to Tom Paisley, the author of the overwrought sleeve notes to the first (and thankfully only) Attila album, Joel and Small left The Hassles – who had released a couple of flop albums on United Artists (*The Hassles* in 1967 and *Hour Of The Wolf* the following year) because they *'were dissatisfied with the sound. They had a dream of a two-man group, with a new and different attack. They wanted the sound to be full-sized, heavy, and to have no middle-of-the-road compromises.'* No 'middle-of-the-road compromises'? Within 12 months of Attila hitting the shelves Joel would release *Cold Spring Harbor*, an album which is a masterclass in middle-of-the-roadness - although that initial solo album almost put the kybosh on his entire career when it was mastered at the wrong speed, leaving Billy sounding, in his words, "like a chipmunk" (the album would be re-mixed and re-released in 1983).

Joel has claimed that he was inspired to start Attila after listening to the British heavy metal bands currently laying waste to America. "Jon and I decide to form a two-man group, really heavy Led Zeppelin, heavy-metal stuff. I figured out a way to wire the Hammond organ to amplifiers to make it sound like a guitar and also to play the bass on the keyboards. I played the organ, the guitar sound, my left had was playing the bass and I played the harmonica and was screaming at the top of my lungs" (*Billy Joel: The Biography* by Mark Bego). Certainly the sound that Joel wrung from his keys was similar to that employed by Deep Purple and Yes, and the bass trick he employed tips more than a nod to Ray Manzarek of the Doors.

As already noted the duo released just one album, the self-titled *Attila* in 1970, and it's just about the most ridiculous, bombastic piece of rock dross you're ever likely to hear. Housed in an absurd sleeve, featuring the Billy and Jon dressed as medieval soldiers surrounded by hanging animal carcasses like a brace of Dark Ages butchers (designed by Richard Mantel, who also did the covers for *The Velvet Underground Live at Max's Kansas City* and the *Divine Miss M*), it was described by Joel himself as "psychedelic bullshit". Split pretty much 50/50 between vocal tracks full of ridiculous lyrics and insane instrumentals, the album features such inspired song titles as **Amplifier Fire Part 1: Godzilla, Amplifier Fire Part 2: March Of The Huns** and **Brain Invasion**. Says Joel: "We had about a dozen gigs and nobody could stay in the room when we were playing. It was too loud. We literally drove people out."

This really is one of the stupidest, most vainglorious projects ever. Joel may try to distance himself from it now but Paisley's confusing sleeve notes herald Attila as *'the most remarkable group on the scene since the Huns sacked Europe. There are only two men in the group, an unlikely number for a conquering horde. But in numbers, the smallness ends. Their sound is their size, so are their ideas.'*

And what ideas the boys had! Have a look at the lyrics to **California Flash** if you don't believe me:

Then he started doing a dance
He said it was imported from France
The girls all fell in a trance
To see the California Flash moving his pants
Taking off his pants...

(*California Flash*, written by William Joel and Jonathan Small. Recorded by Attila on Epic Records. © 1970, Mazur Enterprises Ltd)

Genius! Hardly an obvious precursor to **Just the Way You Are** though, is it?

Attila has been called *'the worst album released in the history of rock & roll'* by critic Stephen Thomas Erlewine, and there are many others who agree with him, including Joel himself, who dismisses Attila as "that hippy shit". *Attila* has its champions, but even if you are one of those that marvels at the fact that this noise was summoned up from the depths of hell by just two people (*'no studio gimmicks, no multiple-track recordings. No extra musicians were called in for the recording session. The sounds you will hear are the same as you would hear live'*, writes a breathless Paisley on the back cover) the idiotic lyrics to **California Flash** and the cod-angst of **Revenge Is Sweet** should be enough to convince you otherwise:

People laughed at me, said I'd never win
Now I turn around and kick your faces in

(*Revenge Is Sweet*, written by William Joel and Jonathan Small. Recorded by Attila on Epic records. © 1970, Mazur Enterprises Ltd)

88

Wake up people! Attila is at the gates! Hardly: despite a glowing review in *Billboard* (*'an exciting album with much chart potential…an amazing album from just two musicians'*) the album did next-to-no business and the band played around 20 shows before imploding. *Attila* was also issued in Japan, complete with obligatory lyric sheet, though goodness knows what Japanese audiences would have made of this mess.

Jon Small now works as a film producer and director specialising in live music: he's worked with Run-DMC, Lynyrd Skynyrd, Garth Brooks and, naturally, Joel himself. Billy is, as we all know, one of the world's most successful singer-songwriters with a string of hits, multi-million selling albums and Grammy awards to his name. Neither of them would credit Attila as a highlight of their respective careers: Joel hates *Attila* so much that he refuses to allow it to be reissued. It has been pirated on more than one occasion and one track – half of **Amplifier Fire** – appears on Joel's career-spanning CD box set *My Lives* (although Joel claims he was not consulted about the track listing for that release and has made it clear that he was less than happy with the collection), so the only way you can currently get to hear this proto-metal masterpiece is by spending a small fortune for an original copy or downloading it illegally.

Or, of course, by perusing the exhibits in our own museum of audio madness.

Black Widow
Come To The Sabbat (1970)

Providing the inspiration for many a European Death metal merchant, Black Widow were one of the more preposterous bands to spring out of Britain's late 60s satanic rock scene. Emulating near-neighbours Earth (who, in August 1969 would rename themselves Black Sabbath and who, for a while at least, would often be confused with our heroes) Black Widow had risen from the remnants of seven-piece psychedelic soul band Pesky Gee!, a group which had recorded a number of unsuccessful singles and an album (known affectionately as *Exclamation Mark*) for Pye in 1969.

Inspired themselves in equal measures by Jethro Tull, local Leicester boys Family* and the teachings of Black Magic witch/occultist Alex Sanders (known to his followers as Verbius), Black Widow scored a minor hit with their first album *Sacrifice*, which included their best-known song **Come To The Sabbat**. A thoroughly ridiculous record, with its stilted flute, dolorous drums and childish chanting, **Come To The Sabbat** sounds like a left over from the soundtrack of a Hammer Films treatment of a Dennis Wheatley novel. You can almost see Beryl Reid and Nicky Henson hamming it up as Vincent Price splashes red paint all over a voluptuous Victorian virgin as vocalist Christopher 'Kip' Trevor encourages his listeners to *'discard your clothes'* and *'join me in my search for power'*.

"I remember that Jim (Gannon) came round to my house," the song's co-writer Clive Jones told British psychedelia website *Marmalade Skies* (marmalade-skies.co.uk). "He was writing a song but had got stuck. I always had a commercial feel. I added the chant and a few other accents and things.

"It's strange but the beginning of the track with the drums and flute was never intended for that song, but as an intro to it for the stage show. Jim clapped his knees for the drum sound and the flute bit just came to me at the time, as easy as that. It took as long to write it as to play it." Bizarrely **Come To The Sabbat** has proved immensely popular in Europe and has been covered by a number of black/death metal acts around the globe.

Black Widow were more famous (or should that be infamous) in Britain for their shocking stage antics - choreographed by members of Leicester's Phoenix Theatre Company and where Kip Trevor would mock-sacrifice a nubile young woman (often Sanders' missus) - than for their recordings. "The controversy over the stage-act was good and bad for us," Jones told *Marmalade Skies*. "It got us lots of publicity. The press all said *'Don't let your kids see this show!'* so of course they all came to see it! The album was released in the States to great reviews and we were due to go over there, but Charles Manson did his black magic murders, and when they saw the publicity about us we were banned from going over."

The stage show, and the success of **Come To The Sabbat** saw the band feted as spearheading the emergent Occult Rock scene – however they quickly eschewed their Black Magic influences in the hope of reaching a larger audience (and not pissing off the Yanks), dumping drummer Bok - chief instigator of their ridiculous satanic posing - and replacing him with Romeo Challenger, who would later become the sticksman in 50s-throwback hit makers Showaddywaddy. Sadly the hoped-for renaissance failed to materialise. "Jim and Kip wanted to drop the Black Magic but I wanted to keep it and make a second album with the same direction," Jones revealed in the *Marmalade Skies* interview, "But they split the band and we became just a Prog rock band like thousands of others. They weren't very nice to work with. They thought they were God's gift and they brought drugs into the band, which totally wrecked it." The hoped for American breakthrough never happened: what did the States, who already had their own ridiculous black magic band Coven, want with a bunch of longhairs from Leicester whose accents they could barely understand?

After a couple of further line-up changes and two more albums (*Black Widow* and *Black Widow 3*) the band imploded. Black Widow included the stupid **Mary Clark**, where the band make the same mistake that Clarence Stacy and Screaming Lord Sutch did on their versions of **Jack The Ripper**, conflagrating a fictional character from a 50s movie with one of the Ripper's actual victims. A final album *Black Widow 4*, recorded in 1972, remained unissued until 2007.

Paul Nashman, the former proprietor of the infamous Nasher's second-hand record shop in Walcot Street, Bath, tells a wonderful story of his own brush with Black Widow's fame. "A fake tanned, balding, somewhat effete middle aged chap came into my shop once and asked if I had any Black Widow records. I started to laugh and told him of how me and my Stockport mates used to do a Northern piss-take of their atrocious **Come To The Sabbat**, and then I broke into an impromptu performance: *'Cum Cum Cum t't Sabbath, cum t't Sabbath, Saytan's thur...'*

"I noticed that he was staring at me rather coldly, whilst politely waiting for me to finish chanting and giggling, and he then told me that it was he who had written that song, and that he'd been in the band. I apologised (a bit) and then we went on to chat for a couple of hours. He was Jim Gannon. Nice bloke." After leaving Black Widow Gannon joined Fox (70s pop band fronted by sultry Australian lead singer Susan Traynor, who performed under the name Noosha Fox, and who had hits with **S-S-Single Bed** and **Only You Can**). Nasher's late and much lamented shop featured on the front cover of the 2002 Van Morrison album *Down The Road*, fact fans.

Three years after Black Widow shuffled off this mortal coil, the pubs and clubs of Leicester began to resound to an altogether different sound.

Often dumped into the catchall NWOBHM (New Wave of British Heavy Metal) grab bag, the bizarre looking four piece (plus their two delightful female dancers) Agony Bag was formed in early 1976 from the ashes of Black Widow. Try to imagine what a Midlands am-dram society would make of the Rocky Horror Show, or what the legendary Kasenetz and Katz (1910 Fruitgum Company, Ram Jam, Ohio Express etc.) were striving for when they decided to launch Furr, the imitation Kiss, and you might get some idea of the look former BW members Clive Jones and Bok were going for. Or maybe they were inspired by transgender punk rocker Jayne County. Who knows: all we can be sure of is that the band's unusual look – dinner jackets, stockings, suspenders, high heels and face paint – can't have made it easy to secure a booking at the Saffron Lane Estate Working Men's Club.

Eschewing Black Widow's infamous satanic stage show in favour of a poorly executed Kiss-in-drag look, after four years of slogging around the Leicester pub circuit the band released their one and only single, **Rabies Is A Killer** backed with **Never Never Land** (both sides of which were written by Jones) on the tiny Monza record label.

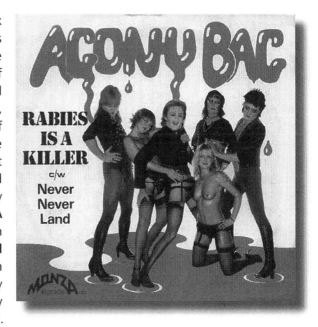

The group made a video to accompany the release, which I urge you to check out (it's on YouTube), if only for the sight of a makeup-caked Jones dressed up in stockings and suspenders swinging from the rafters of a Leicester rehearsal room. He looks for the entire world like Frank-N-Furter imitating a chimpanzee.

Little wonder that, shortly after the recording, bass player Geoff Bevan left the band and joined the fledgling Diesel Park West. Clive and Bok added Ian Watts on guitar and Mick Wright on bass but this new line-up lasted less than two months: the band folded altogether when Clive decided to leave at the end of November 1980. Over the last few years **Rabies Is A Killer** has become something of a cult classic; it should be noted however that the majority of cults are based on nonsense. **Rabies Is A Killer** is fun, dumb punk but a classic it ain't. However the B-side doesn't know what it wants to be. Kicking off with a prog rock guitar intro it moves, Black Widow-style, into chanted group vocals before moving into a weird amalgam of hair metal, falsetto vocals and cheesy keyboard stabs... and there's that wretched flute again. **Never Never Land** is simply abysmal.

Agony Bag were "a most unusual band and well before its time," Clive Jones told Polish metal website *Doomsmoker* (doomsmoker.pl). "It also gave me the chance to write more and do lead vocals. Agony Bag was great fun and we were for sure the only band to have sex onstage and not always with our girl dancers! We did many tours of Germany and have a great fan base over there." This would explain why the tracks were recorded in a German studio and why one chorus of **Rabies Is A Killer** is sung in German.

Agony Bag recorded several other tracks, which were fleshed out with solo recordings by Jones and cobbled together on the 2001 compilation *Feelmazumba*. **Rabies Is A Killer** also recently turned up on the soundtrack of indie horror flick *Jessicka Rabid*. If you'd like to know more about Agony Bag I urge you to check out überfan Phil Mulvaney's website at *agonybag.co.uk*

Kip Trevor had a long association with hit producer Trevor Horn; Bok now lives in France, finding work as an odd job man. These days Clive Jones is fronting a new version of Black Widow and has released several Black Widow archive recordings; he's also been working on his pet project Metalheart, a rock musical. Jim Gannon has been living and working in Australia for the last three decades and is currently playing with show band Soul Agents.

The co-songwriters of **Come To The Sabbat** have not seen each other for a number of years – and Jones likes that just fine.

***

* Family were a huge influence on Black Widow: have a listen to John Palmer's flute on the single version of Family's **The Weaver's Answer** and then compare it to the style employed by Black Widow's Clive Jones. In their earlier incarnation (as Pesky Gee!), the band had already covered the song **Peace of Mind**, which originally appeared on Family's debut album Music In A Doll's House, issued in 1968. Another British band were planning to issue an album in 1968 called A Doll's House, but once the Family album appeared in the shops they changed their minds. The alternative title they used? The Beatles (a.k.a. The White Album). By odd coincidence, an entirely different song also called **Peace of Mind** exists which has been attributed by some to the Beatles. However, although it has appeared on many bootlegs - and sounds remarkably similar to other White Album-era demos, the song (allegedly rescued from the trash outside the Apple offices) has never been acknowledged by any of the band members, their producer George Martin nor by any of their reputable biographers.

Bob Dylan: Crud On The Tracks

I've seen Bob Dylan live several times. I've seen him when he's been so blisteringly brilliant he knocks your socks off and I've seen him when he's been so awful he sounds like an inebriated Eartha Kitt impersonator. His triumvirate of truly great albums – *Bringing It All Back Home*, *Highway 61 Revisited* and *Blonde On Blonde* – stands comparison to *Rubber Soul, Revolver* and *Sgt Pepper's Lonely Hearts Club Band* as quite possibly the most influential sequential three albums of all time.

The man's a bone fide genius: he's even worn my hat on stage (at the Hammersmith Odeon, albeit briefly). I absolutely adore Bob Dylan.

However, as noted in the first volume of *The World's Worst Records*, he's not infallible. **Under The Red Sky**, a ridiculous song which seems to be based on the German folk tale *Hansel and Gretel*, is just appalling. The album of the same name – which followed hot on the heels of the critically-acclaimed *Oh Mercy* – opens with the appalling **Wiggle Wiggle**, a track so desperately awful that the song's author himself hasn't a good word to say about it. Mind you, how can you possibly justify any song that contains a line as jaw-droppingly awful as *'Wiggle, wiggle, wiggle like a bowl of soup'*? Would it surprise you to know that *Time* magazine placed **Wiggle Wiggle** on their list of *The 10 Worst Bob Dylan Songs*, saying that it *'sounds like the theme song to one of those tripped-out television shows beloved by toddlers and drug users'*, and the British rock magazine *Q* – usually so reverential in its' coverage of Dylan - included **Wiggle Wiggle** in their list of *Ten Terrible Records by Great Artists*?

Under The Red Sky was released just days after the Bard of Duluth's second wife filed for divorce and was dedicated to his then-four-year old daughter. It cost a fortune to produce – talents like George Harrison, Slash, David Crosby, Elton John and Stevie Ray Vaughan don't come cheap (unless you call in a few favours, that is) - and it sold appallingly, peaking at just 38 on the *Billboard* charts. Maybe it was Bob's attempt to piss away some of his fortune before the ex got her hands on it.

Dylan apologist Patrick Humphries (in his book *The Complete Guide To The Music Of Bob Dylan*) called it *'proof positive that Dylan had lost it, definitely, permanently, irrevocably'*, stating that the album *'was everything* Oh Mercy *wasn't—sloppily written songs, lazily performed and unimaginatively produced'.* Bizarrely Robert Christgau, reviewing *Under The Red Sky* in *The Village Voice*, believed that 'Under The Red Sky *is Dylan's best album in 15 years, a record that may even signal a ridiculously belated if not totally meaningless return to form'.* The self-proclaimed Dean of American Rock Critics was clearly having a bad day.

Dylan's career has seen myriad highs; but for each peak there has been an equally atrocious abyss to plunder. "I can play those songs, but I probably can't listen to those records, the Great White Wonder told *Rolling Stone* magazine in a 2004 interview. "I was just being swept along with the current when I was making those records. I don't think my talent was under

control." Readers of the same magazine plotted a course through the worst of Dylan in 2013 in a poll for the *10 Worst Bob Dylan Songs*.

Bobby's Christmas album (it's ok, he converted to Christianity from Judaism in 1979 although, confusingly, he continued to follow certain Jewish practices, including participating – even playing – at bar mitzvahs) *Christmas In The Heart* is particularly awful. It might include his Pogues-esque take on the classic **It Must Be Santa** which, to be honest, is quite a lot of fun, but it also includes his vile reading of **O Come All Ye Faithful**, which is introduced by Dylan croaking his way through a verse in Latin like a syphilitic toad*. The girly choir which joins in halfway through does nothing to raise the mood of this deathly dirge, which sounds less like Dylan himself than someone attempting their most half-hearted Bob Dylan impersonation. And if you thought the David Bowie/Bing Crosby version of **The Little Drummer Boy** was just about as bad as it could get you clearly haven't heard Bob's version yet.

With words written by Grateful Dead lyricist Robert Hunter it would be reasonable to expect **The Ugliest Girl In The World**, from the 1988 album *Down In The Groove*, to have some of the psychedelic imagery of Hunter's classic **Dark Star**: instead we end up with probably the most stupid song in the whole of Dylan's gargantuan canon:

The woman that I love she a got a prize fighter nose
Cauliflower ears and a run in her hose
She speaks with a stutter and she walks with a hop
I don't know why I love her but I just can't stop

(*The Ugliest Girl In The World*, written by Bob Dylan and Robert Hunter, performed by Bob Dylan on Columbia Records. © 1987, Special Rider Music)

Down In The Groove is a horrible album. In 2007, *Rolling Stone* rightly singled it out as Dylan's worst: 19 years earlier, on the album's release, they were less damning, praising the unholy mess for its *'simple, heartfelt'* performances and *'strong covers'*, the weaselly hypocrites. Just 10 tracks and a little over half an hour long, there are stories that this album, which also features a perfunctory cover of the Wilbert Harrison/Canned Heat/Bryan Ferry hit **Let's Stick Together**, was recorded sporadically over a period of up to six years and had undergone at least three different track listings before Bobby settled on the final version. That's a little over five minutes of usable material every 12 months! Its 1986 predecessor – *Knocked Out Loaded* – was even more badly received, with critic Anthony DeCurtis calling it *'slipshod, patchwork'*, in *Rolling Stone* and berating Dylan for his *'utter lack of artistic direction'* when compiling *'this conceptual mess'*. However the reviewer, mindful perhaps of how knocking Dylan was akin to putting the boot in to Abraham Lincoln, still felt that *'Dylan sounds fresh and relaxed, singing with a gusto that recalls his best Sixties work,'* the crawler. Even the hardiest of Dylan fans would agree that this back-to-back pairing soundtracks the downright lowest point of his career.

One album that most critics agree on is *Self Portrait*. Unfortunately for the former Bobby Zimmerman they pretty much all agree that it is awful. And who can blame them? Can anyone explain what in the hell was going through his head when he wrote and recorded **All The Tired Horses**? The opening track on *Self Portrait* is three minutes of lush orchestrations with just two lines of lyrics *'All the tired horses in the sun/How am I supposed to get any ridin' done?'* repeated 14 – yes 14 - times by a group of female backing singers. Is it a surprise that reviewer Greil Marcus opened his critique in *Rolling Stone* magazine with the damming sentence *'What is this shit?'* For some unknown reason *Self Portrait* earned gold record status on release - only the second album to achieve that accolade in Dylan's career to date.

Bob has often claimed that *Self Portrait* was a joke. If it were that then the joke backfired miserably. However the idea that Dylan would make a poor album on purpose has never made much sense, and his suggestion that *Self Portrait* was a deliberate attempt to deflect the glare of the spotlight away from him so that he could have some semblance of a family life seems like a lot of revisionist hooey. In an interview given to writer Cameron Crowe for the sleeve notes to the 1985 collection *Biograph*, Dylan finally came clean. *'Self Portrait was a bunch of tracks that we'd done all the time I'd gone to Nashville...and then there was a lot of other stuff that was just on the shelf. But I was being bootlegged at the time and a lot of stuff that was worse was appearing on bootleg records. So I just figured I'd put all this stuff together and put it out, my own bootleg record, so to speak. You know, if it actually had been a bootleg record, people probably would have sneaked around to buy it and played it for each other secretly.'*

Two outtakes from *Self Portrait* (an album that itself was little more than a collection of outtakes) would surface in 1973 on the dreadful *Dylan*; however that mess was put out by Columbia, with no input from his Bobness, after he left the label for pastures new. If Bob hadn't jumped ship the chances are we would never have been subjected to something as awful as his version of the Joni Mitchell standard **Big Yellow Taxi** - at least not until he commenced his seemingly never-ending *Bootleg Series*.

POP

BOB DYLAN—
Self Portrait.
Columbia C2X 30050 (S)
Dylan's first album since "Blonde on Blonde" finds him again in a country way, but in this grand reunion with the Band, Al Kooper and the Nashville bunch, Dylan closes out his own era of searching and sings a mixed bag of pop oldies, "Nashville Skyline" leftovers and new ditties. Best of the 24 new numbers are "Early Mornin' Rain," "Living the Blues," "Copper Kettle" and "Minstrel Boy." Instant gold.

While we're on the subject, why do so many Dylan albums have inexcusably awful covers? Out of focus photos (*Blonde On Blonde, Down In The Groove, Real Live*), appalling illustrations (*Knocked Out Loaded, Oh Mercy, Shot Of Love*) piss-poor,

Self Portrait was reviewed by Billboard as 'Dylan's first album since Blonde on Blonde'. It wasn't. The reviewer forgot John Wesley Harding (1967) and Nashville Skyline (1969), both far better records.

self-indulgent paintings (*Self Portrait, Saved, Planet Waves*) and more. An artist of this stature should not be expected to package his material inside such garbage.

The worst thing that Dylan has put his name to has to be **If Dogs Run Free**, from *New Morning*, an album that was issued just four months after the appalling *Self Portrait*. Featuring ridiculous grunts, whoops and howls from singer Maeretha Stewart (in a feeble attempt at scat that comes nowhere close to the brilliance of, say, Ella Fitzgerald or Louis Armstrong) and jazz lounge piano from Al Kooper, **If Dogs Run Free** is as silly as it is insulting. Dylan doesn't even bother to try and sing, reciting his words as though they had the importance of great poetry. Well, sorry Bob, but lines like *'just do your thing, you'll be king'* or ending almost every line with a word that rhymes with 'free' ain't exactly the kind of stuff we expect from a modern-day Shakespeare, you know. Knocked out in one take, according to the great man himself, and described as *'wretched'* by noted Dylanologist Clinton Heylin (in his book *Revolution In The Air*) and *'banal'* by reviewer Peter James (in his collection of Dylan album essays *Warehouse Eyes*), the only good thing you can say about this horror is that it's childish lyrics inspired illustrator Scott Campbell to turn it into a rather sweet children's book.

In his book *Chronicles Volume One*, Dylan writes: 'I released one album (a double one) where I just threw everything I could think of at the wall and whatever stuck, released it, and then went back and scooped up everything that didn't stick and released that, too". If that is the great man's own summation of the waste of vinyl that is *Self Portrait* and *New Morning* then who am I to argue?

***

*Bob doesn't like being compared to an amphibian. During a speech he gave in February 2015, after he was honoured by the MusiCares charity, he said: "Critics have been giving me a hard time since Day One. Critics say I can't sing. I croak. Sound like a frog. Why don't critics say that same thing about Tom Waits? Critics say my voice is shot. That I have no voice. What don't they say those things about Leonard Cohen? Why do I get special treatment? Critics say I can't carry a tune and I talk my way through a song. Really? I've never heard that said about Lou Reed. Why does he get to go scot-free?"

Screaming Lord Sutch
Lord Sutch And Heavy Friends (1970)

Greatly influenced by the madcap antics of Screamin' Jay Hawkins (and a massive influence himself on Alice Cooper, who he once threatened to sue for stealing his intellectual copyright), David Edward 'Screaming Lord' Sutch* began his performing career at the tail end of the 1950s. With his famously long hair and ridiculous outfits he and his group, The Savages, were known for their frantic stage show: Sutch would leap from a coffin and race around the stage brandishing anything from a twin-headed axe to a mop (christened 'the minge pole' by his band mates), and would often chase members of his audience through the auditorium carrying a crudely-made, but still horrifying, severed head. He soon caught the eye of the maverick producer Joe Meek, who brought him into his Holloway Rd studio, and the brilliant but troubled enfant terrible of production and the outrageous, publicity hungry performer would work together on a half-a-dozen 45s. The best known of these - **Jack The Ripper** (1963)** – would become something of an anthem for Sutch, and he would re-record the song several times during his long and eventful career.

Former window cleaner Dave Sutch was a man of little or no discernible talent, as he would freely disclose himself: *'I'll be the first to admit I'm not the world's greatest singer,'* he wrote in his totally unreliable memoir *Life As Sutch* (HarperCollins, 1991). *'But I am a good rock 'n' roll shouter.'* However those early singles tell us much of what we need to know about

Screaming Lord Sutch: they're charmingly naive, occasionally awkward and delightfully ramshackle. The band is always excellent - many of Britain's brightest stars launched their own careers via membership of The Savages - but Sutch's vocal performances are, at best, limited. Still, as his contemporary Jess Conrad (and a great many others) proved you didn't have to be a great singer to carve out a career in the embryonic world of British rock 'n' roll; a pretty face or a good gimmick would do just as well. The recordings he made with Meek, while not exactly great, are never less than entertaining; although he would continue to record sporadically for the next three decades he would never improve on them.

One of the best - **Monster In Black Tights** (the B-side of his third single, **I'm A Hog For You**) - is a pastiche of the then-current hit **Venus In Blue Jeans**, composed by Meek and co-writer Geoff Goddard:

My monster in black tights
You've got the kind of blood that I likes
I remember the day you dragged me away
And left me on a barbed wire fence - yip! yip!

(*Monster in Black Tights*, written by Joe Meek and Geoff Goddard. Recorded by Screaming Lord Sutch on Decca Records. © 1963, Mirror Music)

Dave Sutch was very good at making the best of what he had. A born entertainer, he quickly realised that if he wasn't much of a singer at least he could extend his fifteen minutes in the spotlight with his outrageous antics - which included launching a pirate radio station, tossing an effigy of Prime Minister Edward Heath onto a burning pyre and letting loose a live bear in the English countryside. When chart success eluded him he decided that the best way to keep his name in the papers was by setting up his own political party - starting in 1963 with the National Teenage Party and later morphing into the Official Monster Raving Loony Party - which, although perceived as a joke, had a couple of surprisingly sensible policies that were later adopted by the mainstream parties and passed in to law: pet passports were his idea, he was partly responsible for having London's Carnaby Street pedestrianised and he campaigned vigorously to have the voting age reduced to 18.

Unable to score a hit record in the UK, in 1968 Sutch moved to America in the hope of making it big there. The following year he went into the recording studio to cut tracks for *Lord Sutch And Heavy Friends*. As he wrote in *Life As Sutch*: '*In all the years I had made singles I had never got round to cutting an album. But when all my old mates who were now with big-name bands started rolling into L.A I saw my opportunity.'* Consequently, although Sutch had been releasing records for 10 years, when it was issued in 1970 *Lord Sutch and Heavy Friends* became his first full-length LP.

Eschewing his horror rock metier for a more contemporary sound, for those infamous Los Angeles sessions Sutch was joined by some of the greats of the burgeoning heavy rock scene - including Noel Redding (bassist with the Jimi Hendrix Experience), guitarist Jeff Beck, Savages' drummer Carlo Little, and John Bonham and Jimmy Page of Led Zeppelin. Page and Sutch had known each other for years: Page had played guitar on Sutch's 1964 single **She's Fallen In Love With A Monster Man** and the pair had become reacquainted after Sutch moved to the States. Beck had appeared on another of Sutch's 1964 singles, **Dracula's Daughter**, and both Beck and Page had been members of Britain's premier white blues band the Yardbirds. It should have been a match made in rock 'n' roll heaven. However Sutch's desire to cut an album that would cash in on the superstar status of his old cronies and launch his career in America would result instead in a hellish cacophony.

A truly terrible record, it's no wonder that most of the people involved tried to distance themselves from *Lord Sutch And Heavy Friends*. Several have claimed that they only agreed to play on the sessions if they remained uncredited, and others insist that they only went into the studio to cut a few demos. Sutch later stated that he wanted to produce "modern rock 'n' roll with the real Zeppelin sound", and the album opener, **Wailing Sounds**, does indeed kick off like a pretty standard Zeppelin-style jam... until Sutch's voice and his banal words - which even name-check Page - interrupt proceedings. It sets the scene for the whole album, a rough and ready psychedelic blues jam with, as Sutch's biographer Graham Sharpe puts it *'self-penned lyrics (which) betray Sutch's limited vocabulary and rhyming ability'*.

Sutch shares authorship of half of the tracks with Page, and the great man is also given a co-producer credit: something he was blissfully unaware of until the disc arrived in the stores. At least one song - **Gutty Guitar** - was a leftover from a 1964 Savages recording session, with most of the original guitar part wiped and new overdubs added by Jeff Beck. It sounds ludicrously out of place: not even Nicky Hopkins' signature piano work can save it.

Page said that he "just went down to have a laugh, playing some old rock 'n' roll, a bit of a send-up. The whole joke sort of reversed itself and became ugly." Although all of Zeppelin caught a show by Sutch during the two-day sessions and even jammed with Sutch and Noel Redding on stage, Page later claimed that he "just did some backing tracks to numbers like **Good Golly Miss Molly**. To cut a long story short, he rewrote all the tunes and he put another guitarist on over the top. He wrote me in as producer, which was very nice of him (but) I wasn't interested in that."

Page's version of events is borne out by the material: he may have been awarded co-composer status, but the songs are hardly original, more a heavy-handed plundering of the catalogues of Little Richard and the Stax and Atlantic labels. **Thumping Beat** and **Union Jack Car** are standard, highly derivative, rock 'n' roll chuggers that steal licks wholesale from a host of earlier songs, and there's little in the way of inventiveness in any of the album's 36 minutes. **Brightest Light**, one of two tracks on the album whose authorship is credited to the mysterious Jay Cee (as in Jesus Christ, who writes crap like this?), might have been listenable if it hadn't been for the ludicrous and already dated Summer of Love lyrics and lacklustre vocal performance; **Baby Come Back** is a shameless steal of Wilson Pickett-like r'n'b riffs and features some of the stupidest lyrics it will ever be your bad luck to hear:

Now she can be awkward, as awkward as can be
If you've ever seen her, well you'd know what I mean
Oh she can be mean, just as mean as can be

(*Baby Come Back*, written by Lord Sutch and Jimmy Page. Recorded by Lord Sutch and Heavy Friends on Atlantic Records. © 1970, WEA International Ltd)

By the time *Lord Sutch And Heavy Friends* was issued, complete with a sleeve featuring Dave leaning against his trademark Union Jack Rolls Royce in his psychedelic finery (including a pair of paisley bell-bottoms which appear to have been made out of his mother's curtains), Led Zeppelin had become international superstars; their second album had been number one in the UK, US, Australia, Spain and Canada and had hit the Top 10 in many other countries. In America and Japan the Atlantic label attempted to cash in on Page and Bonham's newfound fame, with the pair being given more prominence than the good Lord himself on single sleeves: the US 45 release of **'Cause I Love You** features Page alone on the cover. Buoyed by the presence of Zeppelin's dynamic duo the album scraped into the Billboard Top 100 but failed to chart elsewhere. "It was my greatest success," said Sutch, "rising to number 48 on the American *Billboard* charts." It actually only reached number 84, but as Sutch was dyslexic maybe we should let him off.

Critical reaction to *Lord Sutch And Heavy Friends* was entirely negative. *Rolling Stone* magazine said that the musicians on the album sounded *'like a fouled parody of themselves,'* and in a 1998 BBC poll the album was named as the worst of all time. The universal loathing must have affected Sutch terribly: he suffered from depression for most of his life and knowing that his one stab at mainstream success was universally hated would have weighed heavily on his shoulders.

Sales of this wreck of a record were healthy enough though for Atlantic to allow Sutch back in to the studio to record a non-album 45, **Election Fever/Rock The Election**, a dreadful slab of political boogie with another line up of Heavy Friends, which flopped miserably. Although this new band drew on the talents of musicians including Spencer Davies, Adrian Gurvitz (more about him later), Carlo Little and Deep Purple's Nick Simper its failure to ignite the charts is hardly surprising when you consider **Election Fever** contained dreadful couplets like *'the pound in your pocket will never vary/whoever said that, he must be a fairy'*. Lovely.

Undeterred, his lordship went on to produce a follow-up album, *Hands Of Jack The Ripper*, utilising yet a third set of Heavy Friends (Noel Redding, Nick Simper and Carlo Little were the only ones to come along for the ride again), including The Who's Keith Moon and Ritchie Blackmore, who had once been a member of The Savages but was now feted as a rock god thanks to the guitar prowess he was displaying in Deep Purple. This time he didn't bother to kid his mates that they were recording demos: he invited them down to help him during a live residency and secreted recording equipment around the building to capture their performances. Blackmore, who had appeared on some of Sutch's Holloway Road recordings and had been nicknamed Bluebell by David when, as a callow youth he became a member of Sutch's backing band, told interviewer Steve Rosen: "Sutch phoned me up and said 'how do you fancy playing tomorrow night?' I agreed and I came down with (Procol Harum's) Matt Fisher and we just did a night of playing. And I saw the recording equipment and thought *'he's doing it again'*!"

Sutch would make further recordings during the 70s and 80s, but his career was spiralling into a deep decline. The loss of most of his savings on a white elephant of a house and recording studio in Hastings hurt, but the lack of interest in his story from a media he had courted for all of his professional life hurt more. He continued to poke fun at the establishment by standing for any and every election he and his band of like-minded madmen could afford to but, as time rolled on the once outlandish showman became a paunchy has-been and, as his ability to fill concert venues waned his interest in politics started to fizzle out too. The death of his mother, and his increasing dependence on prescription drugs for both crippling headaches and for his depression added to his worries.

He committed suicide in 1999; 32 years after his former producer had ended his life in a similar fashion. His body was discovered by his girlfriend, Yvonne, who found him hanging in the hallway of his mother's home as she opened the front door. Thinking it was an elaborate prank, she took a photograph of his suspended body before the reality of the horrific scene that had confronted her had time to register. It was a sad end to a truly eccentric and colourful life.

***

* Despite what you might read elsewhere, Sutch never was a bone fide lord: although he affected the title for his stage persona, his name always remained David Edward Sutch. Further, although Sutch was a shameless self-promoter he hardy lived a flamboyant lifestyle: he hoarded junk, hated drugs, was utterly devoted to his mum, and was virtually teetotal.

** Sutch usually claimed that he wrote Jack The Ripper, although the writer credit on the label tells a different story: the song was originally recorded in New York in 1961 by its co-composer Clarence Stacy, now an actor and writer.

Jerry Solomon
Past The 20th Century (1971)

'My name is Jerry Solomon. I love to perform.'

Before the middle of 2013 I had barely heard of - nevermind actually heard - Jerry Solomon: he's now become something of an obsession. According to his own short autobiography, Jerry was *'born in San Diego, California and lived in Boyle Heights from age 1-4. Later we moved to West L.A. where I went to grade school and attended Hamilton High. After high school I had a job delivering fur coats. Then I got into show business, singing, dancing, and doing comedy routines.*

'In my 30's I was maliciously given a dangerous drug as a "joke" and suffered brain and heart dysfunction. Over a ten-year recovery period, in the last few years, I've regained to some extent, my former function and am writing a book about my experience.' That book – *A Drug Free Life And A Glass Of PCP* – is available now.

Jerry had dreams of making it as a singer and songwriter, or at least an entertainer of some sort, and somehow managed to get it together to record several singles and EPs during the late 1960s. He paid for the recording sessions himself – funding the first with a loan for $100 from the bank – and, when he could not find a record company who would pay for the tracks to be pressed – he also found the money to issue his first single **Come To The Ball** (credited on the label to Solomon) which came out on January 1, 1966 on Jerry's own Sunlite Records.

Unsurprisingly it failed to sell.

With little or no money – and little or no interest – and unperturbed Jerry followed this initial single by releasing a dozen EPs and 45s on his own Fountain label which, he explains, was *probably the smallest record company in the world.'* The Fountain releases, which began in 1966 with **Seria** backed with **Come To The Fair** (Fountain JS 101), were initially credited to Solomon. Other songs recorded over this period included **Aga Ega** (which a friend told him he used to *'chase away unwanted guests'*), **Oh My Ah**, **Frisco Girl**, **Jet Set '67**, **San Francisco Way**, **Come To The Love-In**, **Press Interview**, **All I Ever Do Is Read 'Dear Abby'** and **Psychic Vibrations**. Jerry was particularly proud of **Frisco Girls**: *'This song came out pretty good,'* he observed in *A Drug Free Life And A Glass Of PCP. 'The beginning…had a certain haunting flavor to it'*. From 1967 onwards his discs were either credited to Jerry Solomon or – on at least one occasion (JS 107, the **Fly Fly Fly** EP) - Jerry Soloman. He recorded at least one single under the name Big Jerry with Mark Bloom and his Combo – **The Virgins/They're Losing Their Virginity** - and also issued albums, including *Past The 20th Century* (1971), *Live At The Show Biz*, and Through The Woods (1973).

Jerry's recordings are all completely insane; he rambles, croons, hoots and shrieks through his material like a crazed psychotic. It's no surprise that the comedian Andy Kaufman – who had seen Jerry perform at the famous Improv comedy club - was reputedly a fan.

Very few copies of these albums exist: so sought after are they that when they do come up for sale it's usually for stupid money. Most come without sleeves: when they do have covers they are usually handcrafted by Jerry himself. Apparently Jerry – who could not get local record shops interested enough in his output to warrant them stocking his records - used to carry around copies of his albums and 45s in a garbage bag, and would try to sell them to anyone who showed the slightest interest.

On most of his later recordings Jerry writes, sings, performs and produces every note: his earlier discs employ a session musician or two to fill out the sound or use a pre-recorded music bed. Through the joys of multi-tracking we can hear – on **Creation 1**, the nine minute opener to *Through The Woods*, for example – Jerry accompany himself on a wheezy harmonium and with a cacophonous recorder before the song breaks down into an almost unlistenable babble of giggling, badly plucked guitar notes and so many overdubbed voices that it becomes a muddy mess. *Past The 20th Century*, probably Jerry's most infamous release, is a mish mash of group recordings and solo performances, with Jerry caterwauling whilst strumming an out-of-tune guitar or running his fingers back and forth over the strings of a piano.

Listening to Jerry is painful and unnerving: this is outsider music which defines the genre.

My idea of having a good time
Is playing chess or Mopa-nopo-ly
Or once in a while
To go on out to a mo-oo-oo-hoo-vie
I guess I just don't fit this modern age

(*I Just Don't Fit This Modern Age*, written and recorded by Jerry Solomon on Fountain Records. © 1970, Jerry Solomon)

According to Mike Ascherman (writing in the essential underground recordings guide *The Acid Archives*) Jerry is a *'real person extraordinaire… with his highly chromatic melodies and overdubbed harmonies, Jerry sounds like a late '50s vocals group from the Twilight Zone. His self-accompaniment consists of a repetitive one-chord (maybe two) guitar strum that predates Jandek and a toy piano that is 'strummed' and sounds like a lysergic zither from the Third Man soundtrack. The songs range from nostalgia for the earlier years of his life to total despair.'*

What's really frightening about these records is that they were recorded before Jerry's mind went AWOL: his life was turned upside down in early 1977, when someone he trusted as a friend gave him a glass full of liquid PCP (Phencyclidine, also known as Angel Dust) to drink. Jerry insists that up until then he had never taken drugs; the man didn't even drink beer. He was 34 years old at the time, and was just about to get his big break on TV, with an appearance lined up on *The Gong Show* (I too was 'slipped' Angel Dust once: it was one of the most frightening experiences of my life. Luckily for me it was a tiny amount and the effects wore off after an afternoon and evening of hallucinatory hell). If he was recording this kind of acid casualty stuff before he fried his synapses, what on earth would have been the results of a recording session during his lost decade?

Now in his early 70s, pretty much fully recovered from his journey into the unknown and calling himself a 'performance artist', Jerry is still desperately trying to carve a showbiz career for himself. He recently auditioned (unsuccessfully), for *America's Got Talent*, singing a self-composed song about Viagra to the tune of **O Sole Mio**. In the past he had his own public access TV show – a couple of uncomfortable-to-watch clips are on YouTube if you are so minded.

If you fancy searching him out, Jerry can still be found busking on street corners in LA. He also regularly appears at open mic and karaoke sessions at LA's famous Farmer's Market *(above)*, performing new songs and old for a small but appreciative audience. And long may he continue to do so.

Sweden: More Than Just Abba

Feted in song by the Stranglers and the Divine Comedy, famous for 70s globe-straddling icons Abba, Europe (the poodle-permed horrors who brought us **The Final Countdown** in all its incarnations, including the horrendous millennium makeover **Final Countdown 2000** and the bizarre New Age reworked **Blue Version**), Roxette, Ace of Base and the Cardigans, Sweden has given the world more international chart hits than any other European country outside of the UK. Those five acts alone have combined sales of more than 450 million units.

The country also gave us Sylvia, of course, whose paean to the package holiday **Y Viva Espana** had thousands of Europeans reaching for the sangria, donning sombreros and pinning up bullfight posters in the mid 70s. In more recent years, we've had the likes of Peter Bjorn and John, Eric Prydz, Icona Pop and the guitar pyrotechnics of Yngwie Malmsteen - and how could we forget Sweden's huge influence on the Death Metal scene with Bathory, Entombed and countless others? The Scandinavian country also begat Rednex, the ridiculous bluegrass-electro studio ensemble that - bizarrely - spent more time at number one in Germany than The Beatles.

As the saying goes, you can't make an omelette without breaking eggs, and you certainly can't secure the amount of hits Swedish acts have enjoyed worldwide without issuing a few duff cuts long the way.

Released by Odeon in Sweden in 1971, **Jolly Jolly Buddy Buddy** and the even more perverse B-side

Molly Cow Teddy Puff (which, even if it is billed as one composition on the disc's label, is clearly two distinctly different 'songs') appear to be the only tracks recorded by the artist known as Reco. Reco's wreckage of a record is sung in what appears to be fake English, a conceit which was also utilised by Daniel Catellano on the ridiculous Italian pop song **Prisencolinensinainciusol** (covered in the UK by comedian Mike Read, and featured in the first volume of *The World's Worst Records*). It's completely unintelligible, but the middle eight goes something like this:

Yollyollyollyollyollyollyolly
Boodyboodybullybullybullybullybuly ba-bloom
Say louielouielouielouielouielouie
Buddybuddybullybullybully is basoom
Boodyboodyboodyboody boom!

(*Jolly Jolly Buddy Buddy*, written and recorded by Reco on Odeon Records (Sweden). © 1971, Nordisk Copyright Bureau)

Both sides start with some seriously funky flute playing, not too dissimilar to the kind of thing that Dutch prog rockers Focus were doing around the same time. It appears that Reco played most of the instruments on the two (or is it three?) tracks, with Ulf Andersson on flute and Ulf Söderholm, a former member of 60's Stockholm six-piece beat group The Telstars, on drums. Both songs were produced by Tommy Hallden who, in the 50s and 60s, fronted his own bands The G-Men and Tommy Hallden and the Rocking' Jupiters. Although he played flute on the single, Ulf Andersson was one of the most sought-after saxophonists in Sweden: he would later play the famous sax break on the Abba hit **I Do, I Do, I Do, I Do, I Do**.

Not much is known about Reco: Swedish website *sunkit.com* has been trying to get to the bottom of this mystery for years. Contributor Magnus Nilsson has corresponded with Reco's drummer, Ulf Söderholm but he doesn't even recall performing on the disc - mind you, if you've played on around 2,500 sessions you're allowed to forget the odd one. "I must admit that I have no memory of this very quirky recording," he told Nilsson. "A crazy recording... this sounds as if we are deliberately playing angular, jerky... much worse than we would normally play in the studio."

Reco was actually a pseudonym employed by one Reijo Kääriäinen, who released a further 45 in Finland in 1978, **Pahalta Tää Kaikki Näyttää/Kuka Mä Oon?** Which translates as something like **All the Evil in the World/**

Who Am I? A bizarre new wave/disco hybrid, there's no mistaking Reco's ranting vocal: rather pleasingly the act is referred to on the sleeve as Kääriäinen and the Geniuses. You'll get no argument here. Described by his family as "a very colourful person," sadly Reco passed away in 2005, a few short years before the world would rediscover his brilliance. Tommy Halden had died four years earlier. Reco left a pile of cassette tapes to his only daughter, a treasury of unreleased recordings. Perhaps one day the world will be allowed to hear them. Reco/Reijo bore more than a passing resemblance to Finnish singer Jorma Kääriäinen, but I'm afraid I have not been able to discover if they were related.

Three years after Reco released his one and only 45, Swedish 'singer' Leif Andersson issued what must rank as one of the most peculiar records of all time. Put out by the tiny September label, his virtually unrecognisable a capella renditions of the classics **Fly Me To The Moon** and **Cheek To Cheek**, are sung (if you could possibly call this awful racket singing) in a nasal, whiny voice and translated into Swedish as **Med Andra Ord** (literally *In Other Words*) and **Kind Mot Kind** respectively.

The story goes that Andersson had originally intended to record the tracks with a full orchestra, but after an argument the musicians walked out on him, leaving him with no option but to perform unaccompanied. I've no doubt, had the gentlemen in question heard them, this brace of badness would have given both Frank Sinatra and Fred Astaire nightmares. It's a horrible, atonal abortion of a record, and it is worth questioning Leif's reason for making the recording in the first place. Maybe this was just one huge practical joke. Just about the only thing that we can be sure about is that this particular Leif Andersson is not the same man who presented the long-running Swedish radio show *Smoke Rings*. That Anderson had one less 's' in his surname. Unfortunately, that hasn't stopped people confusing the two.*

While we're visiting Sweden, let's take time to enter the mad, mad world of Eilert Pilarm - a land where every day is Christmas and everyone spends their evening at a karaoke bar singing Elvis covers. Born Eilert Dahlberg in 1953 in Anundsjö, Sweden, Eilert Pilarm (the name chosen because it had the same initials as his hero) has to be the world's worst Elvis impersonator. In a world full of bad Elvis impersonators, that's one hell of a boast.

The former farm hand and labourer began performing in 1992, almost always to backing tapes, and started to build up a loyal following. TV and radio appearances in Scandinavia and further afield followed (he even appeared on Channel 4's *The Big Breakfast* in 1999) and by 2001 he was the most-booked live act in Sweden. Eilert's TV appearances were, to put it mildly, often rather odd: on many programmes he would turn up, bedecked in an Elvis-ish jump suit, and start cooking,

imitating Elvis at the same time. Kind of like the Muppet's Swedish Chef, but dressed by Liberace and singing a bad version of **In The Ghetto**.

Eilert's obsession with Elvis began when, as a young man, he became ill with an undiagnosed psychosis. He saw Elvis everywhere, heard his voice constantly and even began to believe that he was Elvis: choosing to imitate his hero was a way to defeat his demons. "I used to be Elvis; now I'm Eilert," he says.

He self-released three cassettes - the stunningly originally-titled *Elvis 1, Elvis 2* and *Elvis 3* - before the big time came a-knocking: his debut CD *Greatest Hits* was released in 1996 on MCA, the same year that Eilert finally got to visit Graceland. "I can't work out whether he's brilliant or just incredibly stupid and doesn't realise what he's doing," said DJ John Peel, Britain's much-missed champion of the obscure, at the time, calling *Greatest Hits* one of his favourite albums of 1996.

Peel featured Eilert on his show more than two dozen times, even introducing a special weekly spot *Elvis Is Alive And Living In Sweden*.

Three more CDs followed; *Eilert is Back!* In 1998, *Live In Stockholm* in 2000 and *Eilerts Jul (Eilert's Christmas)* the following year, a collection which often appears in lists of the worst album covers of all time. His rise to notoriety amongst bad record aficionados was complete when he appeared in the Irwin Chusid book (and accompanying CD) *Songs In The Key Of Z*, the must-have guide to the world of outsider music.

In 2002, after performing more than 600 gigs and coming 21st out of 89 in a Presley impersonators contest in Memphis, the Swedish Elvis retired from live appearances. "It's too hard; it's like too stressful," he announced. "Maybe there will be the occasional gig, but no more touring." Interviewed by Tobias Froberg for Swedish newspaper Nöjesbladet, Eilert admitted the reason behind his decision to quit: "It's over. I'm sick. I have pain in my legs and it's not fun". He's released a couple of albums since then, 2003's *Eilert Forever* and *The Best Of Elvis*, was featured in a TV documentary and even left semi-retirement for a year to join social media site Twitter – before disappearing beneath the radar once more.

"I don't think there will be a comeback," he told Froberg. That's a great shame. It seems that Eilert Pilarm, the Swedish Elvis, has left the building.

***

* *Born in Malmo, Leif Anderson was an authority on pre-60s jazz (he detested modern jazz, which he called 'migraine music'), his gruff voice fronting Smoke Rings for almost 40 years: he presented the 1,786th edition of his show on November 14, 1999, three days before he passed away, aged 74.*

The Worst Of Paul Vance

You might not recognise the name of songwriter and producer Paul Vance, but I guarantee that you'll be acquainted with some of the more than 300 songs he's had a hand in. He's written (or co-written) material recorded by Frank Sinatra, Doris Day, Andy Williams, Shirley Bassey, Dean Martin, Ella Fitzgerald, Johnny Mathis and Nat King Cole amongst dozens of others, but he's also co-composed some of the most appalling audio ever to trouble the charts. Still alive today, although he retired from the entertainment industry in the 1980s, Paul Vance specialised in catchy, singalong songs and made a very successful career out of the game: 20 gold records, multiple Grammy nominations and a wall full of framed awards.

Born in Brooklyn in 1929, Vance was one of the leading composers and producers of the bubblegum era. Teaming up with fellow Brooklynite Lee Pockriss he first tasted success with **Catch A Falling Star**, a number two hit on the Billboard chart for Perry Como in 1958 and the first single ever to receive gold record certification. Buoyed by this success, Vance issued a single under his own name, but his saxophone-led tittyshaker **Hey! Now Mary** flopped, Paul's avuncular voice clashing horribly with his dirty rocking rhythm, and he quickly reunited with Pockriss. Almost immediately the pair came up with **Itsy Bitsy Teenie Weenie Yellow Polka Dot Bikini** - which was a US number one hit for Brian Hyland in 1960 and a UK number one in 1990 for Bombalurina (aka Andrew Lloyd Webber and kids' TV presenter Timmy Mallet) - a song Vance has often been known to describe as *'a money machine'*.

After composing a few hits for Johnny Mathis, in 1964 Vance and Pockriss wrote **Leader Of The Laundromat**, a spoof of The Shangri-Las' teen death classic **Leader Of The Pack**. Recorded The Detergents (Ron Dante, Tommy Wynn and Danny Jordan - who just happened to be Vance's nephew), the track's success led Vance and Pockriss to write and release a full-lengthy album: *The Many Faces Of The Detergents*, but that particular success would be short-lived: Vance and Pockriss were sued by Jeff Barry, Ellie Greenwich and George Morton, the composers of **Leader Of The Pack**. Dante would later work alongside Jeff Barry as lead vocalist for The Archies and with Vance as the voice of the first incarnation of The Cuff Links, who scored an international hit in 1969 with **Tracy**.

A few other hits (and near misses) followed, including the utterly peculiar **A World Without Sunshine** by Derrik Roberts, which featured in Kenny Everett's second Bottom 30 (see appendix): Vance and Pockriss composed the theme to the 1966 remake of the hit movie *Stagecoach*, and Paul almost scored a hit as a vocalist when the demo version of the Vance-Pockriss composition **Dommage, Dommage** was issued as a single by Scepter in 1966. Vance and Pockriss formed their own label, Odax, and just missed with their composition **Hot Pants**, recorded by the group Salvage, again featuring the vocal talents of Ron Dante.

In 1972 it all started to go horribly wrong or, depending on your own particular point of view, wonderfully right. Vance and Pockriss penned the sickly sweet **Playground In My Mind**, which was recorded by Bournemouth-born Las Vegas entertainer Clint Holmes - and became a number two hit in the US the following year.*
Based around a kid's

nursery rhyme, Vance's son Philip – who sadly died aged just 44 in 2009 - sang on the chorus of the song: he was just seven years old at the time. **Playground In My Mind** would be the last success for the duo of Vance and Pockriss. Vance changed song writing partners, and life would never be the same again.

Paul Vance's new co-conspirator was Jack Perricone, usually credited as Perry Cone (and not Perry Como). The two of them would write a series of singles characterised by their overblown, melodramatic histrionics, including the huge hit **Run Joey Run** by David Geddes. Released in 1975, Vance's daughter Paula (who, some 15 years earlier, had been the influence behind **Itsy Bitsy Teenie Weenie Yellow Polka Dot Bikini**) sang the chorus this time: a clearly underage girl pleading with her father to save her lover's life.

Daddy, please don't, it wasn't his fault
He means so much to me!
Daddy, please don't, we're gonna get married
Just you wait and see

(*Run Joey Run*, written by Paul Vance and Perry Cone. Recorded by David Geddes on Big Tree Records. © 1975, The Music of the Times)

Unrelated (at least thematically) to the Vance-Pockriss composed Cuff Links song **Run Sally Run**, **Run Joey Run** has got everything: teenage pregnancy, parental abuse and a violent death. It's no wonder that this insane soap opera of a song would reach the Billboard Top Five and provide Geddes (real name David Cole Idema), who had recorded unsuccessfully with a number of labels and had at one point turned his back on music to study law, with his only major hit. His follow-up, produced but not written by Vance, was the peculiarly monikered, revoltingly schmaltzy and excruciatingly awful **The Last Game of the Season (A Blind Man in the Bleachers)**.

Later that same year Vance and Cone pulled out all the stops, issuing what must be one of the worst seasonal singles of all time: **An Old Fashioned Christmas (Daddy's Home)** by actress and singer Linda Bennett. That horror (which gets a brief mention in *The World's Worst Records: Volume One*) is hard to describe without reaching for a bucket to puke into: think traditional Xmas schlock interspersed with fake news reports, off-key whining kids (I believe that we can safely assume that the Vance kids were once again roped in to flesh this particular mess out) and a you-can-see-it-coming-for-miles payoff. It truly is horrible. Although it failed to chart Linda Bennett was no stranger to the recording studio, with albums, TV appearances (including *The Adventures of Ozzie And Harriet, Bonanza, Flipper* and *Doctor Kildare*) and film credits to her name: as a child actress she featured in *The Creature With The Atom Brain, The Seven Little Foys* and *Queen Bee*, the latter starring Joan Crawford at her scenery-chewing best.

Then in 1976 came **Without Your Love (Mr Jordan)**, a revolting song recorded by country singer Charlie Ross - who had previously been the bassist and singer of the moderately successful 60s group Eternity's Children - about a couple who on the surface appear to be deeply in love with each other but who, the listener soon discovers, are both conducting illicit affairs. This horrid record reached number 42 in the US charts (but went to number 13 in the Country Music listings) a moderate success but just about enough to inspire Vance and Cone to pen a follow-up, **Without Your Love (Mr Jordan Part Two)**, issued a year later as the B-side to the Paul Vance - Rupert Holmes co-write **Lady Loretta**.

This time good taste prevailed, and the disc failed to chart. A shame in a way, as **Without Your Love (Mr Jordan Part Two)** is even more ghastly than the original: once again the song is performed as a duet and, as in the original recording, the featured female singer is uncredited. It's unlikely though, given the maturity of the voice in question, that Vance had again pulled one of his kids in to sing on the record.

Shortly after Paul Vance retired from the industry. All was quiet for a number of years, with just the sound of the royalty cheques falling through the letterbox to break the boredom when, in 2006, a widely circulated news story reported that he had died. Needless to say, Mr Vance was not happy. It transpires that an impostor, Paul Van Valkenburgh, had been claiming the authorship of Itsy Bitsy Teenie Weenie and the real writer only became aware of this when a member of his family read his obituary and called up in a panic.

"My phone started to ring from my grandchildren, and each one says, *'Oh grandpa, you're alive'*," he told *Boca Raton Magazine*. "It felt horrible. I told the Associated Press that if they didn't give me a retraction, I would sue their balls off." The scare inspired Paul to begin writing his autobiography, *Catch A Falling Star*. Not everyone was convinced with is story though: "Then my husband's a liar...or (Vance) is a liar," Van Valkenburgh's widow Rose Leroux told the Associated Press. "The more you stir up of this the more you'll smell."

Lee Pockriss died in 2011; Jack Perricone teaches songwriting at the Berklee College of Music in Boston. Paul Vance spends his retirement in the Florida sunshine (the Paul Vance who released the album *The Comforts Of Home* in 2006 is a different person), and I hope he continues to do so for a long, long time.

***

* *Clint Holmes is not, as others have claimed, the brother of fellow WWR miscreant Rupert Holmes (author of the Buoys' hymn to cannibalism* Timothy*), although both are connected to Vance. Like Clint, Rupert was also born in Britain, but with the given name David Goldstein; he would go on to become the lead singer in the Cuff Links (replacing Ron Dante) and would co-write several songs with Vance.*

Ricky Segall And The Segalls, Featuring Rodney Allen Rippy (1973)

A couple of years ago I was invited to appear on *The Squire Presents* podcast to contribute to the then-upcoming Christmas edition. The Squire and I spent a great afternoon chatting about some of my favourite bad Christmas records and he introduced me to some of his. One of the songs he chose - and one I was, until then, blissfully unaware

of - was by a kindergarten-aged moppet by the name of Ricky Segall. The song sounded to me as if it were being performed by Ike Broflovsky, Kyle's adopted Canadian brother (if you don't watch *South Park* you'll not understand that reference: Google it). It was hideous.

Needless to say, I had to track down a copy of little Ricky's one and only album. And I'm so glad that I did.

Ricky Segall And The Segalls Singing Selections From "The Partridge Family" Television Show, to give it its full title, is truly abhorrent. Young master Segall was, at the time, a four year-old child actor who had been drafted in to the hit US TV series *The Partridge Family* to add some light relief to the show – and hopefully distract the audience from the fact that teen heart-throb David Cassidy was preparing to move on to pastures new. Unfortunately the fourth series, the one that introduced his character (Ricky Stevens), would also become the show's last.

All of the songs on the – thankfully short – album are written by Ricky's dad Rick senior and feature Ricky's parents prominently. Rick senior scored a contract as a songwriter with Colgems, the musical arm of the giant Columbia Pictures organisation (and the company behind The Monkees' recorded output), and the album features such top-ranking musicians as noted drummers Hal Blaine and Jim Gordon. It still stinks, and could easily explain why Gordon - who during an illustrious career played with the Everley Brothers, Little Richard, Eric Clapton, George Harrison, the Beach Boys, Frank Zappa, Alice Cooper and countless others - attacked his mother with a hammer before fatally stabbing her a few years later. As I write this, a full 20 years after Gordon (who, at the time of the frenzied attack, was an undiagnosed schizophrenic) was incarcerated, he is still an inmate of a specialist medical and psychiatric prison in California.

Richard Robert Segall III (to give this particular aural offender his full name) was born in New York on March 10, 1969. Now known as the Reverend Richard Segall, these days little Ricky is a minister at The Church On The Way in San Antonio, Texas but he still takes on the occasional acting role. He released his second album, *A Time To Dance*, in 1999 – described as an 'explosive, hi-tech, electronic dance CD'. I'll take Amazon's word for it. Rick Senior would go on to release a 'comedy' album for disco specialist Casablanca: *I Love You Because You're Fat*. I use the word 'comedy' here in its loosest possible sense: *I Love You Because You're Fat* is about as humorous as suppurating herpes. It could easily be responsible for "Weird Al" Yankovic's entire career.

The whole of *Ricky Segall And The Segalls Singing Selections From "The Partridge Family" Television Show* is horrible. **Say, Hey, Willie** – which opens the album and introduces Ricky's parents to an uncaring and uninterested audience – is a 'tribute' to American baseball legend Willie Mays, whose nickname was, apparently, the Say Hey Kid; at a press launch in a New York toy store, the four year-old explained that he liked "baseball, colouring books and girls". **Mr President** is Ricky's stab at a protest song – at least I think that's what it is. You can find your own copy and make up your own mind if you're so inclined. I've sat through this crap so many times now that my brain is starting to atrophy.

And why is the un-adorable little urchin rising out of a giant egg on the front cover? There's a Freudian nightmare if I've ever encountered one.

Little Ricky wasn't the only Partridge Family alumnus to record, of course. David Cassidy had a huge career as a teenybop idol in the

1970s, although his battles with the bottle – which ultimately led to his 2014 divorce – have probably tarnished that image forever. Shirley Jones (the widow Partridge) has made several albums, and Danny Bonaduce - who played Danny Partridge, the family bass player - released a self-titled album in 1973. Though the spectacularly unmusical Bonaduce was credited as lead singer, he has stated that he himself had a very weak voice and that Bruce Roberts - the singer-songwriter who co-wrote the Donna Summer and Barbra Streisand duet **No More Tears (Enough Is Enough)** - provided most of the vocals on the album. Film footage of Bonaduce performing **Feelin' Groovy (The 59th Street Bridge Song)** on US TV attests to his shortcomings. The opening track on the *Danny Bonaduce* album, **I'll Be Your Magician**, in which the pubescent 13 year-old attempts to seduce a woman into making the beast with two backs with him, has to be heard to be believed.

Bell, the company that issued the Partridge Family and Segall discs (but not the Bonaduce album: that dubious honour went to MGM), were adept at manufacturing careers out of nothing. Not long after this trash was foisted on to an unsuspecting public they put out an album by another four year-old recording sensation, Rodney Allen Rippy.

An as-cute-as-a-button black kid with a shock of wiry hair Rippy's album, *Take Life A Little Easier*, features abysmal covers of standards including **He's Got The Whole World In His Hands** and **Candy Man** and is just about the kind of fare you would expect from a child who, on the cover, looks like a stand-in for an oompa-loompa in an African-American version of *Charlie And The Chocolate Factory*.

Legend has it that Rodney, who was coached for his one and only album by his manager Dorothy Day Otis, was able to record a track an hour – literally learning the lyrics from scratch and banging out a take in that 60 minutes. It's hardly surprising then that the quality is questionable, but you've got to admire the child's work ethic...and his chutzpah. According to writer Louie Robinson, in a 1974 edition of *Ebony* magazine, when he was offered a dollar to get a difficult line right during a recording session *'Rodney countered with a request for two dollars. "You see my dad sitting in there," he explained, pointing to the engineer's room. "He's been there all day and he needs the money".'*

Rippy, who also appeared in the classic Mel Brooks comedy *Blazing Saddles* and even stood for mayor of Compton, in southern Los Angeles, in 2013 and 2014 may be unknown outside of his native country but

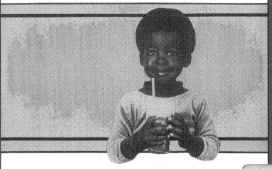

AMERICA NEEDS
RODNEY ALLEN RIPPY

"TAKE LIFE A LITTLE EASIER"

RECORDED BY

RODNEY ALLEN RIPPY

Produced by AL CAPPS for Blue Monday Productions
A Subsidiary of Current Music Enterprises

on Bell 45,481

BELL RECORDS
A Division of Columbia Pictures Industries, Inc.

for one short moment in time he was, as Louie Robinson put it, *'more of a household word than either the former or present vice president of the United States were before their nominations'* and that his *'infectious personality (was) sliding across the*

nation like a new invasion of viral flu'. The communicable disease-like Mr Rippy was snapped up as a three-and-a-half year-old by Jack-in-the-Box, the *'number four fast-food hamburger producer in the country'* for a series of TV commercials – which reportedly proved so popular that they helped the company increase their profits by $33 million. In his heyday (1973, to be precise), the three-feet-seven-inch Rodney appeared with Sammy Davis Junior, Johnny Carson, Michael Jackson and Donny Osmond, and was mobbed by a crowd of more than 4,000 people when he officially launched a line of Rodney Allen Rippy shirts at a Los Angeles department store. There was even a talking Rodney Rippy doll and, at the very height of his fame he became the focus of a McCartney-esque false death rumour.

But fame is a fickle mistress: after appearing in a few commercials for Chevrolet, and in episodes of *The Six Million Dollar Man, The Odd Couple* and *Laugh-In*, television work dried up. By the time the boy had reached the grand old age of 10 he was a has-been, replaced in the nation's hearts by another Lilliputian actor, Gary Coleman. Luckily his parents were smart enough to salt some of his earnings away and easily had enough to pay for Rodney and his siblings to be privately educated.

Now in his late 40s, Rodney runs his own PR firm, Ripped Marketing Group. He also works as the National Director of Marketing at Metro Networks (Westwood One), and is patron of a cancer charity. He still acts occasionally, appearing in David Spade's 2003 comedy *Dickie Roberts: Former Child Star* and starred in the US reality TV series *All Grown Up*, but there's very little chance that he'll be troubling the charts again any time soon.

Uri Geller
The Uri Geller Album (1974)

'Since Uri Geller stepped into the limelight his name, like no other before him, has created either fervent admiration or violent controversies. Scientists of renowned research institutes and universities have now, after exhaustive and extensive tests, come to the following conclusion: There is not a shadow of a doubt that Uri Geller has in fact an extraordinary mental ability, the power of which scientists have neither been able to fathom out nor grasp the extent of its meaning.' - From the original sleeve notes to *The Uri Geller Album*, 1974.

Vilified as a fake by some, feted as a phenomenon by others, Uri Geller is an enigma. Famous for purportedly possessing psychic powers, he has probably garnered more column inches in recent years for his friendship - and very public falling out - with the late Michael Jackson and for his numerous failed attempts at predicting the outcome of sporting events than for his celebrated spoon bending abilities.

Born in Tel Aviv in 1946, he began performing in night clubs in the late 1960s and in 1972, having already gained a huge following in Israel, he moved first to Europe and then to America where his act soon garnered coverage in the national media. By 1973 he was a household name in Britain, with TV and radio appearances by the bucket load, and major articles about him in national newspapers including *The Times, The News of the World* and *The Daily Mail*.

With the amount of media attention even a man without Geller's celebrated psychic abilities would have been able to predict that he would soon start to attract approaches from record company executives. Sure enough, little more than a year after he first came to prominence outside of his native Israel he was propelled into the recording studio to cut his first (and thankfully only) pop album. *Url Geller* features Url's own portentous (and pretentious) poetry put to music by composer and pianist Byron Janis. The result is the *Star Trek* soundtrack of your nightmares: a unique trip inside the mind of a notorious personality which will probably remain unmatched until turquoise jumpsuited New Age nutcase (and self-professed Son of the Godhead) David Icke decides to commit his crazed beliefs about lizards running the world to vinyl.

Geller had known Byron, and his wife Maria (the daughter of Hollywood icon Gary Cooper), for a couple of years. "We first met in the New York director's office of CBS, the TV station, in 1972," the spoon bender recalled, writing for his own website in 2009. "(Maria) invited me to meet her husband at their Park Avenue apartment. Byron and I became soul friends, and we spent many hours playing piano duets, either side-by-side at the keyboard or facing each other across the pair of grand pianos that dominated his flat.

"He taught me to play Chopin, and I reminded him of the tunes to many Hebrew songs. It doesn't take a lot of talent to play duets with one of the 20th century's greatest musicians, by the way — but it does require a wide streak of what Israelis call chutzpah." Janis had a copy of Chopin's death mask on his piano: he later claimed (in his book *Chopin And Beyond: My Extraordinary Life In Music And The Paranormal*) that on one occasion, when Uri was present, *'a clear liquid suddenly started coming out of the left eye of the mask. We froze in shock'*.

Says Uri: "When I was invited to record an album of songs, I naturally insisted I would do it only if Byron wrote the music." Never exactly backwards at coming forwards, it may come as a shock that the utterly shameless self-promoter is surprisingly self-effacing when it comes to claims of vocal prowess. "Promoter Werner Schmidt...originally wanted to do a musical about my life," he wrote on www.uri-geller.com. "(He) brushed off my claims that I couldn't sing... until I opened my mouth to demonstrate. Horrified, he sent me to a voice coach in Zurich - an 80-year-old woman named Lu, reputed to be able to teach anyone to sing like a lark. The best I could manage, though, was a cross between a raven and a frog." Lu encouraged him to take a leaf from actor Lee Marvin's book: instead of attempting to sing he should recite the lyrics in the same way that Marvin had so successfully done on his huge hit **Wandrin' Star**.

Uri is rather proud of his album: "By talking over Byron's beautiful music, putting all the passion and meaning I could into the lyrics which I had seemed to channel from above, I recorded an album that became a sensation. I truly believe nothing like it has ever been made." You're not wrong there, Uri.

"It was so popular that I returned to the studio four times, to re-record it in French, German, Italian and even Japanese." The Japanese version proved particularly popular, with Geller's fans in the land of the rising sun warming to the syllable-by-syllable phonetic translation of his poetry.

The Uri Geller Album sounds exactly like you'd expect it to: ethereal, wispy and fey, with swelling choirs and Liberace-like piano trills. The album's tracks include soppy songs to his children as well as the obligatory hosannas to a higher being. It's all very nice. Featuring a brace of duets with British soul singer Maxine Nightingale, Grammy-award winning artist Beck is a huge fan: "The combination of surging romantic strings and mind over matter (and forks) poetry is a potent one. I picked this up on vinyl in the early 90's and it was a favourite to listen to while we were recording *Odelay*." *Allmusic. com*'s Matt Collar describes it as *'something like Peter Lorre doing a spoken-word album backed by the Carpenters'*. Geller himself is less effusive when discussing his own poetic endeavours. *'I know my poems are not polished literary gems'* he wrote in his 1975 book *My Story*, *'but I feel them deeply. When they come, a force seems to grab me'*.

Several of the limp tracks on this New Age nightmare encourage the listener to try and develop their own psychic powers. On **Mood**, the

127

album's closing track, Geller tells them that they are *'part of a fascinating effect that is really hidden in many of us. But if it didn't happen, please don't be disappointed, because it doesn't happen to everybody. Sometimes it doesn't even work for me'*. Uri could just as easily be describing his own foray into the music business.

In *My Story*, Geller writes that *'When the record did appear in Europe in 1974, it was played over the radio in Switzerland. Sure enough, the station received hundreds of phone calls from people reporting that cutlery and keys were bending in their homes.'* Geller has made a lucrative living from his hypothetical telekinetic powers, and he has been tested and evaluated by many scientists over the decades. He has sued magician, writer and psychic debunker James Randi on three separate occasions over Randi's insistence that Geller's act was little more than stage magic and that his claims to possess psychic powers were fake. Tellingly, Geller lost all three court cases. In 1992 Uri was asked to help investigate the disappearance of Helga Farkas. He predicted that the Hungarian model would be found alive and in good health; in spite of that authorities later discovered that József Csapó and Benedek Juhász, who had kidnapped Helga, had murdered her and disposed of the teenager's body.

Around the time that Polydor (Columbia in the States) were readying *The Uri Geller Album* for release, the world's favourite spoon bender was to have appeared in a movie based on his life. *The Geller Effect* was to be produced by Aussie impresario Robert Stigwood with songs and incidental music by the Bee Gees. The project, which Maurice Gibb later described as "a sort of Star Wars-cum-Love Story" was abandoned, but 20 years later the legendary Ken Russell was behind the direct-to-video *Mindbender*, a film about Geller which co-incidentally did feature the Bee Gees on the soundtrack.

A prolific author, public speaker and personality, in 2007 Uri hosted a TV series in Israel on which he attempted to find his psychic successor: the show went on to be picked up by TV networks in America, Sweden, Turkey, Hungary, the Netherlands and Russia. I wonder if the great man predicted that one?

Uri Geller was reissued on CD in the UK in 1999: the reissue features three extra tracks – all foreign-language versions of **Mood**. In recent years he has released several self-help and meditation CDs; thankfully none of them including material from *Uri Geller* or featuring the spoon bender singing.

***

* Still performing today, Maxine Nightingale released her first single in 1969, appeared on stage in the London production of Hair and went on to have a huge international hit with **Right Back Where We Started From** *in 1975.*

Music And Politics

As a quick scour of YouTube will confirm, politicians around the world seem to believe that one way to prove that they are 'of the people' is to occasionally flex their vocal cords. Barack Obama has done it, Vladimir Putin too; Australian Prime Minister Tony Abbot might consider himself *'too much of a grog-monster'* (Aussie slang for heavy drinker) to put his vocals down in a studio, but that didn't stop him crooning a few bars of Elvis Presley's **Suspicious Minds** during a party to celebrate Australia Day in January 2013. Canadian Prime Minister Stephen Harper serenaded Israel's Benjamin Netanyahu with his rendition of **Hey Jude** during a state dinner in Jerusalem, banging away at a keyboard while he launched gung-ho into the song. Former Italian Prime Minister, convicted tax evader and host of the now-legendary *bunga bunga* parties Silvio Berlusconi paid for his years at college by working as a singer on Mediterranean cruise ships and, in 2011, he co-wrote an album's worth of love songs, *True Love*; wisely Silvio decided to have another man sing his dodgy lyrics. He has, however, been known to put on private performances for the rich and famous. One of Italy's longest serving post-war prime ministers, and one the country's richest men, Tony Blair, Vladimir Putin and George W Bush have all been lucky enough to witness his cabaret act.

It doesn't take much to persuade some fame-hungry people into a recording studio and, as we've seen, many well-known names – including actors, sports personalities, TV presenters and writers – have happily committed their epiglottal warblings to vinyl. With news presenters, golfers, sci-fi authors and topless models all having a crack at the charts is it any surprise that politicians, the very leaders of our establishment, would also want to extend their 15 minutes of fame? The world's best-known singing politicians are all women, although in all fairness the Irish songthrush Dana and Greek singers Melina Mercouri and Nana Mouskouri were all known as performers before they entered the political arena. The same goes for Liberian congresswoman Malinda Jackson Parker, whose brilliant and baffling musical career was featured in *The World's Worst Records: Volume One*.

Former President Bill Clinton may have stuck to blowing a sax, but he was beaten to it by Nigerian senator Pammy Young, who cut several sides with his dance band for Philips West African records in the 1960s. Clinton may not have officially recorded, but over the years many, many US politicians – and a handful of former Presidents - have left the debating rostrum to nip into a recording studio.

Thanks to a recording he made in September 1972 (although it was not issued commercially until 1975), Lyndon B Johnson became the only (former or incumbent) US president to record a single – **Dogs Have Always Been My Friends**. Subtitled *Tales From The Texas Hills*, Johnson's recording was made by Carl Degen, chief of the audio-visual department of Harpers Ferry (an historic town in West Virginia), who was given the responsibility of making a series of film documentaries starring Johnson. Sadly Degen only completed an hour or so of usable footage, filmed around four months before the former president passed away in January 1973: the short snippets which appear on the five track EP are all taken from the film soundtrack.

Johnson had previously issued spoken-word albums (mostly of speeches and addresses to Congress), and even the missus got in on the act: Ladybird was featured on the MGM album *A Visit To Washington With Mrs Lyndon B Johnson On Behalf Of A More Beautiful America*, but this particular recording is a badly read monologue about LBJ's affinity for our four legged friends, including how he and his youngest daughter Luci had rescued a little dog by the name of Yuki. Sold to unsuspecting visitors via the gift shop of his Texas ranch it's dull, dull, dull – until four minutes in when things take a severely weird turn, and Johnson and Yuki perform a howling 'duet' together, making Yuki, as the sleeve notes claim: *'the only dog in history to sing a duet with a President of the United States'*. As bizarre as that is, it also makes LBJ the only US President ever to have 'sung' on record. During his tenure as President, Johnson enjoyed the company of two other dogs, beagles named Him and Her; sadly, neither of them ever performed on disc. Johnson was not the first deceased president to issue posthumous recordings: in 1945, just weeks after he passed away, a collection of five eight-inch picture discs was issued entitled *Great Speeches* by Franklin Delano Roosevelt.

Since then FDR's speeches have turned up innumerable times on vinyl, and the deceased Commander-in-Chief was also one of the stars of the 1956 Folkways Records compendium *The Un-Typical Politician*, a rather odd little album, compiled and narrated by Myles Platt, which consists of various political speeches cut up and pasted together. Unlike the LBJ EP, *The Un-Typical Politician* failed to capture any of the protagonists singing. The outpouring of grief after John F Kennedy's assassination opened the floodgates to dozens of 'tribute' albums featuring the great man. Sadly the closest we'll get to hearing JFK sing is by listening to the many send-ups that were released during his time, principally the 1962 LP *Sing Along With JFK*. Jack, Jackie and the rest of Clan Kennedy were spoofed that same year by comedian and musician Vaughn Meader for his *First Family* album but George Atkins and Hank Levine's *Sing Along With JFK* album took snippets of John F's speeches, added an accordion player and chorus and created the closest thing to a serving President 'singing' as had been heard to date, setting Camelot to music. Promoted as an original cast album, *Sing Along With JFK* was issued by Frank Sinatra's Reprise label. The same technique would be employed in 2004 by the George W Bush Singers for their album *Songs In The Key of W*.

Jack Kennedy's brother Bobby was also spoofed – a year before he too was assassinated – by Comedian Bill Minkin who issued a version of the Troggs' hit **Wild Thing** as Senator Bobby and took it into the Billboard Top 20. Senator Everett McKinley Dirksen, who was lampooned by Minkin on the flip side of the same 45, scored a Top 20 hit himself in 1966 with **Gallant Men**. Again the Senator wisely chose not to sing, although he was accompanied by a rousing choir and suitably patriotic music. Dirksen went on to issue four albums of his particular brand of flagwaving humbuggery, and a surprisingly large number of US Senators have, rather foolishly, followed in his footsteps.

Ohio representative Tennyson Guyer – a former circus performer – issued several albums of political musings and one (the oddly-titled *Attic-dotes Volume IV*) on which he was accompanied by his daughter Sharon (a budding soprano) and pianist Allen Dudley. Virginia Senator Robert Byrd and Mississippi's representative George Cecil McLeod were both pretty mean bluegrass fiddle players and both issued albums, but it would be the Democratic Senator for North Carolina who struck out and scored a bona fide pop hit.

Samuel James Ervin, Jr. (born September 1896) served as Senator for North Carolina from 1954 to 1974. He was instrumental in bringing down two powerful opponents: Senator Joe McCarthy at the very beginning of his career and President Richard Nixon at the very end. In 1954 Nixon, then vice-President, appointed Ervin to a committee formed to investigate whether McCarthy should be censured by the Senate; it was Ervin's investigation of the Watergate scandal in 1972/73 that led to the resignation of his former mentor.

However, although there is no evidence to show that the man was involved in any lynchings himself, in 1956 he helped draft The Southern Manifesto, which encouraged defiance of desegregation and was signed by most the Southern members of Congress. His apologists argue that his opposition to most civil rights legislation was based on his commitment to the preservation of the Constitution, and that he also supported civil liberties by opposing "no knock" search laws, the growing intrusions of data banks and lie-detectors (a machine he branded *'20th century witchcraft'*), the use of illegally-seized evidence in criminal trials, and he played a major role in the defeat of a Constitutional amendment to make prayer in public schools compulsory. So he wasn't all bad, then, or all good. Like most of us.

A native of Morganton, North Carolina, he thought of himself as a "country lawyer", and was well-known for telling humorous stories in his Southern drawl. It was this particular party piece that led Columbia Records to sign him up. His one album - *Senator Sam At Home* - featured

Ervin speaking his mind, telling a few anecdotes and occasionally bursting into song: evidence of which managed to cross the pond when CBS in the UK issued **Bridge Over Troubled Water** as a single in 1973. The track was later re-issued on the Rhino compilation *Golden Throats 2*. *Senator Sam At Home* was, apparently, recorded in the library of his Morganton home.

I fail to understand what was going on in the mind of the CBS executive who thought that this drivel stood a chance of being a hit in Britain. The man was famous in the States, of course he'll sell a few copies, but in the UK he was an unknown septuagenarian doing little more than reading a poem – and reading it badly at that. When performed with emotion, Paul Simon's **Bridge Over Troubled Water** is a great song: recited in stumbling fashion over a hokey backing just doesn't cut it. Scheduled for release in the UK in November 1973, all of the UK copies I have seen have been promos: it's possible that the disc was so poorly received that stock copies were never issued here. In America the album was supported by full-page ads in the trade papers which waxed lyrically about Sam's *'insights into Shakespeare, the Constitution and the Bible'*. William S Burroughs even wrote about the album in *Esquire*.

Sam Ervin retired from Congress in December 1974. He continued to practise law, and his son and two of his grandsons followed him into the legal profession. He died from emphysema on April 23, 1985, aged 88.

Less than a year before Senator Sam 'did' Paul Simon, another member of the House of Representatives had a crack at the charts – only this time the record was not only made by a politician but it was also about a politician. Senator Roscoe Dean's **A Ballad To George Wallace** (backed with **Monday Morning Blues** by Lee Greene and his Shining Knights of Greene) was issued in August 1972 on the tiny GWS (Great World of Sound) label of Miami, Florida. Roscoe Dean Jr - of the city of Jesup - was Georgia's youngest senator, elected to office at just 28 years old in 1963. Governor George Wallace, of course, was also immortalised in song by Ken "Nevada" Maines on the brilliantly odd *The World Of Las Vegas* album (which I featured in *The World's Worst Records; Volume One*). This 45 was issued just months after an assassination attempt - in May 1972 - left Wallace paralyzed, forcing him to use a wheelchair for the rest of his life. Wallace, who died in 1998, is chiefly remembered for his segregationist views, although he eventually renounced segregationism.

Still, apparently, living in Jesup today, Senator Roscoe Dean was indicted on 14 counts of theft – for fiddling his expenses – in 1975, the same year that Governor George launched his fourth unsuccessful campaign for the presidency. The good ol' boy even took his mum to court with him to elicit some sympathy from the bench, but he was still censured by the Senate in 1976 for, amongst other things, claiming mileage from Jesup to Atlanta on days when he was sunning himself in the Bahamas.

Not one to learn from his mistakes, in 1982 Dean attempted to found an illegal drug cartel on the Georgia coast to finance his campaign for governor; unfortunately for him his Columbian drug-running co-conspirators were actually undercover agents from the Georgia Bureau of Investigation. Roscoe Emory Dean, Jr. and John Thomas Bigley were convicted on three counts of conspiracy to import cocaine, marijuana, and methaqualone; Bigley was convicted on one additional count of using a firearm in the commission of a federal felony.

It has even been suggested that he may have been capable of murder: in December 1979, it is claimed, attorney Hirsch Friedman was contacted by a Mr. Weiss, who had been sentenced on a felony conviction in federal court. Weiss stated he had information that Roscoe Dean was involved in a plot to kill Governor George Busbee. Weiss's information was conveyed to the Georgia Bureau of Investigation and the GBI asked Friedman to do undercover work on the investigation into Roscoe Dean's nefarious activities. Friedman was wired up to a concealed tape recorder and, posing as a drug smuggler, discussed the possible sale of cocaine with the Senator.

Mr. Friedman then arrested him.

Bad boy Roscoe was arrested and sent to prison for five years. Released on license after 22 months, his appeal was overturned and he returned to prison in 1985 to serve out the remainder of his sentence.

Luckily there are very few examples of British politicians cutting discs. In the days of the 78 many famous speeches – including those of Neville Chamberlain, Winston Churchill, Stanley Baldwin and even King George V and the abdicating Edward VIII - were issued and sold reasonably well, and more recently Conservative Prime Minister Edward Heath released several albums of himself conducting orchestral works, but outside of very rare (and usually novelty) instances most have stoutly refused to be drawn into battle for a place in the hit parade.

I say most...

The ball started rolling in 1964 when the Conservative Central office issued an EP entitled *Songs For Swinging Voters*. This six-track flexidisc of anti-Labour and Liberal singalongs features two versions of the song **John Citizen** alongside the tracks **Nationalisation Nightmare**, **Four Jolly Labourmen**, **One Man Band** and **Poor Old Jo**, a song

dedicated to Liberal Party leader Jo Grimond. Issued to encourage people to vote Tory in the October 1964 election, the disc only helped further damage the party's standing with the public: Labour increased their majority by an extra 59 parliamentary seats. The credits on the disc do not reveal who appears on the recordings, so I can't tell you if any Conservative MPs actually performed themselves. Never mind: it's still abysmal. Six years earlier Tory leader and current Prime Minister Harold Macmillan had issued a card-mounted flexidisc called *Roll Call for Victory 1958*. Listeners were encouraged to *'play this record and hear his voice'*.

Unsurprisingly few of them bothered. If they had they certainly would not have heard Supermac sing.

Not to be outdone Labour leader Harold Wilson could be heard introducing **Let's Go With Labour**, described in the label as *'the new theme song for Labour Party supporters'*. With lyrics by Dave Carey (based on an idea by Bessie Braddock MP and Wilson's 1963 speech of the same name), the words are set to the tune of **John Brown's Body** performed in the style of the au courant Mersey Beat groups:

In the future, let's go Labour
For the country, let's go Labour
Build a better world with Labour
It's the party that gets things done!

(*Let's Go With Labour,* words by Dave Carey, music trad. Performer unknown. © 1964, The Labour Party)

In the same year that the Conservatives were trying to woo *Swinging Voters* and Labour wheeled out Wilson to introduce their new theme song, musician Brian Lee issued a seldom-seen (and probably even more selom heard) little pop ditty, **The Liberal Song**, on the tiny YL Discs label, backed with a message from Jo Grimond. The disc was produced by John Boyden, better known as a classical music producer; YL stood for Young Liberals and this appears to have been the company's only release. It would be almost two decades before the party would be foolish enough to enter the race for the pop charts again.

Released on the obscure, independent Scotland Video record label, **I Feel Liberal: Alright!** was released to coincide with the Liberal Party Assembly in Bournemouth in 1982. The record consists of excerpts from leader David (now Lord) Steel's speeches set to an electronic music backing written and produced by Scottish musician Jesse Rae and featuring master keyboard player Bernie Worrell. No-one needs to hear Steel – the man lampooned by satirical puppet show Spitting Image as tiny and insignificant – utter the words *'You can help me change the face of British politics/Let's pull our country together instead of tearing it apart'* while the backing vocalists repeat *'Steel! David Steel! I feel Liberal!'* over and over again. It's truly ghastly. After listening to this I certainly don't feel liberal; I feel dirty.

Years later Steel was mocked over his one stab at chart immortality on the TV news quiz *Have I Got News For You*. He insisted that the record was intended to "be fun, tongue in cheek" and even admitted that he thought it had "quite a good tune". Believe me: it doesn't. Not one to let sleeping dogs lie, Steel also appeared on the TV show *Afternoon Plus* with Alliance cohort Shirley Williams performing an updated version of **If You Were The Only Girl In The World** (as *If You Were the Only Shirl...*). Ugh.

There must be something in the water at these Liberal party gatherings: former Transport Minister and Lib Dem MP for Lewes Norman Baker has received much publicity for his band The Reform Club and their debut single **Piccadilly Circus**, a blatant rip-off of the Kinks classic **Well Respected Man**. Another (now former) Liberal MP (and former Cheeky Girl consort to boot) Lembit Opik played and 'sang' (well, recited one line) on the 2002 single **Weekend Rock And Roll Band** by Hank MacGregor and, in 2009, appeared on a charity cover of the S Club 7 hit **Don't Stop Movin'**. But the prize for the worst – and, in hindsight, most bad taste – performance by a politician has to be that of disgraced former Liberal stalwart the late Cyril Smith.

The gargantuan MP for Rochdale (who, since his death has been outed as a child molester) recorded a version of the Laurel and Hardy classic **Trail Of The Lonesome Pine** with diminutive actor Don Estelle – who had previously recorded solo as well as with his *It Ain't Half Hot Mum* co-star Windsor Davies. According to the book *Smile For The Camera: The Double Life Of Cyril Smith* by Simon Danczuk and Matt Baker, the pair polished off this most bizarre of duets in just one take, crammed (and in Smith's case, crouched) in a vocal booth of a recording studio in Rochdale, Lancashire. On completing the recording the ridiculous pair *'high-fived and Don smiled. "That was great Cyril, just perfect".'* Not by any stretch of the imagination could this unholy coupling be described as perfect: Estelle warbles through the tune like the mediocre music hall singer he was while Smith tosses off a quick monologue during one verse of the song and joins Estelle to sing the song's payoff line. It's thoroughly wretched.

UKIP Calypso by The Independents is probably the only political record to have been withdrawn by its author/performer because of a national outcry: shame the same can't be said of some of the other discs featured here. The Independents was a pseudonym for former Radio One DJ and professional Cliff Richard impersonator Mike Read. On October 22 2014 Read turned to the press to announce that he was pulling his own song, a track he had happily been plugging just two days before, following criticism that it was racist. He said that he was sorry for "unintentionally causing offence" with the tune, which he performed in a fake Caribbean accent. Read had defended his song after some objected to his using calypso music to promote the UK Independence Party's anti-immigration agenda. "It was never meant to be remotely racist," he said. "It's an old-fashioned political satire." The song's withdrawal ruined UKIP leader Nigel Farage's hope that the song would reach No 1.

Currently fronting a post-lunch magazine show on BBC Radio Berkshire, the ghastly Read has a history of issuing bad recordings: in 2009 he released – as The Shooting Stars - the dismal single **My Christmas Card To You**. Issued to raise money for charity, I can't imagine the modest royalties this piece of trash would have garnered would have bought many bandages. Read has claimed that **UKIP Calypso** was also issued to raise funds for a charity, this time for the Red Cross and the fight against Ebola. The Red Cross quickly issued a statement saying that they would not accept a penny from the sales of Read's racist rant.

And racist it is. Ignore his pathetic claim that *'you can't sing a calypso with a Surrey accent. I like Jamaicans; honest'* or whatever the twice bankrupt loser said, you cannot escape the fact that any song that contains the couplet *'open the borders let them all come in/ Illegal immigrants in every town'* is a tad less than welcoming to non-Brits. **UKIP Calypso** was not Read's first brush with political posturing: he is a former Tory supporter who, in 2006, entertained guests at a Conservative Conference dinner with a woeful ten-minute political rap!

UKIP Calypso is awful, and you can't help wondering if this was issued with the express intention of its being banned or withdrawn, simply in order to gain more press coverage for the racist, homophobic, right wing nutjobs currently masquerading so successfully as a proper political party.

Read's ridiculous song is not the first to bolster the party faithful: in 2013 Anna-Marie Crampton issued the appalling dance tune **Better Vote UKIP** which sank like a stone. Ms Crampton was suspended by the party soon after over reports that she had posted anti-Semitic comments online. Former Tory and now comedy UKIP supporter Neil Hamilton and his ghastly wife Christine issued a single a few years earlier in support of England's football team – **England Are Jolly Dee** – about which, like anything UKIP-related, the less said the better.

Read's attempts to realise musical greatness go back 35 years. In 1979 he wrote and performed the song **High Rise** under the name The Trainspotters and followed this in 1980 with **My Town** as The Ghosts. He wrote the lyrics to the theme for the TV series *Trainer*, recorded by his idol Cliff Richard as **More To Life**. In 1991 he provided a guest rap on Slade's UK Top 30 hit **Radio Wall Of Sound**. More recently he's had minor chart hits with re-recordings of Hank Mizell's **Jungle Rock** and Mungo Jerry's **In The Summertime** and, in 2005, his song **Grief Never Grows Old** (released by the One World Project, which again included Sir Cliff in its number) actually made the UK Top Five, raising money for charities working with tsunami victims. He's also written music to accompany poems written by John Betjeman and has staged a number of musicals, including *Young Apollo* (a musical about the life of Rupert Brooke); *Oscar* (a 2004 show about Oscar Wilde which was derided by critics and closed after one performance) and *Cliff - The Musical* (which closed after three months, probably because Read took one of the lead roles).

If all that wasn't enough to hate, in 2007 he foisted his Choc Art on the world: 'paintings' made with liquorice allsorts and other sweets – including a reinterpretation of the Beatles' iconic *Abbey Road* and *Sgt Pepper* sleeves that look like they were slung together by a five-year-old. Oh, and he was entirely responsible for having **Relax** by Frankie Goes to Hollywood banned from the airwaves (even though he's since tried to claim otherwise). Would you be surprised to discover that sultan of smarm once worked as an estate agent?

But don't think this phenomenon is the exclusive domain of British or American politicians, for around the same time that Senator Dirkson was spouting off about American troops in Vietnam Liberal statesman Andrew Jones, the youngest member of the Australian House of Representatives, penned a little ditty about every antipodean's right to live in a free, democratic country. Appearing under the perverse title **Shadow Valley And The Iron Triangles** the disc, which starts with a burst of automatic gunfire, is credited to The Young Australians but actually features narration by television executive Rex Heading, perhaps better known in Australia as the creator of beloved children's characters Humphrey B Bear, Winky Dink and Hot Dog.

Issued by Festival Records in 1966 and backed by the track

Too Many Twisted Trails, the disc went to number one in the Adelaide area but Heading's hysterical rant sounded more like a Monty Python sketch that the jingoistic recruiting tool Andrew Jones had hoped for and the record was banned by several radio stations. Fittingly, Jones lost his seat at the next election.

Major Bill And The King

The unfathomable Major Bill Smith is (or rather, was) an incredibly important but now almost forgotten name in the history of American popular music. Based in Fort Worth, Texas, he was responsible for a handful of major (if you'll excuse the pun) hit singles including **Hey Baby** by Bruce Channel (often cited as a chief influence on The

Beatles' **Please Please Me**), Paul and Paula's **Hey Paula** (a US number one in 1963 which, songwriter Ray Hildebrand attests, was directly influenced by **Hey Baby**), and the bad-taste teen-death smash **Last Kiss** by J. Frank Wilson and the Cavaliers. "When Last Kiss came out," he told David McGee of *Record World* magazine, "Everybody told me it was sick. One guy at a radio station said it was the sickest record he'd ever heard. It was sick, alright - sick to the tune of about two million sales!" These three hits would provide enough income to sustain his empire until his death more than 30 years later.

The father of six was born January 21, 1922 in Checotah, McIntosh County, Oklahoma. Unlike 'Colonel' Tom Parker, Major Bill Smith was a genuine officer, serving in the US Air Force during the Second World War.* Stationed near Northampton in England, Bill Smith flew B-17s (also known as the Flying Fortress) on combat missions over Germany; on his 33rd mission he was shot down - for the rest of his life his hands and wrists would bear the scars caused by shrapnel damage - and, after a long spell in hospital, he wound up stationed in Germany, serving there until 1953. Moving into the music industry after leaving the service, after a short period working as a song plugger he set up his own production and publishing company, LeBill Music, and several labels including Le Cam (named after his wife Letitia and his business partner George Campbell), Black Sheep, Charay, Christi, Pharaoh, Soft, Shalimar and Twinkle.

In a showbiz calling than spanned four decades the relentless self-promoter and hustler also had a hand in the early career of the Legendary Stardust Cowboy. The Major took the publishing rights to **Paralyzed**, the Ledge's classic first single, issued it on his own Psycho-Suave label and licensed the song to Mercury. Then things turned sour: the story has it that Major Bill absconded with the tapes of some 50 songs, many of which were intended for the Ledge's first, unreleased, album. Ledge, in a fit of pique, broke into the Maj's office, stole them back and then destroyed the tapes so that nobody (as he told outsider music historian Irwin Chusid), "including Major Bill, could get their hands on my music."

Described as "a klutz and a terrible manager" by Ray Hildebrand (in the book *Setting The Record Straight* by Anthony P Musso) he still managed to produce, arrange and/or write hundreds of tracks during his career. A born showman with a mercurial temper, although quality control was never that important to him he knew (or at least thought he knew) how to sell a song. To the Maj, everything he touched was a *'cotton-picking smash!'* "I ain't the braggin' kind, but I've made 3,000 records" he told Adam Komorowski in an interview for *New Kommotion* magazine (published in 1980); "I got four gold records and a platinum record, which is pretty good".

The Major's career was so long and so varied that there's bound to be a fair amount of crap amongst the gold, but easily the worst of the many releases he was involved with are those on which Major Bill actually performed himself, including **Happy Birthday Jesus**, the sub-Lil' Markie slice of in utero schmaltz **Cry Of An Unborn Child**, and the ridiculous **Freddy, The Disco Frog**.

Happy Birthday Jesus is credited to Major Bill Smith and Nancy Nolte, although poor old Nancy doesn't get much of a look in on the vocal front. Nancy Nolte recorded for Todd Records in 1959 and then went on to release the 45 **Christmas Night** backed with **Christmas Tree In Heaven** for Le Cam the following year. Actor Nick Nolte has a sister called Nancy, who is now an executive with the Red Cross: wouldn't it be wonderful if this were her? On **Happy Birthday Jesus** Major Bill reads a sermon on the true meaning of Christmas over the top of a version of **Silent Night**:

my suspicion is that this disc uses one of those Nancy Nolte tracks as its backing (more than probably **Christmas Night**) - which is probably why she gets a credit here.

The disco craze was responsible for many, many heinous hits and easily some of the worst (and often most tenuous) novelties imaginable. But if you thought **Disco Duck** by Rick Dees and his Cast of Idiots was about as stupid as it could get, you obviously haven't met **Freddy, The Disco Frog** yet. Written and performed by Major Bill with Zane and Hogan, this dreadful disco dirge – an uninspired rip off of the aforementioned **Disco Duck**, was issued on Le Cam in 1978, as the B-Side of **Requiem To The King**, one of the Major's Elvis tributes. Highlights include the Maj mumbling his virtually unintelligible lyrics over the world's worst disco bass line while Zane and Hogan chime in with an endless 'oo-ooh-ohh' backing.

He refuses to play all them crazy frog games
He just want to wait to the sun go down
Then he'll hop on down to the disco in Mudbank Town
Freddie! He cool!
Mighty Freddie, the king of Mudbank Town

(*Freddie The Disco Frog*, written by Smith, Zane & Hogan. Recorded by Major Bill Smith with Zane and Hogan on Le Cam Records. © 1978, Softcharay Music)

It's abominable, but it does lead us nicely in to the really weird part of the Major's story. During the 1980's the cut-price Colonel Parker was going about telling everyone who would listen that the late Elvis Presley was, in fact, not late at all and informed his media contacts that he was now the burger King's de facto manager.

The Maj and Elvis had known each other, briefly, early on in the

King's career - which makes it even harder to comprehend how, more than four years after his funeral, Bill came to be promoting records (and even a telephone interview) which, he claimed, were recorded after the King had apparently left this world for the big burger bar in the sky. Not content with managing Presley's bloated corpse, and not having learned his lesson from the failure of **Requiem To The King** to chart (a record which, confusingly, accepts that Elvis had indeed gone off to meet his maker), Major Bill continued to issue a series of Elvis tribute 45s, occasionally roping in friends like Bruce Channel to help, as he did with the dreadful **The King Is Free** (Le Cam). Ridicule, quite naturally, followed.

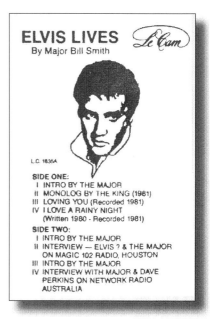

Never one to take criticism lying down, Bill issued a cassette - *Elvis Lives* - containing interviews and songs supposedly recorded by Elvis in 1981, put out a short audio clip of Elvis allegedly recorded live on air (in what he described as 'a conference call') in Houston, released a second cassette, this time credited to The King and Kelli which he claimed featured a post-mortem Presley performing **I Love A Rainy Night** (actually the same recording that had appeared on *Elvis Lives*, with Kelli's vocals dubbed over the top) and - and you have to admire the chutzpah of the man here - in 1993, just a year before his own death, he actually attempted to sue Elvis's estate for perpetuating the lie that he had died in 1977 and from preventing him from promoting his book, *The Memphis Mystery*, about the cover-up surrounding Elvis's faked death. The tapes he touted around were reputedly examined by a voice expert from the Houston Police Department who, it has been claimed, found 35 instances where the voice pattern matched that of known Elvis recordings.

In January 1988 Major Bill issued a single to celebrate Elvis's birthday, **Hey! Big E (Happy 53)**. Still insisting that the King had faked his death so he could live in anonymity, he also claimed that the so-called sightings of Elvis in Kalamazoo in 1988 really were him. One year later he produced the tribute album *Spelling On The Stone* (playing on the conspiracy theorists' favourite 'evidence' that Elvis must still be alive: his name is misspelled on his headstone), featuring the voice of uncredited Elvis-alike Dan Willis, and in 1991 he announced that Elvis would be returning to the world on January 1, 1992, just in time to mark the 57th anniversary of his birth.

"I manage Elvis Presley. I produce Elvis Presley. I am Elvis Presley's spokesman," he told Gary James of *classicbands.com* "Elvis says he's gonna try to come back soon. It will be with The Major and I will be handling the whole damn thing!"

So far as I am aware Presley has yet to reappear (although there is a guy who works down the chip shop who swears he's Elvis). Even if he didn't die in 1977 it's highly unlikely he'll turn up now: he'd be in his eighties. Having said that, there are thousands of people out there who still believe that he never went away: there are, frankly, preposterous claims that Elvis hid in plain sight, being photographed with boxer Muhammad Ali in 1984 and even appearing as an extra in the 1990 movie *Home Alone*!

Outside of his bizarre music career the Maj taught Sunday School and, according to local historian Jerry Adams *'took a great interest in helping the down and outs at the Union Gospel Mission in downtown Fort Worth'*. Smith passed away, at the age of 72, on September 12, 1994. The source of the *Elvis Lives/King And Kelli* tracks turned out to be an earlier tape issued by one Sivle Nora (Elvis Aron backwards; in 1985 singer David Darlock admitted that he provided the voice of Sivle and that he had been hired to 'channel' the voice of Elvis for the performance) and 'produced' by Elvis-isn't-dead conspirator Steven Chanzes. As Major Bill had not received permission from Chanzes to slather the voice of the indescribably awful Kelli Fenton all over his recordings, essentially *The King And Kelli* is a bootleg of a recording issued to perpetuate a fraud.

Since 2012 Chanzes – who insists he knows the 'real' truth of the matter - has been trying to peddle his laughable crap on Ebay in e-book form for $10,000. Unfortunately some gullible Elvis fan will no doubt eventually shell out for it.

In an interesting twist, author Mike Eder (in his book *Elvis Music FAQ: All That's Left To Know About The King's Recorded Works*, Backbeat Books, 2013) claims that poor old Major Bill had been the subject of a con: *'I had been in touch with Smith at the time and after his death I found out that the Major did think he was in touch with Elvis and was duped out of a lot of money.*

'One feels sorry for the elderly Major, who was a tireless promoter with a good sense of humour.'

To be fair, you'd have to have a good sense of humour to peddle some of this crap.

***

* Colonel Tom Parker's real name was Andreas Cornelis van Kuijik: he was a Dutch-born illegal immigrant who had taken the name Tom Parker from the officer who inducted him into the U.S. Army. Discharged for desertion whilst still a private, the man who would become the King's manager was eventually made an honorary Colonel in the Louisiana State Militia by governor Jimmie Davis.

J D Sumner
Elvis Has Left The Building (1977)

Discussing the contributions of Major Bill Smith to the world of bad music and his involvement (however tenuous) in the career of Elvis Presley - brings us nicely on to our next bad record.

No single artist has inspired as many tribute records – literally hundreds, possibly thousands - both during his career and after his untimely demise as the late Elvis Presley. Certainly Elvis must be the second man after Jesus Christ (I'm not counting God here as he's not, nor never has been, a 'man' in the strictest sense of the word) to have so many tonnes of vinyl wasted on rotten recordings of rotten songs by rotten singers and rotten songwriters: there's been enough plastic dedicated to Elvis tributes to double the size of the Great Pacific Garbage Patch. Dire Straits, Alice Cooper, Queen, repeat-offender Tiny Tim (**I Saw Mr. Presley Tip-toeing Through The Tulips**), Kate Bush, Neil Young, Bruce Springsteen...they've all done it. Even U2, that most po-faced and self-aggrandising of groups, churned out a brace of Elvis tributes: the nonsensical and unintelligible **Elvis Presley And America** from the dreadful, massively overrated *The Unforgettable Fire* album and **Elvis Ate America**, from their poorly-conceived, poorly-executed and poorly-received Eno-produced ego-fest *Passengers - Original Soundtracks 1*.

John Daniel 'J D' Sumner (or *His Friend J D Sumner* as he credits himself on both sleeve and label of the tawdry little record) was an American gospel singer, songwriter, and music promoter. Born in 1924, he was a member of a number of vocal groups including the Sunny South Quartet, the Dixie Lily Harmoneers, the Sunshine Boys and the Stamps Quartet, who later became known as J D Sumner and The Stamps. The story goes that Elvis fell in love with Sumner's singing after seeing him perform with the Sunshine Boys when the boy who would be King was only 16 years old. After he became a star he remembered the singer with the incredible range, hiring him to sing at his mother's funeral in 1958, but it would be another 13 years before the pair would finally link up together on record.

Presley hired Sumner and The Stamps as his back-up singers in late 1971, the same year that Sumner issued his first volume of autobiography *Gospel Music Is My Life*. *'Gospel music was designed by Christian people* as a means of reaching the lost', he wrote. 'I wouldn't be on the road as much as I am, staying away from my family, if it were not so. If we can inspire people to live better lives, we've performed a ministry'. Fine words from a man who would later admit to drinking two-fifths (or two standard bottles) of whisky a day and who would

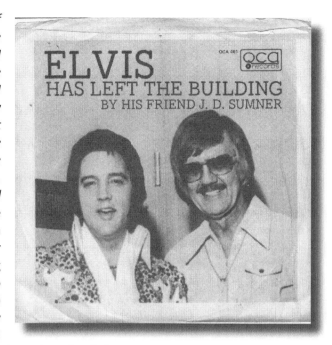

always need a full glass of Scotland's finest near at hand when performing live. He would go on to write – or co-write – several volumes of Christian-themed reminiscences, including 1991's *Elvis: His Love for Gospel Music*.

Sumner and the group toured and recorded with Presley until his death in 1977 (interestingly, the notes on the back of the sleeve of the 45 state that The Stamps only toured with Elvis for four years). Having already done the same favour for Mama Presley, Sumner also sang at Elvis' funeral. Which in no way explains how he released a record as shockingly awful as **Elvis Has Left the Building**, his tribute to his friend and former employer.

The time was 1935, the place Tupelo, Mississippi
God sent this world a baby boy who was born in to poverty
And as a boy he wondered what would be his destiny

(*Elvis Has Left the Building*, written by J D Sumner. Recorded by JD Sumner on QCA Records. © 1977, Gospel Quartet Music)

Sumner, who also provided the bass voice on **Way Down**, one of Elvis' last hits, narrates the story of the King's life and death in the most boring fashion imaginable. Written by Sumner himself (the B-Side **Sweet, Sweet Spirit**, was written by Doris Akers, miscredited as Ackers: Elvis had previously recorded another Akers composition **Lead Me, Guide Me** for his 1972 gospel album *He Touched Me*) it's absolutely horrible: a full five minutes of funereal music and grandiloquent vocals.

One of the first Elvis tributes out of the stalls (other early examples include Ral Donner's **The Day The Beat Stopped**, Ronnie McDowell's **The King Is Gone**, **I Remember Elvis Presley** by Danny Mirror, and Merle Haggard's tribute album *My Farewell To Elvis*), Sumner reads his lines like a gravel-voiced hypnotherapist going through the motions for a particularly boring patient. It's unadulterated rubbish - and this from a man who, for 18 years, held the Guinness World Record for recording the lowest bass note. You'd expect something a little more engaging. Mind you, in the same year as this was released, Sumner and the Stamps also issued the bad-taste album *Elvis' Favorite Gospel Songs (Sung At His Funeral)*.

Sumner, a self-confessed alcoholic who co-founded the Gospel Music Association in 1964 and is credited with being the first artist to customise a coach for groups to travel and sleep in, continued to work right up until his death in 1998. Sumner was well-liked among Elvis aficionados for refusing to air his former boss's dirty laundry in public, so it must have been a bit of a shock for them when he was implicated in the whole sorry Sivle Nora scandal* by fellow backing singer - and fellow funeral chanteuse - Kathy Westmoreland. She states in her book *Elvis And Kathy* (William G Quinn, 1987) that Sumner was not only involved in the scam, but that he asked her to be part of it. She, quite rightly, refused. Sumner is also one of the few people who actually knew Elvis to publicly speak out about the King's legendary drug intake: "He took Quaaludes, sleeping pills and very strong uppers," he told TV host Geraldo Rivera. "He would fire you for using marijuana; he detested cocaine."

J D Sumner was buried on what would have been his 74th birthday. A number of Elvis impersonators turned up for the funeral. One can safely assume that none of them chose to perform a version of **Elvis has Left the Building**.

***

* *Sivle Nora - or Elvis Aron spelled backwards - was the first of many fake Elvii. For the princely sum of $250 singer David Darlock was hired by the Eternally Elvis organisation to record a series of soundalike tracks in an attempt to try and kid people into believing that the king did not cough up his last on the bathroom floor. See the previous chapter (on Major Bill Smith) for more information.*

Los Punk Rockers
Los Exitos De Sex Pistols (1978)

The mid-1970s was a period of massive transition for Spain – and, naturally, for the Spanish people themselves. The death of the hated dictator General Franco in November 1975 ushered in a new wave of optimism and freedom for young people and students, non-Catholics, the politically left-leaning and especially for women. Under Franco Spanish señoras were not even allowed to have a bank account unless their husband was co-signatory; women could not testify in a trial - and they most certainly could not become judges; they were not allowed to become university professors and, should they attempt to leave their husbands, even after suffering from years of spousal abuse, they stood the risk of arrest and imprisonment for 'abandoning the home'. Significantly, the ban on the sale of contraceptives was lifted and, for the first time, Spanish women could chose a method of birth control outside of state or church interference.

Unsurprisingly this openness brought with it a hunger for anything new. *La Movida Madrileña* (the Madrid Scene) saw Spanish cinema, previously

dark and sullen, suddenly come alive with colour and comedy thanks to the outrageous, hedonistic exploits of enfant terrible Pedro Almodovar. Fashions changed, and the clubs of the capital were soon swinging to a new sound, heavily influenced by the emerging punk and new wave scenes of Britain, America and Germany.

It was in to this vibrant (and, occasionally, violent) stew that *Los Exitos De Sex Pistols* appeared: a track-by-track cover version of the entire *Never Mind The Bollocks, Here's The Sex Pistols* album, issued in 1978 by the never-to-be-heard-of-again Los Punk Rockers. It's only natural that Spain's youth would take to the hip anarchy of the Sex Pistols: however why bother to license the original when you could just as easily (and far more cheaply) knock out a swiftly-produced rip-off of the Pistols' only album proper?

Rumours persist that the band playing on the album is Spanish rock act Asfalto, formed in 1972 and, up until that point, best known for their cassette-only release *Tribute To The Beatles*, another note-for-note collection of covers. Having compared the two recordings I can report that there are similarities; I contacted the manager of Asfalto to ask him if any members of the band were indeed involved in the *Los Exitos De Sex Pistols* project: he declined to answer. If it is Asfalto then it's likely that the line-up on *Los Exitos De Sex Pistols* is Julio Castejón (guitar, vocals), José Luis Jiménez (bass), Enrique Cajide (drums) and Lele Laína (guitar). It's this four piece that gigged and recorded as Asfalto through 1977 and 1978, releasing their debut album on the Chapa Discos label in the same year as *Los Exitos De Sex Pistols*.

Whoever it is, and it's unlikely that anyone will ever admit to having been involved in this godforsaken mess, they hardly covered themselves in glory. In fact the whole thing sounds as if some opportunist record exec has glanced vacantly out of his Madrid office window, grabbed the first bunch of leather-jacketed ne'er-do-wells he spied and thrust them into the studio. The band sound like they've had less than ten minutes to learn the material and the vocalist has clearly never heard the original recording, performing a phonetic approximation of John Lydon's agitprop lyrics in a pantomime villain voice. The uncredited producer's attempt to disguise the singer's failings by slathering his vocals with reverb fails abysmally: the uncredited singer sounds like Roland Rat's sidekick Kevin the Gerbil.

The lyrics bear little relation to the original, losing much of the Pistols' anger and angst. Take **Bodies**, for example:

She was a nowhere, a conscious baby
She had a little bondage cash queen
She was an hour ago, she was a lot of cow
Hey! I'm gonna like them all!
Hey! I'm gonna like them all!

(*Bodies*, written by Jones, Cook, Rotten, Vicious. Performed by Los Punk Rockers. © 1978, Universal Music Publishing Ltd., A Thousand Miles Long Inc., Rotten Music Ltd., Three Shadows Music)

The chant '*I'm a lazy sod*' from **Seventeen** becomes '*I'm a lazy seven*'; '*no feelings*' becomes '*and now I feel yuh*'. John Lydon may once have been an angry young man (rather than the butter-peddling, tweed-wearing, *Jesus Christ Superstar*-appearing, upstanding member of the establishment that he's become) but at no time did he ever sing the line '*we're so pretty, oh so pretty, we will cut her!*' **Anarchy In The UK** is certainly anarchic, but for all the wrong reasons. It's an almost unrecognisable parody of itself; punk rock performed by a wedding band, with the bride's tone-deaf grandfather on vocals. It's bonkers and brilliant and, if you have not done so already, you have to hear it.

But buyer beware: original copies of *Los Existos...* are almost impossible to find these days and will cost you around £150 if and when they do turn up for sale. Thankfully the album has been pirated on at least two different occasions, making it accessible, even if it is via the black market. If you're holding out for the real thing then the fakes are easy to spot: the first pirate pressings are missing the Nevada Records logo from the bottom right-hand corner of the front sleeve and the disc's labels are printed in shades of pink. The second batch of copies feature the logo and the correct label colours (brown & orange) but are missing the address of the record company on the rear of the sleeve and use translucent rather than opaque yellow lettering on the front. Both copies feature the date (1978) on the top right hand corner of the rear sleeve. Originals do not.

Half a decade after *Los Exitos De Sex Pistols* hit the supermarket shelves in Spain the London-based punk band The Bollock Brothers issued *Never Mind The Bollocks 1983*, their own primitive electronic version of the Pistols' classic. The album cheekily featured vocals from Michael Fagan, the intruder who broke into Buckingham Palace and entered the Queen's bedroom the previous year. Fagan's version of **God Save The Queen** was also issued as a single: it sold about as well as *Los Exitos De Sex Pistols*...but it's nowhere near as much fun to listen to.

Emerson, Lake And Palmer
Love Beach (1978)

'These guys are as stupid as their most pretentious fans' – Robert Christgau

Has any band ever been so far up its own collective ass as Emerson, Lake and Palmer? Their self-aggrandising website spouts nonsense such as *'Greg Lake is one of the most prominent and popular musicians in the world'*, *'keyboard legend Keith Emerson is one of the most important figures to emerge from the UK rock scene'* and *'dazzling speed and mastery of the drums have secured (Palmer) a place in history'*. Sheesh. They're not exactly backward at coming forward, are they? No wonder that there's an old joke, much repeated by music fans and critics alike, that goes *'how do you spell pretentious? E-L-P!'*

In the field of Progressive (or Prog) Rock, a genre stuffed full of pretentiousness, Emerson, Lake and Palmer are easily the most pretentious of all of them. Forget the ridiculous vocal acrobatics of Thjijs van Leer of Focus; ignore Rick Wakeman salivating salaciously over his keyboard; don't get sidetracked by the self-indulgent noodlings of the various line-ups of King Crimson. And, as hard as it might be, try and avoid being waylaid by Ian Anderson's loquacious lyrics. Universally (and justifiably) hated by critics ELP are, hands down, the worst of them all: they are the Coldplay of the 70s. If you thought that Yes's awful, overblown musical meisterwerk *Tales Of Topograpic Oceans* was the nadir of the genre, you need to remember that ELP is the band that John Peel described as *'a waste of talent and electricity'*. Yes, they may have enjoyed six Top Ten albums and sold in excess of 30 million units prior to their (first) implosion, but we all know that John Peel was seldom – if ever - wrong.

Emerson, Lake and Palmer formed in 1970 when Keith Emerson, the former keyboard player with 60s band The Nice (who had scored a leftfield hit of their own with their over-the-top, organ-driven version of the *West Side Story* showstopper **America**) and Greg Lake, bass player and vocalist with the first incarnation of King Crimson, decided to form a band together. They had been on the same bill several times over the years and had become friends; meeting up in a bar after a show at the Fillmore West in San Francisco they got to talking about the future. Once back in England they began auditioning drummers (including former Jimi Hendrix Experience tub thumper Mitch Mitchell) before settling on Carl Palmer. At the time Palmer - whose shtick was to strip to the waist on stage while never missing a beat – was still playing with Atomic Rooster, the band he formed after leaving The Crazy World of Arthur Brown, but he left to complete the line-up of what would be hailed as one of the first real supergroups*.

In a world defined by excessiveness, interminably long instrumental solos and preposterous, pseudo-intellectual lyrics Emerson, Lake and Palmer were the most preposterous and excessive of them all. "They were not shy people," admitted co-manager John Gaydon in the 2005 documentary *Beyond The Beginning*. "The music, at the time, was pretty weird. It was three guys who were fiercely ambitious, working together to become superstars." The band launched officially that August at the Isle of Wight Festival, ending their set by firing off two antique cannons.

Stage shows featured Emerson – in a stunt Liberace would have been proud of – being spun round in the air, high above the stage, astride a grand piano. In 1977, following the success of their international hit **Fanfare For The Common Man**, the bloated band were touring America with an entourage of 130 people including a full orchestra. A full orchestra! And a choir! 75 extra musicians on the ELP payroll! No wonder they're often cited as one of the main reasons for the musical backlash that presaged the punk rock explosion. As *Spin* magazine put it in 1992 *'ELP were the progenitors and disseminators of the humourless, overblown prog-rock pomp wank that led to the greatest revolution in modern pop history'.* And nothing sums up the pointlessness of their existence better than their ridiculous 1978 album *Love Beach*.

Called *'an appalling attempt at mainstream pop'* by The Rough Guide to Rock, rarely has a record been so out of step with the times. Bored and boring, flaccid and uninspired, *Love Beach* (*'a title I detested'* Emerson admitted in his autobiography *Pictures of an Exhibitionist*) was exactly what the punks were railing against and was deservedly panned in a review by Michael Bloom for *Rolling Stone* magazine: *'Love Beach isn't simply bad, it's downright pathetic. Stale and full of ennui, this album makes washing the dishes seem a more creative act by comparison... that you can hear echoes of the ELP of old simply means that Emerson hasn't learned—or borrowed—a new riff in five years'.*

Everything about this album is wrong, from the bland opener **All I Want Is You** through the dreadful girly backing vocals on **The Gambler** to the cover, which features the members of ELP with their blouses open to the waist, looking to all the world like the Bee Gees. And what on earth is going on inside Keith Emerson's trousers?

The material, which has been so thinly spread over the two sides, consists of five short songs (including the title track, which steals guitar licks from the Beatles), yet another classical jerkfest and a pompous 20-minute suite entitled **Memoirs Of An Officer And A Gentleman**. Recorded at Compass Point Studios in the Bahamas earlier that summer, *Love Beach* was to be ELP's last album of new material for almost a decade and a half. Which is just as well, when the best you can come up with is:

I want your love, with the stars above down on Love Beach
I'm gonna make love to you on Love Beach
Make all your dreams come true on Love Beach
Gonna make love to you on Love Beach

(*Love Beach*, written by Lake, Sinfield. Recorded by Emerson, Lake and Palmer. © 1978, Palm Beach International Recordings Ltd)

Atlantic Records and its chair Ahmet Ertegun saw this steaming pile of disco-funk infected dross as the group's chance to cross over into the mainstream; a misguided attempt by both parties to make something more radio-friendly, in much the same way as the label's other two Prog Rock colossi – Yes and Genesis – would do. Mind you, the company tried the same thing with Ringo Starr, plumbing the nadir of the former Beatle's career with the shockingly awful *Ringo The 4th* – the album that completely destroyed Ringo's up-to-then surprisingly successful solo career.

"We missed the boat on that one," Emerson admits, "Although we tried." The trio have constantly bemoaned the fact that *Love Beach* was recorded under duress, as a contractual obligation. How hard it must have been for the boys to be forced against their wills to decamp to the sun-kissed Bahamas to record this stinker. Famed, even feted for bringing classical and jazz elements to rock, how must they have felt when they presented this collection of middle of the road crap to their adoring public?

One of the big problems with Emerson, Lake and Palmer is that they've never really been a group in the true sense of the word, although they've successfully conned listeners into believing that they are for more than 40 years now. The vast majority of their albums – from their eponymous debut, through the corpulent double album *Works Volume 1* (where each member of the band is given one side apiece as a platform for their pomposity, only coming together for the two tracks which appear on side four) and right up to their last album of new material, 1994's *In The Hot Seat* – simply showcase the talents of three unfettered egos, more often than not working against the group ethic rather than for it. Lake writes his simpering ballads (often with lyricist Peter Sinfield, who started his career with King Crimson and went on to write for Bucks Fizz and Celine Dion); Emerson – desperate to show the world how clever he is – beats the life out of bombastic, faux-classical music on a Hammond organ or Moog synthesiser, thrusting knives between the keys when he wants to sustain notes, and Palmer flails away with eardrum-splitting volume and velocity, sneaking in an excessive drum solo whenever the other two allow him the room. When cajoled, as on *Love Beach*, to perform as a band they failed miserably.

No amount of hindsight can change Palmer's attitude to *Love Beach*. "I always refer to it as the worst album that ELP ever made," he has said. "Not only did the music not really stand up for me, but the album cover I didn't like, I didn't like the whole period of being in Nassau, The Bahamas, I didn't think that it was conducive to the band's way of writing, living, creating, rehearsing, playing…for me it wasn't a great album." Odd then that the Carl Palmer Band should choose to cover the only single released from *Love Beach*, **Canario** (yet another overblown instrumental, this time based on Rodrigo's *Fantasia Para Un Gentilhombre*), on a regular basis.

"I think it is crap," Sinfield told *Impressions* magazine in 1998. "It was bound to be. The band weren't really talking to each other and they were being terrible spoilt brats. I think I wrote nine lyrics, if you count **Memoirs Of An Officer And A Gentleman** as three. I must say, they're not the best thing

I've ever written, but I did my best in the circumstances!

"It was a very odd album. Because when you've got three guys who are really not talking to each other, it's rather stressed circumstances for making a record."

Worn out by years of touring and constantly at odds with each other over which direction their music should take (from the beginning there had been fights over the choice of plugging away at Emerson's neo-classical nonsense or going down a Lake-led, more radio-friendly road), they split acrimoniously shortly after the album was released. ELP would not regroup for more than a decade. "It wasn't like one of those break-ups where there was lots of mudslinging and bitterness," Lake has since said. "We all just felt simultaneously that we'd been pushed too far. We could sense it. It was one of those things. You'd have had to have been there at the time, but you could've felt it: nobody was that keen to play."

When ELP did resurface, in 1985, it was as Emerson, Lake and Powell, with former Rainbow sticksman Cozy Powell perched atop the drummer's stool. Palmer, busy with his own band Asia, declined to take part in that particular reunion, but would rejoin his (former) bandmates later. "When bands have been knocked, when they've had a successful record, when the fans have bought the album and the concerts have been sold out and the critics still knock it... that's one of the biggest factors in breaking up bands in the industry." Palmer told an interviewer at the time. "That had a lot to do with Emerson, Lake and Palmer's split - for one particular member of the band. I am very strong, my personality is very strong. Certain musicians aren't. And there was one person in Emerson, Lake and Palmer who wasn't. I can't tell you who." One shouldn't make assumptions, but the relationship between Palmer, Emerson and Lake is strained to this day: Emerson has played with Lake (in Emerson,

Lake and Powell) and with Palmer (in 3) but Lake and Palmer have not played together outside of ELP. In spite of their many years of friendship, Emerson and Lake would fall out spectacularly with each other in 2010 (see below).

ELP have split up and regrouped more times than The Who, and like The Who they now have released more live albums and compilations than they have collections of new material. "I think there is truth in the fact that the group was pretentious," Lake explained in a 2013 interview for *Rolling Stone* magazine. "We wanted to try and move things forward and do something new and break boundaries. It was important for us to be original."

"It wasn't the journalists that brought down ELP," Lake added, contradicting his former bandmate. "I think it was ELP themselves. It started to fragment when they made *Works Volume 1***. It was a good album, but it wasn't ELP. It was Keith Emerson, Greg Lake and Carl Palmer with an orchestra. Well, with three separate orchestras! The album went platinum, but it wasn't a record that reflected the chemistry of ELP. It reflected the individuals apart from each other. Works Volume 1 was the beginning of the end. After that, ELP never made another really innovative record." Personally, I'd argue that the band have <u>never</u> made an innovative record.

Having steadfastly refused to learn their lesson, the original trio resurfaced in 1992 with the poorly-received *Black Moon*, following that two years later by the even more reviled *In The Hot Seat* which, according to reviewer Marc Loren of *Allmusic.com 'probably shouldn't have been made at all. Clearly, the band's head was not in the game and it shows. To call this a horrible album would be a bit unfair, but it does suffer from a lack of direction, heart, and perhaps most noticeably, a lack of production. This album falls short on so many levels that not even the talents of three phenomenal musicians can save it'.* The last album, blighted by Emerson's health problems, had been recorded in separate segments and pieced together in the studio. It was also plagued by the lack of decent material: it says something about your relevance as a songwriter if the best you can come up with is a cover of Bob Dylan's **Man In The Long Black Coat**. And even then you have the temerity to tack on an 'arranged by' credit. Blech! By 1998 they'd split up again.

In spring 2010 Emerson and Lake embarked on a US tour which was interrupted when the pair had an unholy row after ticket holders had taken their seats (in an Ohio theatre) and the house lights had gone down. Emerson, in *'a personal letter to my fans'* fell on his own sword: *'I must apologise for the very last-minute cancellation of the show in Lakewood, and also of Glenside and Ridgefield shows, and for my absence of an issuance of any sort of statement. I was too distraught and embarrassed to come on stage to perform or even to announce the sudden cancellation myself, and to issue a statement immediately. I now realise fully that the decision had a devastating effect on many including fans, my crew, staff, the promoters and the venues. I realise that I have disappointed my loyal fans.'*

Lake took to his own website to take a shot at his cohort: *'I am pleased Keith has admitted the reasons behind the cancellation, and I trust we can leave it at that.'* Clearly, though, he was far from ready to leave things at that. *'The performance was ready; many of you heard or saw the sound check. Keith has released a statement explaining he felt the need to cancel because of his worry that he couldn't perform up to standard. Keith is not the first performer to have experienced stage fright, and my heart goes out to him. I have dedicated my life to trying to make you happy through my music and nothing saddens me more than to see that you have been disappointed by anything I was involved in. Please accept that these cancellations were entirely beyond my control.'* Fans were more than disappointed; they were outraged at being shabbily treated by two middle-aged men many of them described on fan forums as *'a pair of assholes'*.

The trio's final outing - at least at the time of writing – was a one-off, 40th anniversary performance in London's Victoria Park in July 2010. Here's hoping we've finally seen the last of this particular rock 'n' roll dinosaur, or at least that they'll promise, if they do decide to reform once again, that there won't be a 40th anniversary tour of *Love Beach*.

***

* *Cream is often hailed as the first 'supergroup', but that epithet was only applied retrospectively: only Clapton could be thought of as a star in his own right prior to the band's formation. His next band, Blind Faith, is generally regarded as the first true supergroup, featuring Steve Winwood - ex Traffic and the Spencer Davis Group - Clapton and Ginger baker from Cream and family's Ric Grech.*

** *Works Volume 1, issued in March 1977, was followed, just eight months later, by* Works Volume 2, *a single album collection of outtakes, this time mostly group performances. Several of the tracks on* Works Volume 2 *were left over from their 1973 album* Brain Salad Surgery.

Chainmale Freakout (1979)

Welcome to the weird, weird world of Chainmale, the antipodean performance artist, poet, and musician better known to his family as Michael Freeland.

The leader of the little-known Tasmanian Electro Punk scene, Michael was born in Melbourne in 1952 but grew up in Sydney, his family relocating there when he was four years old. He showed an early aptitude for music and performance, making his first appearances in Gilbert and Sullivan musicals at the Castle Cove Primary School. Pleasingly, an early musical influence was the murderously brilliant Elva Miller: "My father bought a recording of Mrs Miller, not for her singing quality but for her guts. It inspired him, and made him laugh." When he moved on to Glenaeon Rudolf Steiner School Michael was introduced to eurythmy, a form of expressive movement originated by Steiner and Marie von Sivers in the second decade of the 20th century. Primarily a performance art, eurythmy is also used in education and for therapeutic purposes. "I later used eurythmy in combination with classical French mime and method acting to form my own school of performance," he says.

"At the end of 1968, at 16, with ambitions to become an animal collector like

Bob Eustace (left) and Michael Freeland . . . "mime says more"

The mime machines

By ROGER CROSTHWAITE

It was Michael Freeland's love of animals that led him to a life in the theatre.

"I was working as a zoo keeper when I went off on a collecting expedition with Harry Butler," Michael said yesterday.

"I told him that I wanted to make a wild-life documentary and he told me one thing I needed was lots of money, so I immediately thought the best way to get it was in the theatre."

Although his motives were mercenary at the start, Michael soon fell in

love with the theatre life and now has his own theatre group, the Modern Mime Theatre.

The group has only two performers — Michael and Canadian-born actor and mime artist Bob Eustace — and they have put together a brand new program for their show which started at the Bondi Pavilion Theatre this week.

□ □ □

The content ranges from vaudeville-style entertainment such as juggling and fire-eating to the complex subtleties of mime, a format of theatre that Michael refers to as "almost a religious experience."

"You can say more with

'mime than with traditional theatre," he claims.

"You can get across emotionally to people, and of course there are no language barriers."

Michael has proved the universal appeal of mime by performing across the world, from Tennant Creek and Alice Springs in Australia's outback, to London, Cologne, and Amsterdam's Fool's Festival, a gathering of mimes and clowns from all parts of the world.

"If I was on his return from Europe in July of this year that Michael recruited Bob into his group, having worked with him in theatre in 1972.

The show they present covers the full spectrum of theatre, from comedy to tragedy, and all without a spoken word.

"Both agree that m ime is the most challenging aspect of theatre they have yet tackled.

"You have to separate yourself from your body," Michael said.

"And manipulate your body like a machine.

"The art is to use it like a tool."

The Modern Mime Theatre's season at the Bondi Pavilion will run until Christmas Eve, after which Michael and Bob hope to stage the show in other small theatres, taking the ancient art of mime to more and more people.

Gerald Durrell, I left school to become a zookeeper. On returning from a collecting trip in the Outback and in the far north of Australia I took a second job working at night as an assistant stage manager at The Music Hall at Neutral Bay in Sydney.

"This all happened in 1969/70, when Australia was involved in the Vietnam war and Sydney's streets were filled with personnel on R and R. There were demonstrations everywhere: the baby boomer generation were now adolescents and had been totally protected from the financial worries and traumas of their parents and grandparents, who had just gone through two generations of war and depression. I left home and spent several months as a hippy, travelling north and pretending I was Arlo Guthrie, with three chords to my repertoire. I remember going into a pub on the Queensland-Northern Territory border and asking if I could sing for my supper: I got halfway through the first song and a bloke came up and said he would buy me a meal if I promised not to sing another note!"

Unperturbed, and with a belly full of Chicken schnitzel and mushroom gravy, Michael produced a two-man poetry show specifically aimed at children. *Recalled From Childhood* featured the poems Michael had learned from his mother, father and grandmother, and it was here that he got his first crack at fame, of sorts, appearing on the Australian TV show *GTK (Get To Know)* in 1973. "*GTK* was the first of the rock video type shows in the world," he explains. Produced by Aussie television legend Bernie Cannon for the Australian Broadcasting Company (ABC) network, *GTK* "set the pace for all that was to follow. I then went to work in television, at ABC, in staging and floor managing." In his spare time he continued to perform, busking around Sydney before leaving ABC to study drama at the Mechthild Harkness Speech and Drama Studios, where he was trained in mime by Ton Witsel - who himself had trained in Amsterdam and Paris and who had been taught by the celebrated French actor, director and mime artist Jean Louis Barraut. It was there that Michael's passion for mime was born.

"I resurrected *Recalled From Childhood* as a school show, and put together a performance of original poetry at the Stanley Palmer Culture Palace in Darlinghurst. Then in early 1975 I joined the Queensland Theatre Company with their Arts Council Schools Presentation, touring throughout Queensland. I met my first wife while in Queensland, and in late 1975 we returned to Sydney."

Living in a commune in Paddington, a suburb to the east of the city, the couple found that love wasn't enough to keep the wolf from the door and a roof over their heads. With an urgent need to earn some money Michael returned to busking, this time incorporating mime into his act. "That worked well and we began to earn a decent living," he says. "Although it must be remembered that in those days busking was illegal." Being chased by the police became part of the act and Michael worked his occasional brushes with the law into his routine. "We were invited to perform at the Sydney Opera House, in the lunchtime outdoor venue, and also by the Sydney City Council in their Martin Place outdoor venue. This was very satisfying because the very person who was trying to arrest me a week earlier was now carrying my gear and setting it up!"

The birth of the couple's first child forced Michael to reassess his life. "I was 23; I had to improve our situation." Going under the name The Modern Mime Theatre he organised a series of performances in schools and won a four-week contract with the Arts Council of New South Wales, which in turn lead to contracts with arts councils in other states. "I found that I was booked out for two years in advance with three shows a day, five days a week, with one or two evening shows on top of that if I wanted them." In January 1977 Michael performed at the first annual Sydney Festival: he would perform there each year until 1983. His act was going down well: that same year reviewer David Rowbotham, writing in Queensland's *Courier Mail* newspaper wrote that Michael's performance *'speaks volumes for the possibilities of his art. He is a classic entertainer and storyteller.'*

"In 1978, with an 18 month and a six week old baby, we headed over to the UK on our way to the Fools' Festival in Amsterdam. I busked in Leicester Square in London, in Amsterdam, on the steps of the cathedral in Cologne and in front of the Pompidou Centre in Paris. After four weeks we returned to Australia and went back on tour." As his act, and his confidence, grew he added firebreathing and balancing on a unicycle to his act and The Modern Mime Theatre became a duo in July 1978 when Canadian-born actor and mime artist Bob Eustace joined; the pair had been friends since they first performed together in 1972.

MODERN MIME *theatre*

BONDI PAVILION THEATRE
4TH-24TH DECEMBER
Mon-Fri 1.00 p.m and 8.00 p.m.; Sat. 2.00 p.m. and 8.00 p.m.
Tickets 8.00 p.m. and 2.00 p.m. Adults $5.00, Children $2.50
inclusive. 1.00 p.m. Adults $4.00, Children $2.00 inclusive.
(Party bookings available)

It was when Michael and his family got back to Australia that he created the piece of art for which certain people, myself included, will always be grateful: the 7" single **Freakout**. Released under the name Chainmale (Why choose the name Chainmale? "It just seemed like a cool name," he laughs) and backed with the electro-boogie track **Mean Little Woman**, **Freakout** is one of the most unsettling three minutes ever committed to vinyl: Numan-esque keyboards, crying babies, manic screaming and with the words sung and music played in different time signatures to add to the disturbing effect. Odd and disquieting, Michael would incorporate the song into his act, building an uncomfortable and intense mime performance around his lyrics. That performance would later be adapted for use in a video filmed to accompany the single, now available for all to wonder at via YouTube.

"Every year I would take a couple of weeks off at the end of the school year, before the festival season began. The first week I would relax and say how I would retire and never tour again. By the second week I would be thinking that I should be doing something and I would start writing a new show, and by the third week I would be off my tree and that's when my wife would want to kill me!

"We were driving down a lane in the back streets of Hobart and I was jumping out of my skin. We passed a sound studio and my wife said *'why don't you go in and record one of those songs you're always making up?'* So I went in an asked. Nick Armstrong (the studio proprietor) asked what I wanted to record. I went home, wrote out the lyrics, brought them back, and sang them to him with a single beat of my hand on the desk. He looked at me incredulously and said *'is that it?'* I said *'Yeah. If* (renowned Australian musician) *Billy Thorpe can get away with 'mashed potato yeah, oh yeah!' then we'll kill it'*!"

Armstrong asked Michael if he would object to his having his friend Ian Clyne, best known for his keyboard work with the sixties band The Loved Ones, look over his song. "Ian and I met a couple of days later to record it having never met before. He played the sort of thing he thought I would like: it was big, but it was conservative. I said I wanted something with no holds barred; no constraints of convention, just freak out and do what you want. He smiled and said *'this is going to be fun'*. As we were recording the vocals I got excited: my heart started racing and my tempo with it. He tried conducting me but I was gone.

"When we finished he said to me 'you started in 8/8 and you ended up

in 7/8'. I asked if we should do it again. We hit playback and Ian said 'no, it works! You sound like you're freaking out! Hell knows how you'll ever sing it live'. That was the birth of Chainmale. I was around 30, I already had three kids, and in those days rock stars were around 18! I think Ian was around 14 when he was playing at the Wembley Stadium with the Loved Ones."

Issued by the independent Candle Records in 1979, very few vinyl copies of Freakout exist: "I think about 1000 copies were pressed, of which only a fraction made it to the stores. However every now and then someone tells me they have a copy," Michael says. "Did I consider myself a serious singer? I considered myself a serious performer with serious concepts to put forward and humour, confrontation, and sound were the best ways I had of achieving that. I don't think anyone would come to hear my voice for the musical lilt in it, however they might come to experience the theatrical content of it."

In 1980 Michael took his poetry and mime act on a tour of schools around New South Wales and down to Victoria: he continued to perform in Sydney, returned to London in 1987 and would continue presenting his poetry and social conscience one man show at schools in Australia well in to the 1990s. Pieces included *Hate* – inspired by the riots that took place in the UK in 1980 – *Prufrock* (influenced by TS Elliot's *The Love Song Of Alfred J Prufrock*) and his political tour de force *Face Of America*.

"In 1981 I opened a small theatre, The Pits, in Hobart and also financed an ensemble theatre group called Tuk, named after my mother-in-law. I seldom worked in Tasmania but commuted from there to wherever I was performing." Michael's normal routine would see him flying out on the Sunday at around midday, working all week on the mainland and returning on the Friday evening, getting home at around midnight. "Until our eldest child was going to school we all toured together," he says. "However once she was at school commuting was my only option."

Chainmale recorded two further tracks, **Schizophrenic Breakdown** - a jolly little sing-along which appears to be about about crazy people but, as he explains is "actually about the sickness in UK society at the time. An underlying aparteid was developing, as seen in South Africa; the song refers really to the duel or multiple personalities within UK society that manifested itself in the riots" - and the bizarre electro/skinhead anthem **Kickback**, in 1982. Videos were made for **Freakout** and for these two new tracks: the video for **Kickback** – which is listed on YouTube as the *'worst 80s music video'* ever made - features Michael and his young son Joel in skinhead gear, scaring the wits out of anyone who should happen to pass them by. "What we did others got to years later. The subjects of the songs were what ever I was experiencing at the time. The light heartedness in **Schizophrenic Breakdown** is the light heatedness you find in a riot. Everyone participating in a riot is jovial: it's a release. The rage is only for the cameras, when they are given the opportunity to spout about their cause.

"**Freakout** was the only record issued. The problem with the other two videos was getting TV play. **Kickback** had drinking and smoking in, which was against airplay policies, and **Schizophrenic Breakdown** could have upset people who might link it more with the illness rather than with the splitting of the social fabric in the UK into an apartheid similar to that in South Africa. As we already had the videos we put together a pilot for TV by adding some sketches, but I got side tracked with life and with touring."

Michael continued to perform until the mid-1990s. More recently he has become an author, penning two well-received satirical novels – 1995's *Pius Humble* and *The Company* (1996) - under the pseudonym Bogan Gate, a name he took from a small village in NSW. I had assumed that the name change was to avoid confusion between his own work and that of the American author Michael Freeland although, he tells me: "the reason for different names is that you really need independent names for each art form, even for styles within an art form.

So how does the man once known as Chainmale, whose recorded work (thanks primarily to it's resurrection on You Tube) is both feted by people who love it and ridiculed by others feel about his newfound fame? "I think its great," he tells me. "At least it's not mediocre!"

Adrian Gurvitz
Classic (1982)

You can't look at the worst records of the 80s without dipping in to the canon of Adrian Gurvitz, a man who is indelibly etched on our collective 80s memory not only for his guitar prowess, his corkscrew perm and his distressed leather jacket but for performing a pair of the most nauseating singles ever produced.

These days a respected songwriter and producer – he's behind hit songs for Pixie Lott, Hot Chocolate, Eddie Money, REO Speedwagon and a host of others - in the 60s (when he was first known professionally as Adrian Curtis) and early 70s Gurvitz had hits of his own (with his brother Paul an ever-present consort) with The Gun (**Race With The Devil** reached the UK Top 10 and was No. 1 in many European countries) and the Baker-Gurvitz Army. From a music biz background - his dad, Sam Curtis, had been a tour manager for acts including Cliff Richard and The Kinks - he played as part of the Graham Edge Band and would later write **England, We'll Fly The Flag**, the B-side to the 1982 single by the England World Cup Squad **This Time (We'll Get It Right)** – a ghastly record which netted the footballers a number two hit. Predictably I'm reminded of a number two every time I hear that wretched recording.

Born in 1949 Adrian started playing guitar at the age of eight, inspired by elder sibling Paul and the search for solace (according to a short interview which appeared on *totalmusicmagazine.com*) whilst his parents went through a messy divorce. By the time he was 15 he was touring with Screaming Lord Sutch and before he'd reached his 18th birthday he had scored a minor hit with the band Rupert's People: their single **Reflections Of Charlie Brown** made the UK Top 40 and went to number 13 in Australia. To avoid confusion with a certain dinner plate-headed cartoon character, the single was issued in America as **Reflections Of Charles Brown**.

The 60s and early 70s were Adrian's glory years. Working with ex-Hendrix drummer Buddy Miles and former Cream sticksman Ginger Baker kept him busy (both the Buddy Miles Express and the Baker-Gurvitz Army did good business on the live circuit in the States) but sadly by the mid-70s these acts had collapsed and our Adrian couldn't get arrested. A move to

Jet records prompted the release of a brace of rather nasty - and virtually unlistenable – disco-pop albums, *Sweet Vendetta* and *Il Assassino*; he may have dragged half of Toto and Earth, Wind and Fire along with him for the ride, but these sub-Bee Gees recordings did nothing for his bank balance or his credibility (in the UK at least). And no, I don't know why he

went all Italian with the titles either: he was born in Stoke Newington, not Sicily.

In 1982 he moved to Mickie Most's Rak organisation, taking with him the masters for his third solo album, *Classic*. The title track – a twee piece of soft-focus garbage with lyrics so bad they could have been written by Steve Miller – made the Top 10 in the UK and was a sizeable hit around the world:

Gotta write a classic, gotta write it in an attic
Baby, I'm an addict now - an addict for your love
I was a street boy, and you were my best toy...

(*Classic*, written and performed by Adrian Gurvitz on Rak Records. © 1982, Rak Publishing Ltd)

It's just horrible. *'You were my best toy'*? It makes you wonder exactly who - or what - was the object of his affection: a deaf woman, or a Rubik's Cube? Give the man his due though; there aren't many words that rhyme with 'classic'. Although what's wrong with *'Gotta write a Classic, heading back to the Jurassic/Listenin' to Lark's Tongues in Aspic'*? You can have those on me Adrian, should you choose to record an extended version of this drivel any time soon.

A further single – **Your Dream** - was released from the album but failed to make much of an impression on the UK charts, scraping in at a lowly 61. But **Classic** was a fairly major hit and you can understand why Rak, who at that time seemed to be signing just about anybody who could fart in tune – including former chart topper Steve Harley, who issued three flop singles on the label - were happy to indulge him.

And indulge him they did. Buoyed by the international success of **Classic**, and by the bizarre comparisons that their boy was getting to the rock star du jour (according to *Billboard* magazine one cut on the album, **No Fears In The Night**, is a *'high spirited rock anthem recalling the night imagery and dense excitement of Bruce Springsteen'*. I promise you, it isn't. It's a weedy synth fest

whose only nod to The E Street Band is the short – and rather poor – saxophone break), a little over a year later he issued the non-album 45 **Hello Mum**, a record so ghastly it almost defies description, and with lyrics that make **Classic** look like...well, a classic.

This is a tribute song
Through the years you've been so strong
And sometimes you think that we don't care
We're all here today
With these words to say
But they couldn't ever mean as much as you do

(*Hello Mum*, written by A Gurvitz and D Most. Performed by Adrian Gurvitz on Rak Records. © 1983, Rak Publishing Ltd)

What utter, unmitigated rubbish; as sugary as Pixy Stix and about as satisfying, and stuffed with non-sequiturs. If I had presented this morass of misery to my mother she'd have - quite rightly - hit me around the head with it. Put out just in time for Christmas 1983, and issued in a special festive sleeve complete with space for you to write a dedication to your own mother, not even the addition of a dreadful caterwauling kiddie choir could help drag this piece of sentimental crap up the charts. Sales were abysmal - the disc failed to make the UK top 75, peaking at a miserable 80 and vanishing from the charts after just four weeks. It is truly revolting. Thankfully he would not release another single for seven years and would never again score a UK chart entry under his own name.

Now living in Los Angeles, happily married and with four children, someone must have liked Adrian's particular brand of soft rock even if the rest of the right-thinking world finds the likes of **Hello Mum** vomit-inducing. Shortly after he moved to the States he wrote **The Love In Your Eyes**, a number 24 hit for Eddie Money and followed that up with a little song called **Even If My Heart Would Break**, co-written by Franne Gold (a successful songwriter whose hits include **Nightshift** for the Commodores) and recorded by Aaron Neville and Kenny G. **Even if My Heart Would Break** appeared in the Whitney Houston/Kevin Costner movie *The Bodyguard* as well as on the accompanying soundtrack album - a record that would become the top selling soundtrack album of all time - putting more dollars in Adrian's bank account than both **Classic** and **Hello Mum** combined.

Gurvitz was later hired by Walt Disney Records to produce and write songs for their in-house pop puppets, a contract that netted him several gold albums; he also secured a US number one hit for his daughter's band No Secrets. In 2011 he co-founded Buskin Records with tech entrepreneur Jeffrey Evans. Sadly none of the acts signed to Buskin have yet to re-record either **Classic** or **Hello Mum**.

Rene & Renato
Save Your Love (1982)

The funeral of Italian waiter Renato Pagliari took place on the afternoon of August 11, 2009 at the Holy Trinity Church in Sutton Coldfield, in the heart of the Midlands. During the service the congregation could hear his commanding singing voice as his recordings of **Nessun Dorma** and **Ave Maria** echoed through the place of worship. Renato was 69: he passed away after undergoing surgery for a brain tumour. He had been battling illness for several months and, sadly for a man who loved to entertain, towards the end of his life had lost the ability to sing altogether.

Among the hundreds of mourners who had gathered to pay tribute to the popular Pagliari were singer Tony Christie, of **(Is This the Way to) Amarillo** fame, former Manchester United manager and football analyst Ron Atkinson, and a middle aged housewife by the name of Hilary Lester, who turned up to pay her last respects to the man who many had assumed (erroneously) had been her lover in years gone by.

None of this would be of any importance in the great scheme of things if it wasn't for the fact that Pagliari and Lester had once shared the world's stage: the pair had been better known as chart-topping duo Renee and Renato. That day in 2009 would be the last time that the duo – singers on a disc routinely ridiculed as one of the worst singles ever and yet which made number one at Christmas 1982 - would ever be in the same room together. That record was, of course, the infamous **Save Your Love**.

Beating David Bowie, Culture Club and Shakin' Stevens to the top spot, **Save Your Love** spent four weeks at number one and became one of the UK's biggest selling singles, with a total of 16 weeks on the charts. Yet the song's mushy lyrics and the kitsch video which accompanied the release – with the portly Pagliari stuffed into a velour jumper, proffering red roses to a blonde actress miming to Lester's performance – have made it a regular fixture in lists of Britain's 'most annoying' chart records.

Born in to a poor family in the village of Blera, about 50 miles north of Rome, Renato joined the church choir as a boy and, as a young man, won a place at school for professional waiters. After working in several international restaurants he moved to Britain and settled in the West

Midlands, where he married and set about raising a family. Establishing himself in a succession of local Italian restaurants, he soon gained a reputation for bringing in customers, drawn as they were to the well-built man singing Neapolitan airs and operatic arias over the pasta. It wasn't long before he was encouraged to audition for TV

talent show *New Faces*; he won the local heats and made it to the televised rounds.

Catching the attention of songwriters Sue and Johnny Edward, Renato was teamed with session singer Hilary – who had studied at the London Academy of Music and Dramatic Art and whose father and mother had both been performers - to form the duo the Edwards christened Renée and Renato. In an earlier life Johnny Edward had been a member of David Bowie's band The Manish Boys; he had also been a pirate radio DJ and later created, controlled and voiced the robot at the centre of the Mickey Dolenz-directed kid's TV show *Metal Mickey*. He gave Renato and Hilary a song he and his wife had had written and the rest, as they say, is history.

Or at least it would have been if things had run smoothly for the hit makers. However, by the time people started to take notice of **Save Your Love** such a long time had passed between the recording session and the song's chart debut that Renee and Renato had split up, with Lester leaving to join another group. The sudden, unexpected success of **Save Your Love** necessitated the filming of the now infamous video clip where a lip-synching actress by the name of Val Penny replaced the missing-in-action Lester. Hilary was encouraged to rejoin the fold for a handful of TV appearances, and the reunited duo went on to issue several follow-up singles. However, even though **Save Your Love** would top the singles charts in the UK, the Netherlands and Norway and was a top five hit in

Sweden and Switzerland, **Just One More Kiss** barely scraped the top 50, peaking at a miserable 48. The frankly xenophobic, 'Allo 'Allo-style **A Littla Bitta Me, Only You**, and a fifth and final single, **Jesus Loves Us All**, failed to chart at all. Two albums – *Just One...* and *Just One More Kiss* – did similarly poor business.

I had always assumed that a different female vocalist, and not the accomplished Lester, had been employed to screech and scream her way through **It's A Lovely Day**, the ridiculous B-side to the duo's final chart hit **Just One More Kiss**, yet Johnny Edward insists that that was not the case. "I assure you it is Hilary Lester," he tells me. With their light all but extinguished, the Edwards' decided to set Renee and Renato free.

"I think you have to laugh along with it," Hilary told an interviewer in the 1990s on one of the rare occasions that she has publicly discussed her role in creating **Save Your Love**. "You have to take something for what it is. I'll never be ashamed of it, but at the end of the day it was a novelty record." Writer Johnny Edward agrees: "The song was written as a joke, to give the finger to **Save Your Kisses For Me** by Brotherhood Of Man among other tracks that made me chew the carpet."

"Why use 'joke' in a negative way?" he elaborated. "I call it humour. Fun even! Too much pop is far too serious, don't you think?"

After her brief brush with fame and a short stint as a session singer Hilary Lester returned to private life, marrying a stage lighting engineer and raising a son. A short-lived reunion in 1988 spawned the Dutch-only 7" **Are You Lonesome Tonight**. Renato continued to sing, performing on cruise ships and at his son Remo's restaurant, which the chip off the old block named Renato's, in Tamworth, Staffordshire (the restaurant has since been renamed DaQuino Ristorante, in case you decide to go looking for it). He also recorded several albums and in 2002 he was all set to appear in *Second Time Around*, a TV series fronted by Spice Girls manager and American Idol head honcho Simon Fuller, where former chart acts were to be given a second chance at fame. Sadly the proposed series failed to materialise: the similarly themed *Reborn In The USA* aired the following year but did not feature Renato.

Hilary eventually returned to showbiz, and now works as a session singer (she appeared on the soundtrack to *Evita*) and character actress. Prior to her appearance at Renato's funeral she had last been seen in the stage production *Confessions Of A Stay-At-Home Mum*.

After the great man's death the tributes poured in. Many of the UK's national newspapers remembered Renato not only for his one massive hit but also for singing the much-mimicked Cornetto theme: a shame as, according to Remo, the vocalist on the TV ad wasn't his father after all.

Save Your Love – the first ever UK number one single to be entirely independently distributed – has proved surprisingly popular in Sweden, with several cover versions by local dansebands. Less surprisingly, the saccharine-sweet song went on to appear at number 13 in *Select* magazine's *Most Hated Records Of All Time*, and at number five in the *Daily Telegraph*'s 2013 list of the *Worst Christmas Number Ones Of All Time* - which just goes to prove that you can't please everybody.

The Singing Nun
Dominique (1982)

Now, I know some of you will be scratching your heads at this point. **Dominique** isn't that bad a record, you'll say; not only that, but surely it was released in the 1960s? Read on, and I shall explain why The Singing Nun is a worthy exhibit in the arcade of audio atrocity we call *The World's Worst Records*.

In 1963, two years before Julie Andrews would become everybody's favourite convent convert to convert back to a life of lust, and four years before actress Sally Field would take to the televisual skies as *The Flying Nun*, a young Dominican novice known by the name of Sister Luc Gabrielle or Sœur Sourire (Sister Smile) was gambolling up the charts with a jolly little song about Saint Dominic, the Spanish-born founder of her order.

Born Jeanne-Paule Marie (usually Anglicised as Jeanine or Jeannine) Deckers in 1933, a more unlikely pop star is hard to imagine. Jeanine had not always wanted to be a nun. She was groomed by her distant and unloving parents to take over the family bakery and delicatessen, and had briefly worked as a teacher before enrolling in a Paris art school, but she shocked her family by abandoning her classes when she got engaged.

D. A. Chadwick's book *The Singing Nun Story* suggests that her parents endured a loveless marriage and that the relationship between Jeanine and her father. Lucien, was a little more intimate than it should have been, anditseemsthatJeanine grew up in a house where the threat of incest or rape was part of the norm. When her engagement collapsed she suffered the first of what would be a series of breakdowns: both she and her mother, Gabrielle, endured wild mood swings and, although impossible now to confirm, it seems that mental instability ran in the family. In an effort to create some distance between herself and her parents (home life, according to Chadwick, was like *something out of Dante's Inferno'*) her Grandmother paid the entrance fee to allow her to join the Dominican Fichermont Convent in Waterloo, Belgium in 1959. While at the convent she entertained the other nuns by plinky-plonking her simple, nursery rhyme-style songs on her guitar, which she christened Sister Adele.

The Vespa-riding (if the US-made biographical movie of her life is to be believed) Sister Luc Gabrielle's assault on the charts began when her superiors at the convent paid for a few hours of studio time, ostensibly so that she could record some of her songs to raise money for a mission to the Congo as well as spread the word about their order. Recorded at the Philips studio in Brussels, the convent agreed to fund a pressing of 1,000 copies of an eight track 10" album, which was issued in 1961. The A&R people at Philips were convinced that her dainty ditty **Dominique** could be a hit, re-christened Sister Luc Gabrielle Soeur Sourire, and issued it as a 45. The song charted in several European countries in 1962 and, in late 1963, made it across the pond, securing the Singing Nun's (as she was once again rechristened, this time to save embarrassed foreigners struggling with her stage name) place in pop history.

America, still reeling from the assassination of President John F Kennedy – and still a few months away from embracing The Beatles as their saviours – found the sweet-voiced nun irresistible: both the single and her follow up album (called simply *The Singing Nun*) went to number one – with each selling in excess of a million copies in the US alone (by 1967 the single had sold more than three million copies worldwide). Jeanne-Paule/Luc Gabrielle/Soeur Sourire/the Singing Nun signed the rights to the song over to her convent, and in two years **Dominique** made at least $100,000 in royalties for the Belgian brides of Christ (according to a short news item in *Life* magazine). And this was before the sister had set foot outside of her home country. According to an issue of *Billboard* from November 1963 *'Philips has had numerous personal appearance requests from across the country, but the nun wouldn't even consider coming here. In fact, Philips haven't even been able to get a photo of the nun.*

'For the record...the Singing Nun is actually Sister Luc-Gabrielle of Fichermont, 30 years old with blue eyes and blonde hair (the latter of

course hidden beneath her habit). She wears glasses and has been at the convent since late 1959. She is described as 'timid yet independent,' and is a talented artist as well as singer and guitarist. She cannot write music, composes entirely on the guitar, loves Bach, Beethoven and Yves Montand, and enjoys taking long walks.'

The Sister also enjoyed a burgeoning friendship with a young lady by the name of Annie Pécher, whom she met the summer before entering the convent and had reconnected with whilst on a theology course at the University of Louvain. Annie would later become Jeanine's partner.

The first (and, as far as I am aware, only) Belgian single to top the *Billboard* charts, a faithfully-translated English-language version was issued the following year by Mary Ford (of 50s hit makers Les Paul and Mary Ford) and, in 1965, a highly-fictionalised version of Sister Luc Gabrielle's life made it to the silver screen, with the former Miss Deckers portrayed by Debbie Reynolds (Debbie's version of Dominique featured different lyrics to Mary Ford's). So shy was Sister Luc Gabrielle that when she finally agreed to appear on the *Ed Sullivan Show* on January 5, 1964, the father of American TV was forced to send a film crew to the convent to film her slot; five weeks later the Beatles would cross the Atlantic to film their all-conquering performance on the same show and change the world forever. In April she played off against Barbara Streisand at the Grammys for Record of the Year, Album of the Year and Best Female Vocalist. Streisand won Album of the Year and Best Female Vocalist (as well as a brace of other

awards): Soeur Sourire took the statuette for Best Gospel or Other Religious Recording (Musical). Record of the Year went to Henry Mancini.

With the possible exception of the Pope, by the spring of 1964 Soeur Sourire was the most famous catholic in the world. In the same month that she won her solitary Grammy, Philips decided to pump out a quick follow up album - *Her Joy, Her Songs* - but the new collection was unable to repeat the success of her debut. The record came with a deluxe booklet and several art prints of the singing sister's drawings, but by the time it hit the shops America was hooked on The Beatles and sales were a mere fraction of her earlier album.

Still, a veritable crop of fake Singing Nuns sprang up in her wake: Sister Adele ('sung by Madeleine') issued a quick knock-off album via Synthetic Plastics of New Jersey; le Choeur des Enfants de Montmartre issued *The Singing Nun's Song* with an almost-identical cover to the real Singing Nun album and locally-sourced, foreign language versions of her mega hit turned up in Italy, Spain, Brazil and other countries around the world. Tours, EPs for children and more records followed. But as her star began to wane, her relationship with the rest of the nuns in the convent also started to sour.

In 1966 she recorded the inflammatorily-titled album *I Am Not A Star*, again for Philips, under the name Luc Dominique. An expanded version of *I Am Not A Star* was issued in Britain as *Dominican*, but neither version of the album sold. Times were very definitely a-changin': Sister Luc Gabrielle was becoming more and more disenchanted with the convent and, after Philips told her that they owned the name Soeur Sourire, not her, she abandoned that particular persona. The newly-emancipated Sister announced that she agreed with the interview John Lennon had given to journalist Maureen Cleve, in which he made his controversial remarks about The Beatles being "more popular than Jesus".

Sister Luc Gabrielle left the convent in October 1966, before she had taken her final vows. Some sources claim she was booted out; defrocked for her increasingly anti-Catholic beliefs. Reverting to her original name, she declared that she would continue to teach the word of God in a lay capacity.

In April 1967 two British newspapers, *The Daily Express* and *The Daily Mirror*, announced that Luc Dominique had lost the plot altogether, reporting that her latest recording was **Glory Be To God For The Golden**

Pill (the correct title of the song was simply **The Golden Pill**). A jazzy, brass-backed romp in praise of contraception, the song was bereft of her signature strumming style. Released as the title track of an EP in Belgium, it too sank without a trace: original copies are now highly prized amongst collectors. The same year Canadian fans could see an increasingly desperate Luc Dominique perform **Dominique** at a strip club in Quebec.

Luc Dominique may have claimed that she was not a star, but in some parts of the world at least, a star is exactly what she still was. In 1968 a character based on Soeur Sourire was portrayed by Orietta Berti (as Sister Teresa) in the Italian movie *Zum Zum Zum*; the same year she performed a song from *I Am Not A Star* on the Swiss TV show *Carrefour (Crossroads)* in which she sang about the death of her alter ego and the birth of her new identity:

She is dead, Soeur Sourire
She is dead, it was time
I saw her soul fly through the clouds on a flying carpet...

(*Luc Dominique*, written and performed by Luc Dominique on Philips Records. © 1968, Flamingo Music BIEM)

With sales approaching zero, and ostracisation from her convent family all but complete, Luc Dominique abandoned music. "I was never allowed to be depressed," she told an interviewer in 1979. "Mother Superior used to censor my songs and take out any verses I wrote when I was feeling sad." She later claimed that she left the convent after a personality clash with her superiors.

Sadly, Jeanine was poorly equipped for life outside of the convent or out of the spotlight. A book of self-penned poetry and extracts from her journal, *Vivre Sa Verite (Live His Truth)*, flopped and she suffered another nervous breakdown. In 1973 she confessed to her diary that she was contemplating suicide. She was overwhelmed by debt: the Belgian government claimed that Jeanine owed the equivalent of $63,000 in back taxes and the convent, who owned the rights to her only source of potential income, refused to help. Attempts to prove that the rights had been signed over to the sisters proved fruitless, and Jeanine was hounded mercilessly through the courts. Luckily she had Annie; the pair set up home together and they opened a school for autistic children. The lack of money was a constant issue: Jeannie taught guitar and art to earn a few Francs, but it was nowhere near enough to keep the wolf (and the taxman) from the door. Their difficulties were exacerbated by the couple's poor health: along with Jeanine's mental health issues, Annie suffered with crippling osteoporosis.

In 1982, when poor Ms Deckers' money troubles were at their worst and she was becoming reliant on alcohol and anxiety medicine just to get through the day, she returned to **Dominique** in an effort to alleviate her financial woes. However the laughable disco version of her 20 year-old hit (backed with a pointless instrumental version

that carried the hideous title **Dominique (Electronique-nique-nique)** proved a dismal flop, the charm of the original lost under a swathe of synthesiser and Vocoder vocals. It's a horrible, hateful mess, the sort of crap your fat, sweaty auntie would be dancing to in a Benidorm hotel disco. Jeanine was suffering *'breakdown after breakdown'* according to Annie, and the failure of the record (issued as Soeur Sourire once again, after she had won a battle with the both Philips and the convent over use of the name) all but finished her off.

Sister Smile was giving the public very little to smile about. A promotional video, featuring Jeanine in a turtleneck sweater with her pudding-bowl haircut, walking around the ruins of an abbey strumming the ever-faithful Sister Adele, did nothing to help sales. American radio personality Rick Shaw listed the original version of **Dominique** as one of the *10 Worst Pop Songs Of The Rock Era*: one can only guess at what he would make of this abomination. As if an ignominious afterlife in electronic limbo wasn't enough, a decade later **Dominique** would suffer the hell of a handful of techno remixes. Luckily its originator would not be around to see (or hear) this final humiliation.

Pushed to the point of desperation and already having lost their school thanks to the ever-present money worries, in 1985 Jeanine and Annie swallowed a lethal dose of barbiturates, which they washed down with copious amounts of alcohol. Jeanine's struggle to reconcile her faith and her sexuality, along with her failure to reignite her musical career, finally took its toll. Found near to their bodies which, according to Tom Bromley (in his book *We Could Have Been The Wombles*) were found *'in a lettuce field'* was a heartrending note, written by Annie, asking for forgiveness. *'We have reached the end, spiritually and financially and now we go to God,'* it read. *'Jeanine is in constant depression and only lives for me. I live for her. That can't go on. We do suffer really too much... We have no more place in life, no ideal except God, but we can't eat that. We go to eternity in peace. We trust God will forgive us. He saw us both suffer and he won't let us down. It would please Jeanine not to die for the world. She had a hard time on earth.'* The headline in the *New York Post* screamed *'Singing Nun and Gal Pal in Double Suicide'*. Jeanine was 52; Annie Pécher was just 41.

THE "Singing Nun" — whose music brought joy to millions in the '60s — has killed herself in a suicide pact with a mystery woman friend.

The tragedy came 22 years after her smash hit "Dominique" climbed to the No. 1 spot on American record charts.

Although her upbeat tunes — backed by a simple acoustic guitar — racked up millions in worldwide sales, Jeanine Deckers lived in poverty in her final years.

Police in Wavre, Belgium, found her body yesterday morning, along with the body of her roommate. The pair apparently had shared a fatal dose of sedatives.

Friends said Miss Deckers, 52, and her friend had been depressed over government spending cuts that had forced the children's home they ran to close.

Known as Sister Luc-Gabriel before leaving the Dominican order in 1966, she was called "Sister Smile" in the French-speaking world.

In a 1966 interview, she said she had left the Convent of Fishermont after seven years "to be closer to the people."

"I found my habit was a barrier, a shell that made

By RANSDELL PIERSON

communication difficult," she said.

"The music is my way of revealing something alive. I sing because I believe in Christ and want to reveal the living Christ to living people."

Despite her departure from the sisterhood, she maintained her strong religious ties, wearing a crucifix during world-wide performances of her devotional hymns.

The songwriter named her beloved guitar "Adele" and used it to raise funds for lepers and poor people in underdeveloped nations.

Her soothing tunes were a velvet contrast to the '60s rock tunes of groups like the Beatles and the Rolling Stones.

Like the Beatles, she became familiar to American audiences through appearances on the Ed Sullivan Show.

Jeanine Deckers — known to millions as the "Singing Nun" — performs her hit song "Dominique" at the height of her career.

Jeanine and Annie were buried together in Cheremont Cemetery in Wavre, the town where they spent their final years. The inscription on their tombstone reads *'I saw her soul fly through the clouds'*, a line from **Luc Dominique**. "Would I do it all over again?" Jeanine once agonised over during an interview. "That's not a good question. You can't. You can't do it all over again." In 1993 Jeanine was the subject of a British documentary *Kicking The Habit*: three years later an off-Broadway play, *The Tragic And Horrible Life Of The Singing Nun* played fast and loose with Jeanine's life and its camp comedy was dismissed as tasteless by critics; despite the panning a musical version followed. In 2009 *Sœur Sourire*, a Franco-Belgian biopic starring Cécile de France as Jeanine, was released to critical acclaim.

In a sad and somewhat ironic twist to this already sad story, unknown to the pair the very day that they took their lives the Belgian Society of Authors, Composers and Publishers (SABAM) awarded Jeanine almost 600,000 Belgian francs in unpaid royalties, around six times the amount that she owed and easily enough to clear her debts.

In 2014 Cristina Scuccia, a 25 year-old nun from Sicily, won the Italian version of the televised singing contest *The Voice*, singing joyous, gutsy versions of anthemic pop songs, Here's hoping that the church treats her better than her poor predecessor.

Gerty Molzen
Walk On The Wild Side (1985)

Gerty Molzen, a German cabaret star of the 30s and 40s, found fame performing comic songs during the Second World War: she as one of that incredibly rare band of artists who performed for both Adolf Hitler and for the British troops. Decades later she enjoyed a second spell in the spotlight performing her off-kilter versions of current and recent pop hits – including the song that bad music aficionados worldwide treasure her for: **Walk On The Wild Side**.

Born in the North German fishing port of Flensburg in 1906, Gerty Margarethe Molzen was the daughter of a ship owner; her own mother was the daughter of a pastor. To the horror of her very proper parents she turned out to be a bit of a tomboy: "I would much rather have been a boy and worked hard to fit in with the other young boys," she later admitted. "I was always in the thick of things."

Gerty's father decided that his wilful daughter needed to find a respectable career path, and so he sent her off to study voice, first in Berlin then later in Munich and Milan. Her first appearance as a singer took place in St. Mary's Church, Flensburg in 1930, although her career proper started in 1931, performing opera at the Salzburg Festival. Within two years she had joined an opera company in the German city of Koblenz. There she sang in Verdi's *Forces Of Destiny*, Mozart's *The Magic Flute* and more. The 1934/35 season saw her move 200 kilometres south to Saarbrücken, and the popular and versatile singer found work for the next few years both in Germany and throughout Europe.

In 1938 she crossed paths with Gustaf Gründgens, one of Germany's most famous and influential actors and a visionary theatre director. Gründgens recognised Gerty's comic ability and suggested that she move away from opera towards comedy, cabaret and parody. When the war broke out, Gerty was enlisted to entertain the troops: rather than give them operatic arias, she would strap on an accordion and perform comic songs instead. Gerty continued to perform after the war. Gründgens, her bisexual and politically left-leaning mentor, had avoided persecution by the Nazis and had even attempted to enlist (he was a favourite of Goebbels and had been included on his famous list of artists who were exempt from military mobilisation) but was imprisoned for a time by the Russians. Gerty, however, went from entertaining German troops to performing for Allied servicemen stationed in the newly-bifurcated country. "My life constantly alternated between cheerfulness, joy, sadness and melancholy," she once explained.

Her first single, *Die Roty Lilly* (**The Red Lily**), was issued in 1962 (she had previously recorded the song **Auprès De Ma Blonde** in 1938 while with Gründgens: her performance is featured in the movie *Der Schritt vom Wege*) and she had her first major movie role, in *Hamburg: City Of Vice,* in 1964. She also wrote around half a dozen books, based on her experiences and on her memories of her hometown. Gerty became well-known on German TV in the 1970s, appearing in a number of popular series, including *Das Kurheim (The Sanatorium), Hamburg Transit, Bismarck von Hinten, oder Wir Schliessen Nie (*the oddly-titled *Bismarck from Behind or We Never Close)* and *Kreisbrandmeister Felix Martin (District Fire Chief Felix Martin).* In 1977 she appeared in the Wim Wenders movie *The American Friend.*

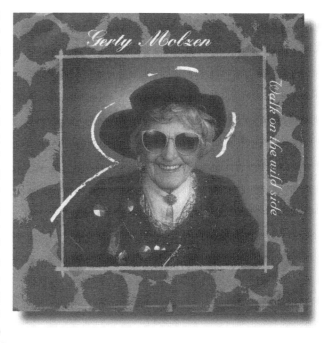

At the grand old age of 79, after more than 60 years in the industry and with four distinct careers (author, actor, opera singer and cabaret performer) under her belt, she was 'discovered' by producer Gerd Plez. It was Gerd - who had previously found fame with the German pop band Hong Kong Syndikat - who persuaded Gerty to join him in the studio to record a version of the Lou Reed classic **Walk On The Wild Side** for possible single release. Her performance is unique - and thoroughly diabolical.

Dubbed 'rock-oma' (or Grandma-rock) by the German press, Lou's tale of transsexualism, drugs, male prostitution and oral sex - which was based on many of the people he met during his time at Andy Warhol's Factory - is transformed into a hopeless, hysterical mess as the soon-to-be-octogenarian Gerty mangles Reed's lyrics, struggles with the language and slurs his words. In Gerty's world the coloured girls don't go *'do, do-do, do-do'*, but *'double-u do, double-u double doo'*, but despite that there is a certain charm in the way she croons *'valk on ze vilde side'*.

Although it failed to hit the Top 50 in the UK it proved popular in gay clubs, where Gerty's camp value was enhanced by DJs segueing her version into Reed's recording. With her stumbling performance, Dietrich on downers voice and 80s pop sensibility what's not to love?

She wasn't the first artist to cover the classic: Australian singer Duffo (who had a minor hit in the UK in 1979 with **Give Me Back My Brain**) issued an electronic version in 1981; bands including The Strokes and The Arctic Monkeys have performed the song live; saxophonist Jimmy Castor released an instrumental version; Eurythmics main man David A Stewart teamed up with French chanteuse Vanessa Paradis for another adaptation and French band Coco M issued a dance version of the song in 1987. But none of those could hold a candle to Gerty's wacky reading.

A modicum of international fame followed the release: Gerty appeared on *The David Letterman Show* in the US and on the popular Irish TV programme *Gay Byrne's Late Late Show*; she performed live on stage in London (at Peter Stringfellow's nightclub The Hippodrome), in New York and in Vienna, and released further singles - including her versions of Culture Club's **Do You Really Want To Hurt Me** and the Troggs' classic **Wild Thing** (*Vild think, you make my heart sink/You make everythink gravy, vild think*). She was followed to New York by a German film crew for the TV special *I'm Not Beautiful, I Am Much Worse (Ich bin nicht schön, ich bin viel schlimmer)*, appeared in several more movies and made a name for herself as a character actress in TV dramas. In September 1986 she was awarded the German Federal Cross of Merit (similar to an OBE or Damehood) for *'exhilarating and restorative services to young and old people'*; shortly after that she landed a recurring role, as Frau Hinnerksen, in the long-running television drama series the *The Country Doctor (Der Landarzt)*. Unfortunately Gerty's newfound fame would not last long.

Following her final television role, in which she sang the James Brown song **This Is A Man's World** whilst lying on her death bed, this amazing woman passed away on August 31, 1990 leaving no children and, after her funeral on September 7 her ashes were scattered at sea. A posthumous 22-track compilation, *From Flensburg To New York - Songs From 60 Years On Stage*, which collected her best known work alongside several previously unreleased recordings and a handful of live tracks, is available from her official website, *gertymolzen.com*

If you ever fancy visiting Flensburg you can rent an apartment in Gerty's former family home; a rare opportunity to walk in the footsteps of a truly original artist.

Starship
We Built This City (1985)

"Oh you're shitting me; that's the worst song ever." - Grace Slick

The 80s was an awful decade. It began with the murder of John Lennon and went downhill from there. Sure there were some good things – REM, the first three Frankie Goes to Hollywood singles, *Non Stop Erotic Cabaret*, the birth of the Pixies, **Enola Gay**, **Ghost Town**, **Love Will Tear Us Apart** and plenty more – but it also gave us the Stock, Aitken and Waterman music assembly line (see the chapter on **I'd Rather Jack** for more on those particular malefactors), the LinnDrum, **Shaddup You Face** and this travesty, **We Built This City**.

To fully appreciate the circumstances behind the dreadful **We Built This City** we have to go right back to a pre-Summer of Love San Francisco, 1966 to be exact, when a then-little known young model and singer named Grace Slick left her band The Great Society to replace Signe Anderson in up-and-coming acid-folk act the Jefferson Airplane. The band had already issued their first album, *Jefferson Airplane Takes Off*, but it was the addition of Slick's powerhouse vocals and the two songs she brought with her – **White Rabbit** and **Somebody To Love** - that propelled the group towards stardom.

Grace Slick has not always made the most sensible or informed career moves – with the possible exception that is of deciding, in 1989, to withdraw from the music scene altogether because, as she candidly put it: "all rock-and-rollers over the age of 50 look stupid and should retire". In 1968, when Jefferson Airplane performed **Crown Of Creation** on TV show *The Smothers Brothers Comedy Hour*, she dolled herself up as Al Jolson and ended the song with her fist raised in the air in a Black Power-style salute. I'm sure she had the best of intentions in making her gesture of solidarity with the black counterculture, but she came across like the ignorant posh girl she was (Slick's father was a high-profile banker who sent his precious daughter to finishing school).

Her alcoholism directly contributed to the band fracturing in 1972, and in 1978, according to Jefferson Airplane's official website, Grace was dragged off the stage of a local San Francisco game show after abusing the contestants. Predictably her attempt to lace President Nixon's tea with acid failed when she was prevented by security from entering the White House.

In 1974 former Airplane member Paul Kantner teamed with Grace Slick to officially launch Jefferson Starship with their first proper album *Dragonfly* (their pair had previously used the name for the concept album *Blows Against The Empire*): a third ex-Airplane member, Marty Balin, also appeared on the album and later became an official member of the group. However Slick's near-legendary alcohol intake was spiralling out of control and, after a disastrous show in Germany in 1978, when a drunken Slick shocked the audience by swearing, making sexual references and repeatedly asking, *a la* Basil Fawlty "Who won the war?" Kantner fired her from the group, Balin left and Kantner hired male vocalist Mickey Thomas. That same year, in an interview with *People* magazine, she admitted: "I started drinking heavily at 16 - anything I could get my hands on. My headmistress thought I was drinking orange juice - actually I was getting smashed on screwdrivers."

By 1981 she was back in the fold, but three years later Kantner left his own group and took the rest of the members to court, insisting that they drop the word 'Jefferson' from their name. Our Gracie, the only member of the original Jefferson Airplane line-up still with the band, and her compadres continued as Starship - Slick's slick, yuppified, big hair,

synth-led pop band which, almost immediately, scored two American number one hits. And it's one of those hits - which spent 15 weeks on the *Billboard* charts and sold in excess of a million copies domestically - that we're dealing with here.

This idiotic piece of drivel, with its nonsensical lyrics and clichéd synthesiser stabs, should never have been a hit, and it wouldn't have troubled the charts at all if it had not been for the rise of MTV; the channel featured the video for **We Built This City** in 'heavy rotation', airing the fetid clip over and over again. How in God's name would this rubbish have got to number one in the US, Canada and Australia otherwise? *'Marconi plays the mamba'*? What is that supposed to mean? That Guglielmo Marconi, the father of radio, couldn't distinguish between a stringed instrument and a snake? Four writers and not one of them knew the difference between the mambo, a dance, and a venomous reptile? That this rubbish was co-written by repeat offender Bernie Taupin should come as no surprise. And then they dress it up in a sleeve featuring the band posing as *Miami Vice* extras. At least radio announcer Les Garland, who improvised the DJ voiceover section of the record on the spot when visiting a Starship recording session, refused payment for his role – asking instead that any money due him be donated to charity.

Blender magazine ranked this karaoke classic as *'the worst song ever'*, with editor Craig Marks stating that the track *'is a real reflection of what practically killed rock music in the '80s'*. VH1 included it as one of their *50 Most Awesomely Bad Songs...Ever.* An online poll for *Rolling Stone* magazine named **We Built This City** as *'the worst song of the 1980s'*, and, in 2004, Channel 4 included the song in its *100 Worst Pop Records Of All Time* special. They programme's compilers should think themselves lucky that they did not flip it over, as the B-side is even worse. **Private Room** is a boring, pointless and interminable instrumental

'Someone's always playing corporation games', Grace sings: the lyrics of **We Built This City** claim that the band is anti-corporate rock, but in fact the opposite is true. This garbage is the epitome of corporate rock, music that is commercially successful but creatively bankrupt. There isn't a single ounce of originality here, no trace of the threat that Jefferson Airplane once posed to the nation's youth. This record is about as rock 'n' roll as Pat Boone. *'To the Woodstock generation',* wrote *Rolling Stone,* the enormous success enjoyed by Starship *'seemed like the final nail in the coffin of their youth'*. In 2012, during an interview with *Vanity Fair,* Grace admitted: "It's embarrassing. In the 80s we weren't writing our own songs. I like to write my own stuff or have the band members write their own stuff, and we weren't doing that.

"I was in my 40s and I remember thinking, God, this is just awful. But I was such an asshole for a while; I was trying to make up for it by being sober, which I was all during the 80s, which is a bizarre decade to be sober in. So I was trying to make it up to the band by being a good girl. Here, we're going to sing this song, *'We Built This City on Rock and Roll'*. Oh you're shitting me; that's the worst song ever."

Two years later Starship would score another international hit with the miserable **Nothing's Gonna Stop Us Now** which, unbelievably, went to number one in the UK and the US. You'd think with that much success that the band's future would have been secure, but within 12 months Grace Slick had left to rejoin Jefferson Airplane.

There have been so many different incarnations of Jefferson Airplane/ Jefferson Starship/Starship and so on since then (including a brief, uncredited reappearance from Our Gracie on the 2008 album *Jefferson's Tree Of Liberty*) that it's impossible to keep up. In 2015 Paul Kantner was still taking a riding crop to his section of this particular dead horse (Jefferson Starship), playing tiny venues in British backwaters in 2015, whilst at the same time Mickey Thomas was doing the rounds of slightly larger venues Stateside as Starship. Confused?

In 2014, after the track was used in a TV commercial for mobile phones, this hideous pile of poop once again became a hit, reaching number 25 in the UK charts. It seems that, in some dark corner of the globe, someone is still playing corporation games.

Tiny Tim
Santa Claus Has Got The AIDS This Year (1985)

With his white pancake make-up, rouged cheeks, lank hair and enormous, Cyrano-like nose; wearing a gaudy suit, clutching a battered ukulele and emitting a shrill, falsetto cry Herbert Buckingham Khaury, a.k.a. Tiny Tim, was one of the 60s least likely superstars. Born in New York in 1932, Tiny was a bizarre creature who suffered from an undiagnosed strain of Obsessive Compulsive Disorder (showering and brushing his teeth as often as six times a day), wore adult diapers (not from necessity) and was fanatical about personal cleanliness. When he married his first wife, Miss Vicky, in front of 40 million viewers on *Tonight With Johnny Carson*, he insisted that the new Mr and Mrs Tim remain 'pure' after their wedding.

"Tiny insisted we remain virgins until after we were married," the former Victoria Budinger told *Star* magazine in 1995. "He admitted later that even though he'd never slept with a woman, he'd had sex with men. Nothing happened between us sexually for six months. Throughout the time we were together, we had sex just enough to have had a daughter." The girl was named Tulip, after her father's biggest hit, 1968's Top Twenty **Tip-toe Thru' The Tulips With Me**. Tiny was 37 when they wed; Miss Vicky was just 17. Alongside the Beatles' first appearance on the *Ed Sullivan Show* and the 1969 moon landings, their wedding was one of the most watched televisual events of the 1960s. Tim and Miss Vicky would later launch their own record label, the rather brilliantly-named Vic-Tim Records: after they split Tiny would go on to launch a second label, the less-than-subtle Toilet Records.

A devout Christian who detested drugs and bad language (but who liked a beer or three), Tiny's metier was turn of the century vaudeville songs and Tin Pan Alley standards. As a child he spent most of his time in his bedroom listening to, and devouring, 78 rpm recordings by Rudy Vallee, the Paul Whiteman Orchestra (featuring a young Bing Crosby) and Billy Murray. His reward for the hundreds of hours of devotion would be an encyclopaedic knowledge of these early recordings and an enormous repertoire to draw from. There were three main reasons why he sang, Tiny once confessed to *Newsweek* magazine: "The first is to give thanks to God for the gift he gave me. Number two is to cheer people whether they are young or old, with a song of the past or present. And number three, perhaps above all, is because of all the lovely women who, because of their beauty, cause my heart to overflow with joy." Tiny sure did love the ladies, chivalrously referring to them as 'Miss' and often penning songs to his favourites – or 'classics' as he called them. He even awarded an annual trophy to his preferred classic.

Described by one reviewer as having *'hair like Rasputin and hips like a lazy housewife'*, the half-Lebanese, half-Polish Herbert was a living, breathing archive of long-forgotten songs. He began performing in 1950, when he won a local talent contest, but he would have to wait until 1965 to get his big break.

Whilst appearing at the New York club The Scene Mo Ostin, president of Frank Sinatra's Reprise label, and fellow record company executive Stan Cornyn, caught Tiny's act. The pair had gone there after a tip-off from Pete Yarrow of Peter, Paul & Mary, who had long been a champion of Tiny and had previously used him in the movie *You Are What You Eat*. *'A strange long-haired freaky fellow walked up to the front of the room,'* recalled Cornyn, writing for *www.rhino.com*. *'Freaky because this guy wore white-ish makeup. He carried a shopping bag with a ukulele in it. Without tuning it, he just started to sing. His voice was falsetto! Like imitating Shirley Temple or like he was some castrato.'* Ostin offered Tiny a recording contract on the

spot and, when he found out that Tim had already worked with Reprise producer Richard Perry on a one-off 45 for Blue Cat Records (**April Showers**) the pair were reunited and ushered into the studio together to cut Tiny's first proper album.

Tiny's genius was well-served with three hit albums on Reprise (the Top Ten hit *God Bless Tiny Tim, Tiny Tim's Second Album* and the Grammy-nominated *For All My Little Friends*), and he would make dozens of TV appearances, including a semi-regular spot on the hit show *Laugh In*, 20 appearances on *Tonight With Johnny Carson* and an hour-long special on Australian TV. He enjoyed the patronage of The Beatles (making a guest appearance on their 1968 Christmas record performing **Nowhere Man**) and he even had his own board game - *Tiny Tim's Game Of Beautiful Things*. Equipped with a voice that could switch from soprano to baritone with ease, Tiny was probably the only hit artist who was able to duet with himself - as he did successfully on his versions of **I've Got You, Babe** and **Daddy, Daddy, What Is Heaven Like?** He even recorded **Fill Your Heart** four years before David Bowie would cut the definitive version for the brilliant *Hunky Dory* album. Tiny's version inspired Bowie to search out the obscure first album by Biff Rose, the song's co-writer: David would go on to perform several tracks from *The Thorn In Mrs Rose's Side* in the years before he became Ziggy Stardust.

But not everything in Tiny's career went smoothly.

Recorded way back in 1962, *With Love And Kisses From Tiny Tim - Concert In Fairyland* was put out in 1968, when he was at the height of his fame, by the tiny Bouquet label. The recordings were originally due to be released credited to Darry Dover and the White Cliffs, one of the many stage names Herbert used ("I've been Larry Love, Emmett Swink, Judas Foxglove and Darry Dover," he told *New York* magazine) before settling on the moniker Tiny Tim, a joke as he stood a full 6'1" in his socks. As Larry Love, the Singing Canary, he had been a fixture at Hubert's Museum, a basement freak show on 42nd Street, performing for tourists next to the flea circus. "I was booed for years and years," he once revealed when discussing his early years. "I went from dive to dive and from bar to bar all over New York and New Jersey."

The songs on *With Love And Kisses From Tiny Tim* were transcribed to tape without overdubs or retakes during one session at a club in Greenwich Village, New York City (Tiny's first professional performances were, according to him, when he "Got paid ten dollars a night in 1962 in

Greenwich Village at a place called the Café Bizarre"). For this release the 12 songs were slathered with the noise of an overly eager audience, laughing, clapping and cheering away in a vain attempt to pass this rubbish off as a new live concert. Unfortunately the audience tape loop lasts for about 30 seconds, which means that your  listening pleasure is quickly ruined by the same raucous whistling three or four times in each song. Despite containing early versions of Tiny Tim classics, including **On The Good Ship Lollipop** (which would be issued by Bouquet as a 45 around the same time that Tiny's re-recorded version also appeared in the shops), it's shockingly bad; Tim's management slapped a lawsuit on Bouquet, and the company was forced to withdraw the album, but not before it had sold many thousands of copies.

"It may be the worst record ever produced," Tiny told author Harry Stein (for his 1976 book *Tiny Tim*). "In those days, I'd sometimes sing off-key on spite." It's no wonder Richard Perry, the producer who worked with Tiny from **April Showers** thorugh to the early *For All My Little Friends* sessions (and who would later weave his magic with Harry Nilsson and Ringo Starr), is often quoted as saying that *With Love And Kisses From Tiny Tim* was the album that killed Tiny's career.

I guess you can't really blame the former Mr. Khaury for that, but he's certainly fully responsible for another utterly reprehensible recording: **Santa Claus Has Got the AIDS This Year**.

Although his 15 minutes of fame was pretty much up by the beginning of 1970 he continued to record sporadically right up until his death. In 1977 a down-at-heal Tiny was defaulting on his child support payments and couldn't even afford the cab fare to pay for his first visit to his estranged wife (then working, according to *New York* magazine as a go-go dancer) and daughter in three years. A brace of albums planned for 1981 (*I Won't Dance* and *Tell Me That You Love Me*) failed to materialise but several others would see the light of day, including the well-received *Girl* (with Brave Combo), as would a number of 45s – some good, some mediocre at best. However controversy rages amongst his dedicated army of fans about what must be the most offensive record in his oeuvre.

He won't be yelling out ho! Ho! Ho! Ho!
But he'll be screaming out no! No! No! No!
He's lying sick in bed, call the doctor there instead
Santa Claus has got the AIDS this year

Each season he is full of pep and vim
But now the AIDS have got the best of him
The nurses all look sad, 'cause Santa's got it bad
Santa Claus has got the AIDS this year

(*Santa Claus Has Got The AIDS This Year*, written and recorded by Tiny Tim. © 1985, The Estate of Herbert B. Khaury)

It has been claimed by a number of sources – including the author of the song himself - that **Santa Claus Has Got The AIDS This Year** was written in 1980, two years before the term AIDS began to be used in conjunction with what was then still known by many as 'the gay plague', yet the song first appeared as the B-side to his obscure 1985 single **She Left Me With The Herpes**. Recorded live in a hotel bedroom, the song received wider coverage when it was included on the 1995 album *Songs Of An Impotent Troubadour*. In the sleeve notes to that album, a collection of self-composed songs written over a period of more than 45 years, the producer says he became aware of the song in 1984 - well after the acronym AIDS was in common use.

Tiny claimed that his tune was about Santa's over indulgence on Ayds (a meal-replacement chocolate bar popular with slimmers in the 1970s) but that he couldn't use the name Ayds as it would have led to copyright infringement. Personally I think that's bull. Tiny said that he "wrote this way before Rock Hudson...around 1980," but there is no evidence at all, bar a single revisionist quote from the late ukulele-playing minstrel, that this song is not about the disease which has wiped millions of people off the face of the earth. It's a shocking aberration: Tiny was known for his gentlemanly way - he went out of his way to be as courteous as possible

- yet the lyrics of this horror make it perfectly clear that poor old Santa is lying in bed stricken with a terrible illness, not that he has to dash off to the lavatory every few minutes with rampant diarrhoea because he's binged on slimming treats. Still, it is what it is - a truly bad-taste piece of work by a titan of outsider music and truly worthy of a place here in The World's Worst Records' museum of the malodorous. **Santa Claus Has Got The AIDS This Year** was listed at number seven in Dr. Demento's *11 Worst Song Titles of All Time*.

During his brief period in the spotlight Tim reckoned he earned between two and four million dollars. Unfortunately, many of his business associates (*'a succession of sleazoid agents'* as Irwin Chusid put it in *Songs In The Key of Z*, his essential guide to the world of outsider music) took advantage of his naïveté, leaving him with little money, and forcing the man who once commanded $50,000 a night into a succession of smaller and smaller gigs: at one point he was even touring America with a circus. That didn't stop him entering the race for Mayor of New York in 1989, although he soon backed out and decided to support Rudolph Giuliani instead. The campaign had been his manager's idea "and I just went along with it - but it never seemed to catch fire," he told a reporter from the *New York Daily News*.

Tiny gave his last performance at the Women's Club of Minneapolis in November 1996. Accompanied by his third wife (Miss Sue) he was taken ill whilst performing his signature song (he had insisted on performing even though he'd recently had a heart scare, was battling diabetes and had stumbled and fallen on his way to the gig) and he collapsed as she was trying to help him back to their table. He was rushed to the Hennepin County Medical Center where he died an hour later. After his previous heart attack, during a ukulele festival in Massachusetts two months earlier, the self-proclaimed Impotent Troubadour said: "I am ready for anything that happens. Death is never polite, even when we expect it. The only thing I pray for is the strength to go out without complaining." Tiny was buried at Lakewood Cemetery Mausoleum, Minneapolis.

As Miss Sue told *The Seattle Times*: "He went out with a big bang. Very theatrical. That was his way, to collapse in front of hundreds of people." And her thoughts on that controversial record? "Tiny never judged people," she told Scott Michaels of finddeath.com. "He thought that homosexuality was wrong, but he was not repulsed or outraged by it. He knew that *'there but for the grace of God go I'*. He was always around all kinds of people, and accepted everyone."

Bette Midler
The Wind Beneath My Wings (1988)

I'm willing to accept that this next choice is contentious. I fully understand that there are some people who find this song moving, and I appreciate too why it has become one of the most popular pop songs to be employed at both weddings and funerals. I'll even go so far as to say that I 'get' how the pseudo-religious sentiment has led to the lyrics of this particular song being reprinted, mantra like, in Hallmark-style books of sickly-sweet 'thoughts for the day' and in dozens of guides for sermon writers.

But I still hate Bette Midler's version of **The Wind Beneath My Wings**. Just thinking about the syrupy racket makes me want to barf.

Born – shortly after the end of the Second World War - into a Jewish family in a mostly-Asian part of Honolulu, the young Miss Midler was named after the actress Bette Davis (although the two women pronounced their names differently: Midler the single syllable 'Bet', Davis 'Betty'). She studied drama (for less than a full academic year) at the University of Hawaii, and got her first acting break in the 1966 Julie Andrews/Richard Harris movie *Hawaii*, playing a seasick passenger. Although she went uncredited, *Hawaii* the money Bette earned as an extra on funded her passage to New York, where she soon found stage work: within 12 months of her arrival in the Big Apple Midler had joined the cast of *Fiddler On The Roof* on Broadway. After three years with *Fiddler* she began singing at the Continental Baths, a notorious gay bathhouse in the basement of the gothic Ansonia Hotel (also on Broadway), accompanied by pianist Barry Manilow. Manilow would go on to produce her first album, *The Divine Miss M*, which was released in 1972 and earned Midler a Grammy award for Best New Artist.

Huge success would follow: platinum albums, mega hit movies, sell out tours – Midler soon became one of the most recognised faces in showbiz. It's a bit of a shame that today that face appears to have had so much botox and filler injected in to it that she now looks as if she's stuck her head in a wasps' nest (although she's never admitted to having had plastic surgery, her countenance is unnaturally wrinkle-free for someone who will soon begin her eighth decade on the planet). In 1988, at the pinnacle of her career, she took on the role of C C Bloom in the hit comedy-drama movie *Beaches* – and recorded the film's malignant anthem **The Wind Beneath My Wings**.

Co-opted or downright plagiarised by dozens of quasi-religious quacks for their own self-published poetry anthologies, **The Wind Beneath My Wings** was originally recorded not by Bette Midler but by the whistling Kenyan-born troubadour Roger Whittaker. Written by Jeff Silbar and Larry Henley (who, sadly, died shortly before Christmas 2014 – co-incidentally while I was writing this. I do hope the two incidents are not connected) in 1982, the song has become a bona fide standard, recorded by more than 200 artists. Silbar was a career songwriter with several country hits under his belt; Henley had been a singer. It is Larry Henley who provides the falsetto vocals on the 1964 hit **Bread And Butter** by The Newbeats.

The song writing partners recorded a rough demo of their new song – an upbeat, guitar-led version – which they then passed on to their publisher, Bob Montgomery of House Of Gold Music, and promptly forgot about. Montgomery loved the song, but felt the arrangement was wrong. Over a weekend he rearranged the piece, giving it the ballad setting we all know today. "We both had tears in our eyes," Silbar has since said. "Bob had taken our demo and produced a new version which truly showed the potential of the song". It would take a year of relentless plugging before Montgomery found – in Whittaker - someone willing to sing the sentimental ballad. Cover versions by Sheena Easton, Lee Greenwood, Lou Rawls, Gladys Knight & The Pips (as **Hero**), Perry Como and others followed. Then, in 1988, Marc Shaiman - Midler's musical director - suggested that she record the song for her upcoming movie Beaches. Midler was reluctant at first: "I said, *'I'm not singing that song,'*" she told The Times in 1999, "But the friend who gave it to me said, *'If you don't sing it I'll never speak to you again'*, so of course I had to sing the damned song. Whatever reservations I might have had I certainly don't have any more."

"I heard a demo, with Bette singing it," recalled Silbar. "I was blown away by her version and its impact in the movie. I felt Bette had recorded the definitive version of the song." Midler's recording went to number one on the Billboard chart and also became a huge international hit. Since then many other artists have recorded **The Wind Beneath My Wing**s, including Willie Nelson, Kenny Rogers, Judy Collins and Shirley Bassey. It has won seven ASCAP Awards, including one for Song of the Century.

After **The Wind Beneath My Wings** Midler scored another huge hit with the maudlin – and more overtly religious - **From A Distance**. Shortly after that she was offered the lead in *Sister Act*, turning it down because she felt uncomfortable making fun of nuns. The role, as we all know, went to Whoopi Goldberg, riding high after the massive success of *Ghost*. Midler had to contend with being awarded a Golden Raspberry for Worst Actress in *Stella*, her misfiring remake of the 30s Oscar-winning melodrama *Stella Dallas*.

However, as interesting as that all is, none of this explains why I hate this record. Maybe it's the saccharine sentimentality. Perhaps it's the misappropriation of passages from the Bible, a book peppered with plenty of eagles/wings/rising up metaphors. It could be that the damned disc was always being played on the jukebox every time I walked in to the Golden Cross in Cardiff in the 1990s, or it might even be that the song could be construed as being quite mean spirited and selfish: *'It must have been cold there in my shadow/To never have sunlight on your face'*, but no. Most of my anger is reserved for exactly three minutes and 35 seconds into this monstrosity, when the Divine Miss M hits a note so preposterously awful that it quite literally sets my teeth on edge. *'Fly, flyyyyy, flyyyyy awayyyyy'* she brays, sounding like a donkey with distemper. That's why I detest **The Wind Beneath My Wings** – because that one note offends me so very, very deeply.

Not that any of the recording's creators will give a fig. "The most rewarding thing for me is to hear people tell me what the song has meant to them," says Silbar. "It is a tremendous feeling to know that I had a part in creating such a special song." A poll in 2002 established that **The Wind Beneath My Wings** was the most-played song at British funerals. Perhaps that's what I hate about it: maybe it's simply the fact that I'm getting old, I'm attending more and more funerals and they're all soundtracked by this wretched record.

Elton John
Give Peace A Chance (1990)

In a career that spans five decades Sir Elton John (born Reginald Dwight, in London in 1947) has sold more than 300 million records, making him one of the best-selling artists in the world. He's also one of the most famous people on the planet and one of the world's richest musicians: he was ranked as the third highest earning musician in 2014 by *Forbes* magazine, amassing £62 million ($100 million) in that year alone.

He also holds a special place in hearts of Beatles fans, playing piano for John Lennon, Ringo Starr and George Harrison, and singing **Hey Jude** with Sir Paul at the Music for Montserrat concert in 1997, making him one of only three people (the others being Eric Clapton and percussionist Ray Cooper) to have played with all four solo Beatles. He also famously aided the reconciliation of an estranged Lennon and Yoko Ono in 1974 after what would turn out to be Lennon's last live performance, as Elton's guest, at Madison Square Gardens in 1974. John and Elton were close friends: John played on Elton's covers of his compositions **One Day At A Time** and **Lucy In The Sky With Diamonds**, and Elton repaid the favour by banging the keys on John's US number one hit **Whatever Gets You Through The Night**.

John Lennon's assassination, in December 1980, would leave an indelible mark on Elton: in 2013 he revealed to *Entertainment Weekly* that when he performs **Empty Garden**, a song he wrote as a tribute to his late friend, he makes sure he doesn't catch a glimpse of the images of the former Beatle that appear onscreen behind him for fear of bursting into tears. *'I don't look back when I'm playing that song - if I see the footage of John, I get choked up and it's too hard to get through the song. I miss him so much. He was a force of nature, and you don't get many of those. And you sure as hell miss them when they leave.'*

Which makes his utterly bizarre cover version of Lennon's anti-war anthem **Give Peace A Chance** so stupefying. Issued in 1990 in a handful of countries as the B-side to the hit **Club At The End Of The Street**, this peculiar performance features Elton adopting a range of voices and accents (including reasonably passable imitations of camp British comedy icons Kenneth Williams and Frankie Howerd), while snatches of his 1998 hit **I Don't Wanna Go On With You Like That** play in the background. It is, frankly, ludicrous.

One can only assume that our Reg thought that it would be funny, a Goons for the 90s perhaps. The lyrics bear little more than a passing association with Lennon and McCartney's original, and Elton's references to TV puppets Rag, Tag and Bobtail would confuse anyone under 40 or not au fait with children's television programmes in post-war Britain. It is telling that the track – surely the only recording under the sun to include mentions of Scottish trombone player George Chisholm, sub-four minute miler Roger Bannister, Madonna and Max Bygraves - was made (according to biographer Philip Norman) in December 1988, while Elton was still, as he acknowledged in an interview he gave to NBC's Matt Lauer in 2012: "the biggest junkie there was." To make a recording this bad you would have to be smacked out of your head on something.

Give Peace A Chance was John Lennon's first solo single (credited to the Plastic Ono Band), recorded on his extended honeymoon in 1969 and reaching number two in Britain and number 14 in the US, and Elton is not alone in releasing an awful version of the song. Mitch Miller and the Gang (see the chapter Mama Will Bark) issued their version as the closing track of their 1970 Atlantic album *Mitch Miller And The Gang Peace Sing-Along*. One of the most influential figures in American popular music during the 50s and 60s, Miller's sanitised version of Lennon's counter-culture hit is as bland as they come. Miller's version has several howlingly bad lyrical transpositions, my favourite being when Mitch sings 'rabbits' instead of 'rabbis'! Louis Armstrong's perverse rendition appeared on his 1970 album of pop covers *Louis Armstrong And Friends* and was released as a posthumous UK A-side (on Phillips in 1971) with a re-recording of his huge hit **What A Wonderful World** on the flip. Then there's the Hot Chocolate Band's take on the song, released on the Beatles' own Apple Records in 1969 (Apple 18): an abominable, cod-reggae mess with stupid lyrics and idiotic, fake-patois vocals. Who could have guessed that with a slight name change the group would go on to score at least one chart single every year in the UK between 1970 and 1984? U2 have performed the song live more than two dozen times: Yoko Ono has revisited the song too, with new versions appearing in 1991 and 2008.

Elton, who had performed a more traditional version of **Give Peace A Chance** while on tour in 1970, admitted that he "came very close to dying," during his years of addiction. "I'd have an epileptic seizure and turn blue and people would find me on the floor and put me to bed, and then 40 minutes later I'd be snorting another line.

"When you take a drug and you take a drink and you mix those two together, you think you're invincible." Lennon, of course, had his own battles with booze and drugs, and the pair would often party together. On one occasion, as Elton revealed to *Rolling Stone* magazine, the pair were "stoned out of our minds on coke at the Sherry-Netherland hotel," when someone came a-calling "at two in the morning".

"It took me five minutes to get to get the door because I was so paranoid, but it was Andy fucking Warhol! I said, *'It's Andy Warhol,'* and he (Lennon) said, *'Don't fucking let him in! He'll have a camera and everything!'* So we just waited for him to leave." In his 2012 memoir *Love Is The Cure: On Life, Loss And The End Of AIDS* Elton admitted that he finally stopped using cocaine and abusing alcohol after he met Ryan White, an Indiana teenager who contracted AIDS through a blood transfusion. When Ryan died in 1990, Elton was forced to reconsider his own mortality. "I was just in and out of a drug-fuelled haze in the '80s. I did nothing to help people with AIDS," he said. "I was a gay man who really sat on the sidelines."

Since then, of course, Elton has done amazing things, setting up the Elton John AIDS Foundation, a non-profit organisation which supports innovative HIV/AIDS prevention, education, care and support services for people living with HIV/AIDS and which has raised over $200 million to support HIV/AIDS programmes in fifty-five countries around the world.

It would be remiss of me if I didn't give a brief mention to Elton's biggest international hit, his hideous, coffin-cradling remake of **Candle In The Wind**. Acknowledged by the *Guinness Book Of World Records* as *'the* *biggest-selling single since UK and US singles charts began in the 1950s'*, and second only in sales to the Bing Crosby perennial **White Christmas**, this hateful rewrite of what had been a pretty, heartfelt tribute to the sad life of actress Marilyn Monroe was issued in 1997 to mark the passing of Diana, Princess of Wales. It's little wonder that Hong Kong-born but New Zealand-based 'singer' Wing Han Tsang chose this particular version of the song to cover on her hysterically awful 2009 collection *Beat It!*

The Reynolds Girls
I'd Rather Jack (1989)

One hit wonders The Reynolds Girls are the exemplar of everything that is wrong with manufactured pop music. Their sole chart entry, the 1989 Top Tenner **I'd Rather Jack** is, quite rightly, routinely outed as one of the most irritating – and most awful – records made, reaching number 53 on BBC Three's rundown of the *Most Annoying Pop Songs Ever* and 91 on Channel 4's list of the *100 Worst Pop Songs Of All Time*.

The British charts of the late 1980s were dominated by the names of three men – Mike Stock, Matt Aitken and Pete Waterman (SAW): probably the most successful writing and production partnerships of all time, with in excess of 100 UK top 40 hits (including seven number one singles in 1989 alone) and sales of 40 million. Not bad for a brand that began with female vocal duo Agents Aren't Aeroplanes and their dire Frankie Goes to Hollywood rip-off **The Upstroke**.

It's estimated that the trio earned around £60 million before Aitken left the fold in 1991. Waterman and Stock finally called it a day - rather acrimoniously as it turns out - in 1993 after a few more Top Five chart placings for acts including antipodean diva Kylie Minogue, the World Wrestling Federation and American pop singer Sybil. Things did not fare well for the three former friends once the hits dried up: in 1999 they were facing each other from opposite sides of a court room, with Stock and Aitken claiming that Train Set Pete owed them a fortune in royalties. The pair lost and Stock, in a fit of pique, branded Waterman "a buffoon" who "thinks talent is blond hair and big tits", a thinly-veiled reference to Waterman's reviled late night TV show *The Hitman And Her*. His book, *The Hit Factory* (New Holland Publishers, 2004) is a bitter commentary on the way the multi-millionaire was so badly treated by Waterman and the music industry at large.

There are few – if any – production teams that inspire the downright disgust regularly demonstrated towards SAW. That's probably to be expected though for a company that, as music critic Alex Petridis noted in a 2005 article in *The Guardian 'churned out records like fast food: cheap, disposable, unwholesome, identical. Beating off stiff competition from the Chernobyl disaster and the Ethiopian famine, they were voted*

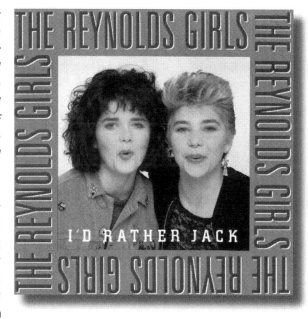

the second worst thing about the 80s (Margaret Thatcher pipped them). Phil Spector may have recently garnered a similar level of opprobrium, but he had to be charged with murder first.'

They were never going to be critical darlings, having begun their career producing Hi-NRG anthems for gay discos with John Water's favourite drag queen Divine, Hazell Dean and Dead or Alive. Even today when, in a post-modern nostalgic sense, it's actually pretty cool to like those floor-filling classics (and who doesn't love **You Spin Me Round**, **You Think You're A Man** or Bananarama's version of **Venus**?) there is so much to hate in the SAW canon. No amount of ironic revisionism can justify the horrors that were Sinitta's ridiculous **Toy Boy**, FKW's awful remake of Rick Astley's number one hit **Never Gonna Give You Up** or any of a number of cuts from the fetid Aussie cheese factory that was Kylie and Jason. Their label PWL (Pete Waterman Limited) also licensed material from the hateful Dutch dance act 2 Unlimited (*no, no/no, no, no, no/no, no, no, no/no, no – there's no lyrics*), but nothing is as vile as **I'd Rather Jack**, which Petridis calls *'Stock Aitken & Waterman's God Save The Queen... less a song than a kamikaze act of provocation, designed to upset as many people as possible in the space of three minutes. Everyone from the Rolling Stones to Radio 1 DJs and programmers - everyone, in fact, who isn't Stock, Aitken and Waterman - gets it in the neck over a thumping house beat.'*

Golden oldies, Rolling Stones, we don't want them back
I'd rather jack than Fleetwood Mac
No heavy metal, rock 'n' roll, music from the past
I'd rather jack than Fleetwood Mac

(*I'd Rather Jack*, written by Stock, Aitken and Waterman. Released by The Reynolds Girls on PWL Records. © 1989, All Boys Music)

207

Originally of Irish descent, Linda and Aisling Reynolds hailed from Litherland, a suburb of Sefton in Liverpool, and were just two of the nine Reynolds siblings. Although legend will have it that the girls were plucked from the streets, the truth is far more mundane. Linda had trained as a hairdresser before getting the performing bug (one of the other Reynolds kids, Debbie, had appeared in the Channel 4 soap opera *Brookside*) and 16-year-old Aisling dropped out school to join her in a pop career. They approached Waterman with a demo tape while he was filming in their hometown, and he was impressed enough to invite them down to the PWL Studios (a.k.a. The Hit Factory). A quick shopping trip to Primark and Claire's Accessories later and the girls were off to London in their padded denim jackets to record I'd Rather Jack.

Bizarrely the hit-making trio saw this piece of nonsense as their great protest song. I'd Rather Jack was Aitken's (the chief culprit) response to the music critics who ignored or ridiculed their young pop acts, and to the radio DJs who concentrated on playing older, more established bands rather than the soulless, mechanised pop pumped out by SAW. "It is about snobbery, people who are up their arse in music," Waterman once said of the track. He was no fan of the national radio station either: "Radio One (is) out of order," he told *Roadblock* fanzine in 1995. "It's ego maniacs playing stuff they want to play, not what the public wants to hear."

"I'd Rather Jack was a tongue-in-cheek record about the changes that were going on in radio at the time," Waterman has said. "We wanted to knock that so we wrote this record. I'd met the girls at a show and thought *'we may as well use these two'*." He obviously wasn't paying a lot of attention to his protégés: when the girls appeared with Waterman on *The Hitman And Her*, miming to their single and skipping around the stage waving their arms around in a rough approximation of dancing, he introduced them as "the Reynolds Sisters".

A hastily-recorded video – filmed in Liverpool and featuring several of the sisters' siblings – was rushed out to help promote the disc, which managed to make it into the Top Ten of the official the UK singles charts. The girls were sent out on a round-Britain PA showcase (loftily titled *The Hitman Roadshow*) with other SAW acts including Big Fun and Halo James, and they even got to support SAW's second-biggest act – former Australian soap star Jason Donovan. "It really is a good atmosphere," Aisling told *The Liverpool Echo*. "All the bands are equally brilliant but Big Fun are incredible - they are going to be bigger than Bros!" Now that's an accolade! Reflecting on their hit, Aisling told the newspaper: "It's not about nuclear waste. It's got a great beat, there's humour in it, and it's now, it's today!"

According to media interviews the girls gave at the time, Aisling liked sleeping, chocolate, reading and had to do a lot of *'complicated things'* to keep her big hair big; elder sister Linda liked telling bad jokes, and liked INXS (although not Michael Hutchence's then-current look: "His new haircut isn't very nice" she said. Let's hope her stinging critique didn't trouble the singer too much). Both girls detested being asked if they really hated Fleetwood Mac. Said Linda: "I think they're quite good at what they do really. They just suited the idea of the song, mainly because their name rhymes with jack." No shit, Sherlock!

It was Waterman who was convinced that he could give these two spectacularly average singers a song and turn it into a hit - and it was a shame-faced Waterman who had to admit that he got it wrong. "It was the only record we put on Top of the Pops that went down the next week," he later claimed. It didn't: it was at number 17 the week the Girls appeared on TOTP and would eventually peak at Number Eight. "You can't get the public to buy something that they don't believe in, and they never believed in the Reynolds Girls. If this had been Mel and Kim it would have been Number One." Kim Appleby disagreed. "The Reynolds Girls thing was awful," she told producers for the ITV documentary *The Hit Factory - The Stock, Aitken And Waterman Story.* "They (SAW) deserved the backlash from that."

The Reynolds Girls parted company with Stock, Aitken and Waterman after just one single, allegedly after they became *'too big for their boots'*. With the backing of their dad Walter they released the Mel and Kim-esque **Get Real** on their own label (Renotone) which failed to chart. Linda would later resurface in the band HYPE, who did moderately well on the club circuit and toured with Take That but failed to score any chart success. Around 2005 a rumour began to circulate that one of the girls had died, either in childbirth or from cancer. Luckily for their fans (and for the girls themselves) this proved untrue: both girls were still alive and well, and both were happily married with children.

In 2012 *The Liverpool Echo* reported on a search to find and reunite the siblings for a celebratory concert to mark the 25th anniversary of Waterman's PWL company and to appear in the aforementioned ITV documentary. Steps, Jason Donovan (along with a 'surprise' appearance from his erstwhile squeeze and on-screen wife Kylie), Sinitta, Sonia, Rick Astley, Bananarama, Brother Beyond and many others were all due to appear in the Hyde Park spectacular, but the outdoor extravaganza was cancelled. When the former stars of Waterman's Hit Factory did finally reconvene – indoors at the O2 Arena in London's Docklands later that year – the Reynolds Girls were conspicuous by their absence.

Not even the rose-tinted glow of nostalgia could polish this particular turd. Still, not everyone hated it: Japanese boy band Litomo Seinentai covered it and, in 1990, Brighton-based punk outfit Peter and the Test Tube Babies also covered the song for their PWL 'tribute' album *The Shit Factory*.

Duran Duran
Thank You (1995)

Duran Duran was a worldwide synth-pop sensation: a massively successful leviathan of a band whose juggernaut of fame swept aside all comers. Formed in Birmingham in 1978, by the end of 1980 they had settled on their classic five-piece line-up and were signed to EMI records, the company keen to bag itself one of the biggest bands on the emerging New Romantic scene. Within 12 months the group had scored four UK hit singles and a Top Five album. International fame and outright hysteria soon followed for the five pretty young men from the Midlands.

But how does a band that huge go from being the biggest worldwide phenomenon of the 80s to becoming one of the most reviled acts of the 90s and issuing an album that has been ridiculed by fans and critics alike?

Celebrated by *Q* magazine as the *Worst Album Of All Time* (in a 2006 readers poll) and called *'stunningly wrongheaded'* by *Rolling Stone*, *Thank You* was a sorry, misguided effort by the band - down to a trio from their five-piece heyday - to pay tribute to some of their influences: not that the average Durannie would see a link between the poppy **Planet Earth** and the hip-hoppy **White Lines**. Yes, that's right: amongst the treasures that *Thank You* yields are despicably awful covers of Grandmaster Melle Mel's anti-drug hit, the rap classic **White Lines** and Public Enemy's police-bating **911 Is A Joke**. You'd have to hope that someone involved in this aural abortion thought the whole project was a joke, but not the oh-so-serious Simon Le Bon and his pals. As Robert Webb writes in his book *100 Greatest Cover Versions 'it's hard to see who, exactly, the album was aimed at'*.

Thank You was, according to contemporary reports, originally conceived as a light-hearted tribute to the band's influences, in the vein of Bowie's *Pin Ups* or Bryan Ferry's *These Foolish Things*. Some of the tracks were recorded while the band was on tour promoting their previous album (*Duran Duran* a.k.a *The Wedding Album*), however conflicts within the band and with Capitol/EMI created delay after delay, and mixes of the tracks were ordered and rejected on more than one occasion by the label. "We wanted to bring a different energy to familiar songs," bassist John Taylor told *Billboard* magazine, "while also playing proper tribute to those who have given us the inspiration to make music. Those albums were perfect examples of how that can be accomplished." He's right: both *Pin Ups* and *These Foolish Things* are fine examples of how to breathe new life into old favourites. Unfortunately for Taylor and his cohorts, the only life that *Thank You* breathes is a last gasp death rattle.

Even having the original perpetrators of **White Lines** along for the ride couldn't save Duran from ending up with a whole lotta egg on their collective faces; Le Bon's white bread vocals are no match for the grittier, street-wise Grandmaster Flash (who, despite being  credited on several international releases, did not appear on the original version) and Melvin 'Melle Mel' Glover (who very much did). A staggering 20 different mixes and edits of **White Lines** were released to help sales of the single (which reached number 17 in the UK) - issued across a multitude of 12" singles, CD singles and promo-only vinyl versions. *Spin* magazine hit the nail well and truly on the head when their reviewer described the track as *'more like a soft drink commercial than an anti-drug rant'*.

911 Is A Joke has to be one of the worst things on the album, and therefore one of the worst things a member of Duran Duran has ever been involved with, although it's hard to separate this horror from the ridiculous cover of the Temptations' classic **Ball Of Confusion**. Personally I despise their version of the Door's gorgeous **The Crystal Ship**, but **911** and **Ball** are so stupid they almost defy belief. I wonder how the Public Enemy guys felt about this, having their angry anthem - a song which is fiercely critical of the longer response times taken by US emergency services visiting black neighbourhoods - trodden all over by a bunch of middle class white boys who know absolutely nothing about the problems trying to get an ambulance in New York. Again *Spin*'s James Hannaham is full of opprobrium: *'they say they covered it because they knew it would piss people off, but coming from a band devoid of rebellion it sounds as convincing as Amy Grant covering GG Allin. And not as funny.'* The Japanese CD edition of *Thank You* featured two extra tracks – limp covers of David Bowie's **Diamond Dogs** and the Velvet Underground's **Femme Fatale**.

It's not all awful: the version of Lou Reed's **Perfect Day** is a perfectly fine - if a bit bland - note-for-note retread of the original, but turning the great **Watching The Detectives** by Elvis Costello and the Attractions into a poor, UB40-esque parody is unforgivable. Re-reading Led Zepplin's **Thank You** (hardly the greatest track in the respected Zep canon) into something that *'sounds like the band is covering Chris DeBurgh'* is simply shoddy. Hannaham describes Le Bon's vocals as *'an excellent impression of Robert Plant being catheterised by a shrimp de-veiner'* – and who am I to argue?

Duran Duran were not the first band to pay homage to their roots (and they sure won't be the last) however I'd posit that - with the penultimate song on the album, **Drive By** - they are certainly one of the very few acts so outrageously conceited as to pay tribute to themselves. **Drive By** is essentially an introduction to the track **The Chauffeur** from the band's 1982 album *Rio* which segues in to a version of the original song - meaning, in essence, that the out-of-touch (and probably off their heads) band are indeed doffing a collective cap to their younger selves.

In a bizarre turn of events, many of the acts patronised on the disc have spoken kindly of the band's efforts. Bob Dylan is reported to have said that their version of **Lay Lady Lay** is *'the best yet. It beats mine by a country mile'*; Led Zeppelin guitarist Jimmy Page has described **Thank You** as *'exceptional'* and the late, great Lou Reed was quoted as saying that Duran Duran's version of **Perfect Day** was *'the best cover ever completed of one of my own songs'*. High praise indeed: I assume he hadn't heard Gerty Moltzen's version of **Walk On The Wild Side** at that point: leaps and bounds above this mechanical rehash.

By the time *Thank You* appeared in the stores the band had lost any enthusiasm they once had for the project. Videos were made for both

White Lines and **Perfect Day** but they received little exposure: a damning indictment of the material when you consider how large a role MTV played in breaking Duran Duran in America, bombarding their audience with their early videos. John Taylor was particularly frustrated with a Capitol-mandated tour of radio stations and festivals to promote the release – band mate Warren Cuccurullo also went on record to say that *'it's not exactly the kind of tour we initially wanted to do'* - and stormed off stage several times over the course of the five-week expedition. After a final show at the Irvine Meadows Amphitheatre in California, where most of the audience walked out and those that stayed booed the band's lacklustre performance, Taylor left the band. He would not rejoin until 2001.

Coldplay
X&Y (2005)

There are not enough expletives in the English language that I could employ to adequately describe how much I hate Coldplay. Seriously. Pompous, bombastic and unbearably smug, Coldplay are, without question, the worst thing that has ever happened to rock music. Coldplay records are bought by people with no taste and no talent: the kind of people who think that wearing a comedy tie or cartoon character socks to work singles them out as the life and soul of the office. Well, it doesn't. You can't buy a personality. Unfortunately this hasn't stopped millions of people worldwide from purchasing CDs by the dull, whiney Chris Martin and his hateful mates. This is music for people who don't like music: safe, antiseptic suprmarket fodder.

Admittedly most of my ire is directed towards singer, guitarist and keyboard player Martin. It's coloured by the stupid names given by him and ex-wife Gwyneth Paltrow (conscious uncoupling my arse) to their poor children (Apple? Apple? It's a child, not a computer, you pillock. He even had the audacity to rope the poor girl in to sing backing vocals for him when she was still just nine years old), and influenced by their shameless theft of an iconic Kraftwerk riff for **Talk**, one of the many singles from the band's abysmal 'difficult third album' *X&Y*, the record I have chosen as a prime example of their hideousness – although to be fair I could have picked almost anything from the group's oeuvre. Incidentally, Chris Martin admits that he wrote a begging letter in

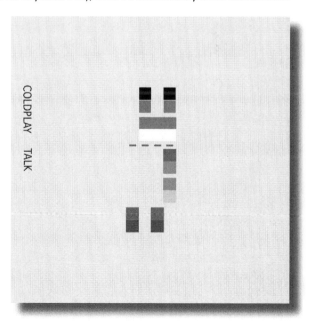

COLDPLAY TALK

schoolboy German to Kraftwerk mainman Ralf Hutter in order to secure his permission to use the melody of **Computer World** for the track. That's how pathetic this band is. Most globally giant acts would employ a manager, a lawyer or at very least a decent translator: not Coldplay. Martin loves to play the role of the 'man of the people', yet the multi-millionaire Hollywood A-lister is about as close to being one of the plebs as Pluto is to the sun. Then there's that weedy, reedy falsetto voice and the insipid lyrics. Chris Martin is a middle aged, middle class man with the world on his plate, but in his songs he expresses all the complexity and emotion of a teenager who has run out of Clearasil.

I hate him.

From their breakthrough hit **Yellow,** a miserable rip-off of Radiohead's **Fake Plastic Trees** (although Martin insists it was actually written as a Neil Young pastiche) to their latest album *Ghost Stories* it's been blatantly obvious that Coldplay are not happy being Coldplay – they really want to be the arch and artful Radiohead, the beloved (and much missed) REM or the planet-straddling U2. So in thrall of Radiohead was he in their early days that (it is said) the dictatorial Martin once banned the rest of the band from taking cocaine because he heard that's what Thom Yorke had done. Radiohead copyists they may have hoped to be, but in reality their trajectory has been more akin to that of pompous stadium fillers and former Irishmen U2. Although the best of their material sounds no better than a collection of rejected Radiohead B-sides, their management and producers decided that the route followed by Bonio and Co was the way for their charges to go: who needs credibility when you can have shed loads of money? Why else would they team up with Brian Eno, the keyboard genius who was once so vital a part of the brilliant Roxy Music but who had more recently become better known as the producer who saved U2's career? Martin's cold heart must have been broken when the Dutch-for-tax-purposes Paul Hewson called him "a wanker" on Jo Whiley's Radio One show, going on to say that the singer is "obviously a completely dysfunctional character and a cretin".

It might not be so bad if all of their songs didn't sound the bloody same: low-key acoustic intro, swelling keyboards, grandiloquent orchestrations, the obligatory quiet bridge and the thoroughly overblown ending. It's a formula that has worked again and again, but even the most formulaic of musical acts knows that you have to throw that formula out of the window or at least mix it up a little now and again. And it does all follow a formula: in the Coldplay office, affixed to the wall, is a 10-point plan which includes such rules as *'albums must be no longer than 42 minutes'*, *'production must be amazing, rich, but with space'* and *'always keep mystery: not many interviews'*. Then there's that wretched voice. Chris Martin's tone is, at best, a miserable, fetid whine which slithers around the melody like an incontinent drunk on a particularly bad karaoke night.

As *The Independent*'s music critic Andy Gill wrote when forced to review their fourth album, the abominable *Viva La Vida* (or, to give that particular steaming heap its full, ridiculously affected name *Viva La Vida Or Death And All His Friends*): *'They're sort of the anti-Sex Pistols, an act that repulses not through outrage, bad manners and poor grooming, but through their inoffensive niceness and emollient personableness. Their music sounds like Radiohead with all the spiky, difficult, interesting bits boiled out of it, resulting in something with the sonic consistency of wilted spinach.'* Coldplay are pop's embodiment of Tony Blair blandness, and entirely responsible for the glut of copyist bands that followed in their wake: Snow Patrol, Athlete, Keane, the Script and so on. Keane especially deserve your disgust here: the group's main man Tim Rice-Oxley knew Martin at university: Keane had already formed, at that time playing under the name The Lotus Eaters. Rice-Oxley had toyed with the idea of renaming his band Coldplay, before deciding that the name was too 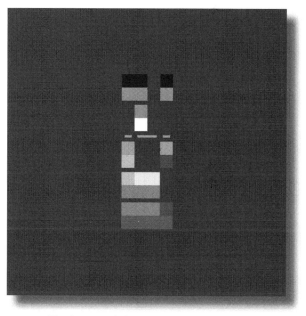 "depressing". Martin, however, liked it...and the rest, as they say, is history.

'Am I part of the cure, or am I part of the disease?' the miserable Mr Martin sings on **Clocks**, from second album *A Rush Of Blood To The Head*. If only it had been a bunch of fists to the head instead we might have been spared almost two decades of this drivel. Is it any wonder that *The New York Times* labelled them *'the most insufferable band of the last decade'*?

Chris Martin plays a clever game, constantly putting his own band down, agreeing with his critics and posing as the most personable, self-effacing gent you could hope to meet. However methinks he doth protest too much: his whole career, his every move is entirely calculated. Yet for all his right-on, do-good, fair-trade faux-politicking he's not averse to throwing a wobbly or punching the odd paparazzo. His split from the deadweight Paltrow (rumoured to have been so despised by the rest of the band that they referred to her as Yoko) is probably the only thing he has ever done right: the actress was voted the most hated celebrity in Hollywood in a 2014 *Star* magazine poll.

The Hardest Part, from the rotten *X&Y* – an album inexplicably awarded nine out of ten by the NME - is easily one of the worst things ever committed to vinyl. The lyrics are no more than a collection of clichés, with little or no relation to each other outside of the fact that they rhyme:

And the strangest thing was waiting for that bell to ring
It was the strangest start
And I tried to sing, but I couldn't think of anything
And that was the hardest part, oh, oh

(*The Hardest Part*, written by Berryman, Buckland, Champion, Martin. Recorded by Coldplay on Parlophone Records. © 2005, Universal Music Publishing)

It took four, university-educated men to come up with that garbage? What's even worse than the dreadful lyrics to this turgid rubbish is Martin's deluded belief that it compares to one of the greatest singles of all time. In a *Guardian* article published to coincide with the album's release, writer Craig Mclean wrote that '**The Hardest Part** *is a steal from REM's* **Losing My Religion**, *so blatant that the band almost didn't include it'*. What a shame that they didn't have the courage of their convictions.

Martin, who had carefully cultivated a friendship with REM front man Michael Stipe, would ruin the Athens, Georgia band's appearance in London during Oxfam's Make Poverty History shows the same year by running on stage and gurning like a demented loon during **Man On The Moon** (and, being that I was in that audience that night, I'd cite that particular incident as the point my unabashed hatred of Coldplay began). "The one great thing about being famous," he told *Rolling Stone* magazine, "Is that I get to meet people who I respect. Our relationship is akin to a dog and its master. I'll always look up to him." Now I'm fortunate enough to have met Michael Stipe, and I believe that there is absolutely no way the man would ever respect someone who followed him around like a stray puppy. Martin's friendship with Stipe was an enormous influence on the direction of *X&Y*. Unfortunately, instead of modelling this limp lettuce of a record on *Life's Rich Pageant, Document* or any of REM's great works they instead decided to try and emulate the overblown and over-played *Automatic For The People* but ended up producing something more akin to *Around The Sun*, the lowest point of REM's otherwise-exemplary career.

X&Y also contains the turgid **Fix You**, a song which sounds as if it were specifically written to accompany a 30-second advert for cheese, mobile phones or building societies and which has mutated into the inspiration-less TV producer's go-to ballad. This particular piece of pap has provided the soundtrack to pivotal plot moments in *Extras, Glee, Scrubs, The Newsroom, The O.C., Without A Trace, Cold Case* and countless other shows. If ever a song was over-exposed, it's the repellent **Fix You**. *X&Y* is the rock bottom of a rock career whose long and winding road is flecked with bottomless potholes of mediocrity. **What If?**, another track from this clunker of an album, highlights Martin's inexcusably awful, dejected teenager lyrics better than almost anything else in their repertoire:

What if I got it wrong?
And no poem or song could put right what I got wrong
Or make you feel I belong?

(*What If?* Written by Berryman, Buckland, Champion, Martin. Recorded by Coldplay on Parlophone Records. © 2005, Universal Music Publishing)

Oh, grow up you cock!

I started to write this in the same week that their latest collection, *Ghost Stories*, was released (May 2014). Widely believed to be a collection of thinly veiled references to his disintegrating marriage (It's this album that features a young Apple Martin on backing vocals), *Ghost Stories* was savaged by British online rock music and pop culture magazine *The Quietus*. *The Quietus* allowed their notorious poison pen Mr Agreeable, who once described imbecilic new-folk fakers Mumford & Sons album Babel as '*septic f***ing horseshit*', to savage the album in an expletive-laden rant which contained no less than 93 uses of the word f***ing (their asterisks, not mine). '*Ghost Stories is from its arse to its f***ing elbow, one, long stagnant f***ing pool of premium grade f***ing cockwash! I would rather chew off my f***ing scrotum than ever listen again to* *this boneless f***ing melange of morose f***ing piss-shit!'*

Mr Agreeable's opinion of *Ghost Stories* is somewhat out of step with Coldplay's own assessment. Speaking to Jo Whiley during the two-year recording sessions (will this band never learn? Jo Whiley is not your friend), guitarist Jonny Buckland laughingly admitted that "there's only so far you can go without becoming pompous and a bit overblown." That ship, Mr Buckland, has well and truly sailed.

In a radio interview in December 2014, Chris Martin hinted that the next Coldplay album might well be their last. Let's hope so.

Black Out Band
Video Games (2006)

One of the most singularly annoying things that is ever likely to assault your eardrums, **Video Games** was released in 2006 by the Black Out Band (a.k.a. the Black Out Kids). Long before anyone had ever heard about Justin Bieber, the Black Out Band found their own unique way to express pre-teen angst - and it didn't involve attacking the paparazzi, urinating in hotel flowerpots or crashing expensive sports cars.

Not to be confused with the Welsh post-hardcore (whatever that is) outfit, the Black Out Band were three precocious, middle-class boys from Virginia: Hunter Watson on vocals and lead guitar, Tug Hunter on bass and drummer Matthew Salutillo. Hunter and Matthew had been practicing together for a while, playing cover versions of songs by Daniel Powter (the Canadian singer who scored an international hit with **Bad Day**) and Weezer amongst others. One day in school Matthew heard Tug giving a report about his hobby and he suggested that Tug join him and Hunter at one of their jam sessions. Hunter and best friend Matthew were 11 years old when they recorded **Video Games**; Tug was the old man of the group at 12.

Sounding precisely as you'd expect a trio of whiny children to sound, apparently this ghastly racket started life when the boy's music coach Dennis Decreny (not a teacher you understand; daddy had the money for a private coach) found that the boys would rather be playing with their XBoxes than learning the chord sequence to **Three Blind Mice**. "Each time I turned my head during a practice, the boys were playing video games," he says. Coach, as he was no doubt known to the youngsters, told Hunter - who began learning piano at the age of five before progressing to the guitar - that he ought to write a song about his obsession. The following week, with assistance from his band mates, Hunter had the chorus and first verse.

The three boys worked out the basic melody but it was left to Mrs. Watson to come up with the rest of the words. The boys recorded several more songs - including the original compositions **Graffiti**, **6th Grade King** and **Recess Blues** - lined up some low-key local gigs during their summer vacation and set up their website – now defunct but which laughably compared the tiresome threesome to Neil Young. Mr. Watson founded his own record label, Chapman Records, and started to push their merchandise – including Black Out Band t-shirts and the **Video Games** CD single – onto a none-too-eager public. He also insisted that his charges take their fledgling career more seriously. "We work on our rehearsals whenever we can," said Hunter, "mostly between baseball and soccer on Saturdays, and if we've got our homework done, on Wednesday and Friday evenings." It's The Shaggs all over again.

According to the press release that accompanied **Video Games** *'the single elicits laughter and nods of recognition each time a new crowd hears it - from kids as well as their forty to fifty-something parents'*. Really? I can't see anything to laugh at. *'The video utilises 75 screaming adolescent fans and was shot inside a historic theatre by a local production team that previously worked on several Beyoncé videos,'* it goes on to claim. The truth was a little more prosaic: Matthew's mum Wendy organised the video shoot, and the audience consisted of 30 local school kids hopped up on free pizza and sugary soda. Still, it looked like Black Out Band were on their way to the big time. Hunter, Matthew and Tug continued to play shows at the boy's school and set about writing songs for their debut album, several of which promised to *'reflect the childhood influences in their lives'*. The band cobbled together a set featuring their original material and a bunch of crowd-pleasing favourites, including the Monkees' **I'm A Believer**, Bob Marley's **Lively Up Yourself** and the Ramones' **Blitzkrieg Bop**. "Our hope is to get really big and have a lot of fun while we're doing it," said Hunter who, according to the band's bio, is *'Mick Jagger cool'*. "We just want to make kids happy listening to our music".

"I burst out laughing when I heard it," said one mother who was in the audience at the first public performance of the song. "It was such a relief to know that other families are struggling with what the limits are. We still argue about it, but now we joke about it too." The big shame is that the rest of the public was not quite as eager as Jerry and Judy Watson had hoped. Hunter's parents might have thought

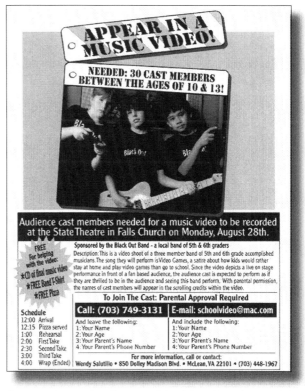

that the Black Out Band was going to be the next big thing, but the world clearly disagreed.

Outside of a few random local radio and TV appearances and the occasional live show – as their official biography revealed *'time constraints limit gigs to school assemblies and local invites at coffee houses and community festivals'* - by 2008 it was all but over. In 2010 the band launched an official Facebook page, which acted as a repository for their old videos, a place to hawk their old crap and somewhere to make the occasional 'joke' about AIDS*. Oh, and to make false claims about **Video Games** being awarded a Grammy. A second single, the digital-only **Louie Louie**, was all but ignored, and the scheduled album – which would have included all of the previously-mentioned titles as well as **ADD** and live favourites including Neil Young's **Rockin' In The Free World** - has yet to materialise. As a school friend of the boys reported at the time: *'Tug is real quiet and Hunter is pussy-whipped pretty badly by his girl. Oh yeah, and they each get ripped a new one every day for the video.'*

Hunter, Tag and Matthew will be approaching their 20s now and, no doubt, are as embarrassed as hell for having produced this miserable diatribe. Or maybe not: for, when all is said and done, these three young men have written and recorded their own music and have performed it in front of hundreds of people, which is a damn sight more than most of us. If you want more, the band's MySpace page is still up and running. Hunter's elder brother Teddy is now the lead singer in indie band Stargroves.

***

* *'Hope to bring the "lost" Black Out Band songs here to Facebook soon before MySpace dies from AIDS.' Posted on Black Out Band's official Facebook page by the page admin on March 25, 2012.*

BrokeNCYDE
Bree Bree (2010)

Crunkcore, according to the fount of all knowledge that is *Wikipedia*, is *'a musical genre that combines crunk hip hop with the vocal style of screamo'*. No, me neither. Okay, it didn't take a great leap to work out that 'screamo' was simply emo performed by vocalists who, because they can't sing, resort to screaming their lyrics, but I had to look up 'crunk'. Unfortunately I'm not much the wiser, although it's got something to do with drum machines and the misuse of autotune.

According to contributors to the usually infallible *Urban Dictionary* crunkcore is a *'musical genre that is regarded by all but its small demographic as one of the worst ever conceived. It has been rumoured to have been invented by the band BrokeNCYDE'* or, indeed, crunkcore is *'what happens when fans of the Jonas Brothers figure out that they can swear. It generally combines bad electronica with faux-teenage-angsty screaming, but may also include elements of bad hip hop and rap. It is to be consumed only in comical doses'.* That really does tell you about as much as you

need to know - apart from the simple fact that it is just plain awful. Maybe I'm too old to appreciate it, but I find a bunch of whiny, middle-class brats screaming about having sex to a hiphop beat is about as appealing as ebola.

And you don't get more middle-class and more whiny than BrokeNCYDE (broke inside – geddit?), a four piece from Albuquerque, New Mexico who

- whilst tarted up like some kind of Manga nightmare - have produced four albums of the most annoying, unlistenable, sexist nonsense imaginable. Just take a look at the lyrics to their song **Kama Sutra**, from their 2010 album *Will Never Die*:

I need a freak bitch, with some nice tits,
Flick her titty like a motherf***in' light switch.

Rubbin' on my dick make a motherf***er hard.
Slap her on her face she like 'oh my God!
I never seen a dick that big before'.

(*Kama Sutra*, written by Tristan Krause, performed by BrokeNCYDE on Break Silence Recordings. © 2010, Break Silence/Suburban Noise Group)

This is the group that Warren Ellis (the British comic book author, not Nick Cave's right hand man) pilloried as "a near-perfect snapshot of everything that's shit about this point in the culture". Fronted by David 'Se7en' Gallegos, the band's name is often abbreviated to bc13, or possibly *bc13 motherf***ers* as the silly children inform us at the start of one of their most infamous 'songs' **Bree Bree**. My guess would be that the epithet bc13 was affected because young David as just 13 years old when he formed BrokeNCYDF (with his mates Michael 'Miki' Shea, Anthony 'Antz' Trujillo and Julian 'Phat J' McClellan); *BC13* was also employed as the title of one of their EPs.

If you've ever wondered what noise a pig emits as it faces the horror of the butcher's blade, **Bree Bree** will answer your question. Beginning with the sound of a teenager projectile vomiting into a rubber bucket (or an assimilation of that noise) while someone else plays an ocarina, this unintelligible assault on the ears appears to be about the pleasures bisexual bestiality - or something like that: Se7en screams lines over and over again about pigs that need hot girls and hot boys but definitely don't want to get cut (the band employ a youngster in a pig costume as a mascot, also dubbed Bree). Golly, but that boy must have a sore throat; I hope his mummy keeps a packet of Strepsils in her pocket.

The whole thing sounds like a South Park spoof. "The screaming in our music always came second to the beat," Se7en claims in the band's official biography. It's a great shame then that the 'phat beats' the band lay down are usually hidden behind a wall of painfully sexist, ear-shattering noise.

Would it astonish you to know that BrokeNCYDE seldom get an easy ride from the critics? The unnamed author of a January 2010 Tech Eye column in the *Warsaw Business Journal* attempted to describe their music by asking his readers to *'imagine an impassioned triceratops mating with a steam turbine, while off to the side Daft Punk and the Bee Gees beat each other to death with skillets and spatulas. Imagine the sound that would make. Just try. BrokeNCYDE is kind of like that, except it also makes you want to jab your thumbs into your eyeballs and gargle acid'.* In a review of their second full-length album *I'm Not A Fan, But The Kids Like It!* The New Musical Express stated that *'even if I caught Prince Harry and Gary Glitter adorned in Nazi regalia defecating through my grandmother's letterbox I would still consider making them listen to this album too severe a punishment. And she's just had new carpets put in. It's like having an autotuned, crack-addled Cher with a hard-on bearing down on you singing, "Let's get freaky".'* The instigators and the leaders of new genres are often abused by their peers, only to be accepted in to the fold when time or taste proves their significance, but *I'm Not A Fan, But The Kids Like It!* was ranked by the users of *rateyourmusic.com* as number two in the list of *The 10 Worst Albums Of The Last 25 Years* – and it seems unlikely that history will cause us to re-evaluate the importance of BrokeNCYDE.

By subjecting yourself to the horror of BrokeNCYDE you have reached are the absolute lowest point in music: in all fairness to the band's critics they really are that terrible. The video for **Freaxx** might have had almost 10 million views, but how many of those were from young people desperate for something decent to listen to rather than from kids looking for a laugh? Summed up as *'the perfect shitstorm of the worst in contemporary American music'* by *OC Weekly* magazine, YouTube views did not translate to CD sales – *I'm Not A Fan, But The Kids Like It!* Made a brief appearance in the *Billboard* charts at 86 and very quickly vanished.

In much the same way that the Parents Music Resource Centre (PMRC) came about as a reaction to the kind of language and imagery being used in heavy rock and hip hop, BrokeNCYDE inspired a group of concerned Christian parents to band together and campaign against the band. Mothers Against BrokeNCYDE handed out flyers at their shows, Westboro Baptist Church-style, condemning the band for encouraging underage female fans to send them nude pictures of themselves for their online 'slut pit' (the existence of which the band have categorically denied) and for glorifying date rape, heavy drinking and something called *'teen sexuality pregnancy'*. It's just about enough to make you warm a little

BROKENCYDE?

MORE LIKE MORAL GENOCIDE!

DONT LET YOUR CHILDREN LISTEN TO RACIST, SEXIST, PEDOPHILIC, AND DEMEANING MUSIC THAT GLORIFIES UNDERAGE SEX, HARD DRINKING AND 'GETTING CRUNK', AND UNPATRIOTIC VIEWS!

- DID YOU KNOW MEMBERS OF THE MUSICAL ACT 'BROKENCYDE' ENCOURAGE UNDERAGE FEMALE FANS TO SEND NUDE DIGITAL PHOTOGRAPHS OF THEMSELVES TO THE BAND MEMBERS WITH THEIR NAMES AND HOME PHONE NUMBERS WRITTEN ON THEIR CHESTS, AND POST THEM ON A PUBLIC INTERNET FORUM CALLED "THE SLUT PIT"?
- DID YOU KNOW BROKENCYDE HAS A SONG CALLED "THE ONLY GOOD PRESIDENT IS A WHITE PRESIDENT"?
- DID YOU KNOW BROKENCYDE HAS A SONG CONTAINING THE LYRICS "IM A SLIP YOU A DRINK YOU THINK IS PEPSI, THEN ILL SLIP MY C*** IN WHEN YOU GOOD N' TIP'SI. B**** I AINT GONNA CALL AGAIN, NOW ITS MY BROS TURN, HE DO YOU AGAIN", ENCOURAGING DATE RAPE?
- DID YOU KNOW BROKENCYDE HAS A SONG CONTAINING THE LYRICS "F*** YOUR PARENTS, F*** THE PRINCIPAL, SMOKE WEED ALL DAY THEN LETS DO COCAINE. TAP YOUR SISTERS A** THEN PUSH HER OUT OF THE CAR WHILE WE DRIVE AWAY, LETS EAT AT FRIENDLYS BUT THEN NOT PAY, IM GONNA GET THE WIZARD SUNDAE"?
- DID YOU KNOW BROKENCYDE HAS A SEGMENT OF THEIR LIVE PERFORMANCE WHERE YOUNG GIRLS GET ON STAGE AND PULL DOWN THEIR PANTS TO "SHOW YO COOCH, WIN A SMOOCH"

TAKE BROKENCYDE ALBUMS AWAY FROM YOUR CHILDREN, AND DO NOT ALLOW THEM TO ATTEND THEIR "CONCERTS" IN YOUR TOWN AS THEY ARE A BREEDING GROUND FOR DRUG USE, UNDERGROUND FIGHT CLUBS, UNDERAGE DRINKING AND TEEN SEXUALITY PREGNANCY. FOR MORE INFORMATION VISIT WWW.MOTHERSAGAINSTBROKENCYDE.NET

to the otherwise hateful little ticks. There's no trace of Mothers Against BrokeNCYDE these days: if I didn't know any better I'd posit that the group was invented by the group's management to garner a few extra column inches.

Perhaps unsurprisingly a subgenre of this emo-screamo nonsense, known as Christian Crunkcore (CC), soon sprang up - although when you consider that pretty much every crunkcore song ever is about getting underage girls drunk and then sexually assaulting them I'd guess the well of lyrical inspiration for CC acts must be pretty near bone dry, as can be heard in the material produced by chief CC act Family Force 5 – a stupendously stupid band which tries to marry crunk imagery to Christian idolatry and fails on an epic level.

In a 2009 interview with *The Quietus* Se7en whimpered that "everyone's hating on us...I have absolutely no idea why". Perhaps he should have a listen to some of his own lyrics. How about *'Look at how she shakes that ass/She drops it to the floor/Girl you're such a dirty whore'* from the tender love song **Sex Toyz**, *'Let's go get messy girls/Come on bitch, you know you want this'* from their breakout hit **Freaxx** or *'I got two bad bitches from Tokyo/And they ride my dick like a rodeo'* from **Teach Me How To Scream**? I do hope these young men don't kiss their mothers with their potty mouths.

BrokeNCYDE are pretty much broken altogether these days: the band now boasts just two members, Se7en and Miki. Se7en has reinvented himself and, at the grand old age of 21, issued his first solo album *Psycho*, under the name Sev N@sty. The boy may have become a man, but with 11 hellish hip hop and screamo tracks, *Psycho* proves that his 'music' has yet to mature.

Chief Kooffreh
She Will Cut Your Balls Off (2010)

'Profoundly talented with a deep sense of entertainment', according to his own publicity, Chief Kooffreh is the outsider musician for the 21st Century. He's misguided, quite possibly deluded, but resolutely ploughing his own anomalous musical furrow – aided and abetted by social media, YouTube, music download sites and more - no matter what the rest of the world may think of his eccentric efforts.

Outsider is a term that is used to describe the output of musicians (and I use that word in the loosest possible sense) who are not part of the mainstream music industry; usually these musicians write music that, as the all-knowing *Wikipedia* puts it *'ignores standard musical or lyrical conventions, either because they have no formal training or because they disagree with conventional rules'.* Few outsider musicians achieve anything resembling mainstream popularity; however there is a small but appreciative market for outsider music, and many of these performers manage to maintain a cult following – Jerry Solomon, the Shaggs (both discussed in previous chapters), Daniel Johnson, Jandek, Wesley Willis, Hasil Adkins and our old friend the Legendary Stardust Cowboy (featured in *The World's Worst Records Volume One*) included. Many of the outsider musicians profiled in Irwin Chusid's essential book *Songs In The Key of Z* have suffered years of torment, both physically and mentally. Chief Kooffreh is just freakin' nuts.

Kooffreh Bassey Kooffreh was born in Calabar, Nigeria; his official Facebook page would have you believe that his current place of residence is New York. It isn't. He lives in Lawrence, Massachusetts with his wife Elizabeth Tampol Kooffreh (who he respectfully refers to alternately as *Queen of Asia* and *International Long Hair Model*) and his extended family. He often boasts that he is a *'voting member of the Grammys'*: the only qualifications needed to vote at the Grammys is to have *'creative or technical credits on at least six commercially released tracks'* and to stump up your annual $100 membership fee. In May 2014 the Chief had more than 50 albums available through *cdbaby.com*, although two years earlier - in a blurb to accompany the release of his album *International Great Star* - he claimed to have issued *'95 musical recorded albums, 2010 tracks, 250 videos. Officially Chief Kooffreh is the artist with the largest catalogue of published recorded music in the history of the North East of the United States'.*

Chief Kooffreh, like many outsider musicians, has a very distinctive style: the vast majority of his 'songs' feature the Chief rapping over a cheap, pre-recorded drum track (think 80s Casio keyboard) with the minimum of musical accompaniment. This back-to-basics approach has allowed the Chief to amaze the world with his prolific song-writing prowess. For his 2012 track **Sexy Beyoncé And Sexy Lady Gaga** he really pushed the boat out: the drum track is almost drowned out by a two-second, nine note highlife guitar loop (which, over the course of the six minute, five second-long song is repeated a maddening 18,150 times), the sound of dogs barking, the chimes of Big Ben and someone randomly banging away at an anvil. Well, I assume it's an anvil: it could just as easily be his empty head.

The Chief's catalogue contains some seriously barmy titles: **Bad Policemen Out Of Control Bully, Abuse, Wicked Brutality (evil! Put A Stick Into A Man's Butt Ass/anus)** (sic), for example. Then there's the tongue-twisting **Biggest Worldwide Tribute To Michael Jackson, Whitney Houston And Amy Winehouse 4 Billion Fans Download Worldwide (Parts 1-4)**; or how about **Women In Love With A Hot 5th Grader Man** and his 2014 'hit' **Princess Stella Oduah – Minister Nigerian Aviation (Parts One And Two)** which, naturally, featured wailing sirens and the Chief's signature *'This is Chief Kooffreh, for my millions of fans!'* introduction. The homemade video for the song, like most of his videos, features endless footage of fireworks, film of a dancing waters display (seemingly captured on an iPhone in a North American shopping mall) and plenty of buxom beauties including, as always, his own wife. Oh, I almost forgot **Orgasm Milk Shake**.

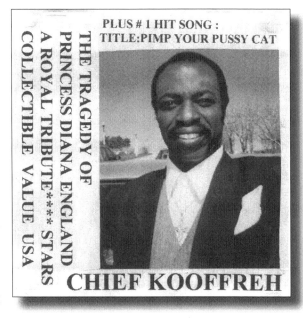

In 2011, possibly in homage to the late Robert Palmer's iconic **Addicted To Love** video, the Chief issued a series of bump-and-grind videos featuring The Queen of Asia thrusting against an electric guitar. Tasteful.

And boy, does the Chief love the ladies! He's composed songs in honour of female film stars, female musicians, female politicians and, of course, Britain's Queen of Hearts Diana, Princess of Wales.

A lovely flower, Princess of Wales
The shining star of English kingdom
We miss you-oh
We miss you-ohhh
We miss you-oh
English angel!

(*Princess Diana Of England/Accident or Pushed?* Written and recorded by Chief Kooffreh. © 2011, Chief Kooffreh)

He claims that his songs have influenced government policy on everything from gay rights to police brutality and even unemployment figures. He has suggested that the US government would save a fortune in aid by giving every American free education and $1 million, and he predicted the end of the world in 2013, claiming that *'the Mayans missed it by one year'*. I'm writing this at the tail end of 2014, and despite what the good Chief may think the world still appears to be turning.

She Will Cut Your Balls Off is, perhaps, the Chief's most infamous song – with the possible exceptions of **Tragedy Of Princess Diana England** (pretty much the same song as the aforementioned **Princess Diana Of England/Accident or Pushed?**) and the many different versions of **Michael Jackson We Miss You (Important Song)**. In an effort to confuse and confound his *'millions of fans worldwide'* (a phrase he employs again and again with no attempt to justify the outrageous claim), Chief Kooffreh often issues the same song several times under different titles, or under its original title on different albums. **She Will Cut Your Balls Off** appears on the albums *Paris Gold, Oprah Vs. Eskimo Sarah Palin, Broken Promise, Pimp Your Pussycat* and so many others that trying to catalogue them all is making my head spin. Under one of its many alternative titles (in this particular instance **Rihanna & Pi Daddy Will Cut Your Balls Off Chris Brown Ghetto**) it also appears on 2009's *Top Album* and, as **She Will Cut Your Balls Off Flush It Quickly Down The Toilet** on the 2010 collection *Love Sex*.

You cheat on her, you lie to her, you play around, you f*** around
You kick her face in
She will cut your balls off
Wait 'til you sleep
She will cut your wee-wee off
Cut your dong off...

(*She Will Cut Your Balls Off*, written and recorded by Chief Kooffreh. ©
2011, Chief Kooffreh)

So concerned is the Chief over what his *'millions of fans worldwide'* might
be inspired to do after listening to any one of the great many versions
of **She Will Cut Your Balls Off** that he issued the following disclaimer:
*'Please women! It only for entertainment. I AM NOT RESPONSIBLE FOR
ANY WOMAN AFTER LISTENING TO MY SONG DECIDED YAH it is time to
cut off the balls of his cheating no good husband or boyfriend. Again
chief Kooffreh is NOT responsible for any situation in which a woman cut
of the balls of her man. A MAN WAKING UP WITHOUT HIS DONG CAN
COLLAPSE. Women buy the cd and let your man hear it as a WARNING
shot. Warn him first that the DONG MAY BE COMING DOWN'* (sic). He
followed the 'success' of **She Will Cut Your Balls Off** with the heart-
warming tale **Viagra Will Cancer Your Balls**. The last track featured on
the albums *Sweet Asian Girl* (a tribute to his beloved Queen of Asia)
and *Love Sex*, both of which also contained the salacious, squalid and
downright sleazy **Kiss The Pussy Cat**:

Lick their juice, eat the pussy
Oh eat the pussy cat – right!
Pound the pussy, pound the pussy cat
Bang the pussy cat – right!
Eat their box

(*Kiss The Pussy Cat*, written and recorded by Chief Kooffreh. © 2011,
Chief Kooffreh)

The Chief's entire canon is worth checking out. Who else would open
an album of yuletide songs (his 2008 collection *Carols Of Christmas*)
with the 14 minute track **Oprah Winfrey Commits Suicide If Obama's
Presidency Fails**? Like I said, utterly freakin' nuts.

A God-fearing man who uses his celebrity status to raise awareness of
the *'really bad leaders who have made Africa poor'*, when not making

music or running his *Celebrity News Network* website (basically photos of him, his wife, actresses with suspected eating disorders and politicians caught doing the dirty), Mr Kooffreh works as a substitute teacher, specialising in mathematics, business studies and English. His avowed aim in the music biz is to *'reach the*

STAR OF MICHAEL JACKSON 7

CHIEF KOOFFREH

total number Elvis Presley have' (sic), or issue 180 albums. That's easily achievable, and he may have already done that by the time you read this: when your entire catalogue consists of you howling over a simple drum beat accompanied by an air raid siren that shouldn't be too taxing.

Robin Thicke
Paula (2014)

Has a fall from grace ever been quite as spectacular as that experienced by American-Canadian singer-songwriter Robin Thicke? Just how does a man go from having one of the biggest international hits of 2013 to releasing an album described by *The Guardian* as being *'the biggest musical flop of the decade'* and selling *'fewer copies than the worst record of 2013'*?

The son of soap opera actors, Robin Thicke had been slowly building a decent career for himself since he entered the music biz at just 14 years old (in 1991), working with 50 Cent, Usher, Pink, Will Young and others. Everything was going well; he was friends with Will Smith, he starred in the TV show *The Real Husbands Of Hollywood* and his albums were doing very nicely, thank you. He wasn't setting the world alight, but his star was definitely in the ascendant.

Then he issued **Blurred Lines**.

Thicke's track **Blurred Lines** – on which he performs with singer/producer Pharrell Williams and rapper Clifford Joseph Harris Junior (better known as T.I.) - topped the charts in 14 countries and sold almost 1.5m copies in the UK alone. Yet the song that propelled him so stratospherically to musical stardom may also have been the cause of his downfall. The backlash generated by the song's sexist lyrics, the misogynistic portrayal of women in the accompanying video and the, frankly, x-rated performance by Thicke and former teen sensation Miley Cyrus at the 2013 Video Music Awards (the event that launched the word twerk into the lexicon) presaged a downward spin that he may never recover from. Whilst the career of former *Hannah Montana* star Cyrus took off like a rocket, Thicke's fizzled and spat like a sparkler dumped in a bucket of water. Thicke was named *'the most sexist person of 2013'* by the End Violence Against Women Coalition. Everything he did sunk like a stone.

His next two singles, **Give It 2 U** and **Feel Good**, barely made a dent in the *Billboard* charts, peaking at 25 and 37 respectively; three of his four subsequent releases failed to crack the UK Top 40. Then the family of Marvin Gaye decided to sue him, claiming that **Blurred Lines** ripped off Gaye's classic **Got To Give It Up**; the lawsuit was settled in the Gaye family's favour. Shortly after that came the news that Thicke's relationship with actress Paula Patton was on the rocks – their shaky nine-year marriage was hardly helped by a flood of photos and news stories in the tabloid press documenting his serial philandering.

Thicke became obsessed with trying to win Paula back, but the woman who had been his consort for 21 years was having none of it.

So what do you do when the flowers, the phone calls and the public shows of affection aren't working? Why, you record a whole album of sickly, syrupy love songs to your estranged missus, name the whole package after her and hope that will do the trick for Mrs Thicke. Unfortunately it didn't. Nor did it do the trick with his fans, who abandoned Team Thicke in their thousands.

The album *Paula* was preceded by the desperate ballad **Get Her Back**, which peaked at a miserable number 82 on the *Billboard* charts and was accompanied by a bad taste, and downright creepy, black and white video. When musicians split from their partners they tend to produce some of their most amazing, personal and often angry music: the aforementioned Marvin Gaye and *Here My Dear* is a case in point. Andy Partridge of XTC and the bilious **Your Dictionary** and **How Do You Sleep?** (John Lennon's scathing attack on Paul McCartney) spring to mind as fine examples of the genre. However what we get from Thicke on *Paula* is track after track of miserable, self-inflicted-wound licking and 'poor little me' posturing.

It's absolutely miserable. *Paula* positively drips with obsequiousness as, in ballad after ballad, Robin boo-hoos about poor little Robin. This isn't an album about a man's love for his wife: his oleaginous lyrics are all about how awful life is for him now that she's gone. It's an exercise in what several US reviewers have called *'tiresome self-flagellation'*.

The scant few up-tempo tracks in this self-love fest can't hope to drag this mess out of its mire of melancholy. The lyrics are insufferable, sexist garbage, as this verse from **Lock The Door** eloquently shows:

Don't leave me out here in the cold
Oh turn the porch light on
At least open the doggy door
Throw a friend a juicy bone
Baby please give me a little hole

(*Lock the Door*, written and recorded by Robin Thicke on Star-Trak/ Interscope Records. © 2014, Star Trak Entertainment)

As Hannah Ellis-Petersen wrote in *The Guardian* in July 2014: *'with 530 copies sold in the UK, 550 sold in Canada and fewer than 54 sold in Australia, Robin Thicke's latest album Paula has become the laughing stock of the music industry in just one week'*. In the United States - Thicke's biggest market - the album entered the charts at number nine and sold 24,000 copies - a far cry from his previous album, which debuted at number one and sold 177,000 in its first week. Paul Scaife, of music industry internet resource *Record Of The Day (recordoftheday. com)* said the album had flopped because "his problem, apart from the questionable music and the theme of the album, is that people didn't like Robin Thicke, they liked **Blurred Lines**."

Actually Paul, not everyone liked **Blurred Lines**. Along with the previously mentioned campaigners for female equality, almost two dozen Student's Unions in the UK have banned the song from University and college campuses. "It promotes a very worrying attitude towards sex and consent," Kirsty Haigh of the Edinburgh University Students' Association explained. "This is about ensuring that everyone is fully aware that you need enthusiastic consent before sex. The song says: 'You know you want it'. Well, you can't know they want it unless they tell you they want it."

When a beleaguered Robin took to Twitter to discuss his career with fans the publicity stunt backfired horribly: he was crucified. Hundreds of people used the *#askthicke* hashtag to poke fun at poor Robin; hundreds more used it as an opportunity to call him out on his treatment of women.

It was a PR disaster (although not as funny as when Susan Boyle's people took to Twitter to celebrate #susanalbumparty). *'Is your next 'hit' just a lyric sheet, with a Rohypnol Sellotaped to it?'* asked one Twitter user; another wondered *'did you really write a rape anthem as a love song for your wife and are you still wondering why she left you?'*

"The album is exactly what happens when you lose the love of your life," Thicke said in an interview about Paula with internet-based hip-hop radio station *Hot 97*. Well that might be true Robin, but the pathetic sales for *Paula* should be convincing proof of what happens when you royally screw up and discover that very few people out there actually like you or are willing to put up with your misogynistic crap. You're almost 40, for God's sake. Grow up.

Paula Patton, Thicke's wife and muse, filed for divorce on October 3 2014, citing *'irreconcilable differences'*. I should imagine the public humiliation caused to the poor woman by having her name permanently fused to the dreaful *Paula* would be reason enough for any judge to agree to terminate their marriage.

Appendix

Kenny Everett's Second Bottom 30

As the original Bottom 30, broadcast in 1977, had proved such a hit with the public, on April 4 1980 the legendary Kenny Everett aired his second run down of bad records, as voted for by listeners of his Capitol Radio programme *The World's Worst Wireless Show*.

30: Bob Monkhouse - I Remember Natalie
29: The Neasden Connection - Tchaikovsky's Piano Concerto No. 1
28: Herbie Duncan - Hot Lips Baby
27: Elvis Presley - Old MacDonald
26: Helpless Huw - Still Love You (In My Heart)
25: Shirley Ann Field - It's Legal
24: Paul Henry - Benny's Theme
23: Nola Campbell - Searching For My Baby
22: Nick Coltrane - Igger-Dagger
21: Sam Finch – Trees
20: Tony Blackburn - Here Today, Gone Tomorrow
19: Pat Campbell - Mother Went A Walking
18: Cathy Berberian - Help!
17: Tommy Vance - Summertime
16: Jess Conrad - Hurt Me
15: Melody Suggs - You Gone Stomped On My Heart
14: Jim Reeves - Old Tige
13: P.J. Proby - Only You (And You Alone)
12: Derrik Roberts - A World Without Sunshine
11: Leonard Nimoy - Where Is Love
10: True Taylor - True Or False *(True Taylor was an early pseudonym used by Paul Simon. Kenny erroneously credited the recording to Simon and Garfunkel)*
9: David Hamilton - Just Like That
8: Jack Warner - You Have Got The Gear
7: Mrs Olivier Schönke - Snowmobile Romance *(a Halmark label song-poem: Mrs Schönke is the composer, not the artist. Ken made the same mistake during the first Bottom 30 with Adolph Babel's My Feet Start Tapping)*
6: Red Sovine - Teddy Bear

5: Terry Costello - The Perfect Human Face
4: William Shatner - Lucy In The Sky With Diamonds
3: Steve Dahl - Unhappy New Year
2: Jag - If You Walked Away (B-side: the flip was called I'm Nearly Famous Now)
1: Reginald Bosanquet - Dance With Me

The winner, former ITN newsreader Reginald Bosanquet, appeared on the show to discuss how he came to record the sublimely terrible **Dance With Me**, and to accept a makeshift award from Kenny. As Reggie revealed: "A very nice man called Barry Norman asked me. I said 'look, I'm tone deaf, I can't sing and I've got no sense of rhythm'. And he said 'you're exactly the chap we want'". He also revealed that the song was recorded in just one take.

Bibliography

The following publications and articles provided crucial information for *The World's Worst Records: Volume Two*. My sincere thanks to all of the authors, editors and publishers involved.

100 Greatest Cover Versions
- Webb, Robert: McNidder & Grace, 2012
A Drug Free Life And A Glass Of PCP
- Solomon, Jerry: Jerry Solomon, 2012
Acid Archives, The
- Lundborg, Patrick (Ed): Lysergia Publishing, 2013
Billboard (various issues)
- Prometheus Global Media
Billy Joel: The Biography
- Bego, Mark: Thunder's Mouth Press, 2007
Blender magazine, May 2004
- Alpha Media Group
Boca Raton Magazine, January 2012
- Boca Raton Magazine/ Margaret Mary Shuff (Publisher)
Captain Quirk: The Unauthorized Biography Of William Shatner
- Hauck, Dennis William: Pinnacle Books 1995
Chopin And Beyond: My Extraordinary Life In Music And The Paranormal
- Janis, Byron with Maria Cooper Janis: John Wiley & Sons, 2010
Chronicles Volume One
- Dylan, Bob: Simon & Schuster Ltd, 2003
Complete Guide To The Music Of Bob Dylan, The
- Humphries, Patrick: Omnibus Press, 1995
Ebony magazine (various issues)
- Johnson Publishing Company
Eddy Arnold: Pioneer of The Nashville Sound
- Streissguth, Michael: Music Sales Ltd, 1997
Elvis And Kathy
- Westmoreland, Kathy: William G Quinn, 1987
Elvis Music FAQ: All That's Left To Know About The King's Recorded Works
- Eder, Mike: Backbeat Books, 2013
Frank: The Making Of A Legend
- Kaplan, James: Little, Brown 2010
The Guardian (various issues)
- Guardian Media Group

Hit Factory: The Stock, Aitken And Waterman Story, The
 - Stock, Mike: New Holland Publishers Ltd, 2004
Impressions magazine, Issue 6
 - Whetmore, Liv G (Editor): Trilogy Publishing 1998
In Their Own Words
 - DeMain, Bill: Praeger Publishers, 2004
Jimmie Rodgers: The Life And Times Of America's Blue Yodeler
 - Porterfield, Nolan: University Press of Mississippi, 2007
Legendary Joe Meek: The Telstar Man, The
 - Repsch, John: Cherry Red Books, 2001
Life magazine (various issues)
 - Time Inc.
Life As Sutch
 - Sutch, Lord David & Peter Chippindale: HarperCollins Publishers, 1991
Mama Loved The Ways Of The World
 - Bonomo, Joe: The Normal School, 2013
The Man Who Was Screaming Lord Sutch
 - Sharpe, Graham: Arum Press, 2005
New Kommotion Issue 23
 - Komorowski, Adam (editor): Shazam Promotions, 1980
New York Magzine (various issues)
 - New York Media, LLC
New York Times, The (various issues)
 - The New York Times Company
New Yorker, The September 27 1999 (*Meet the Shaggs*)
 - Orlean, Susan: Condé Nast, 1999
Newsweek (various issues)
 - Newsweek LLC
NME (various issues)
 - IPC Media
OC Weekly, December 2010
 - OC Weekly LP
People magazine (various issues)
 - Time Inc.
Picures of an Exhibitionist
 - Emerson, Keith: John Blake Publishing 2004
Q magazine (various issues)
 - Bauer Media Group
Re/Search 14: Incredibly Strange Music Volume 1
 - Vale, V & Andrea Juno: Re/Search Publications, 1993
Record World magazine (various issues)
 - Record World Publishing Company, Inc
Revolution In The Air
 - Heylin, Clinton: Constable, 2010
Rolling Stone magazine (various issues)
 - Wenner Media LLC

Rough Guide To Rock, The
 - Buckley, Peter (editor): Rough Guides/Penguin, 2003
Setting The Record Straight
 - Musso, Anthony P: AuthorHouse, 2007
Sinatra! The Song Is You
 - Friedwald, Will: Da Capo Press, 1995
Singing Nun Story. The : The Life And Death Of Soeur Sourire
 - Chadwick, D A: Createspace, 2010
Smile For The Camera: The Double Life Of Cyril Smith
 - Danczuk, Simon and Matt Baker: Biteback, 2014
Songs In The Key Of Z: The Curious Universe Of Outsider Music
 - Chusid, Irwin: Chicago Review Press, 2000
Spin magazine (various issues)
 - Spin Media
Star magazine (various issues)
 - American Media, Inc.
This Is My Story: Bennie Hess
 - Kettner, Klaus & Tony Wilkinson: Rockbilly Music Association, circa 1995
Time magazine (various issues)
 - Time Inc.
Tiny Tim
 - Stein, Harry: Playboy Press, 1976
Uri Geller: My Story
 - Geller, Uri: Praeger Publishers, 1975
Village Voice, The (various issues)
 - Voice Media Group
The Wanderer: Dion's Story
 - Dimucci, Dion and Davin Seay: Beech Tree Books, 1988
Waylon: An Autobiography
 - Jennings, Waylon and Lenny Kaye - Chicago Review Press, 2012
We Could Have Been The Wombles
 - Bromley, Tom: Penguin Books, 2006
World's Worst Records: Volume One, The
 - Bullock, Darryl W: Bristol Green Publishing Limited, 2013
Worst Rock 'n' Roll Records Of All Time, The
 - Guterman, Jimmy and Owen O'Donnell: Citadel Press, 1991

Index

Album titles in italics

Acknowledgements

It's impossible to write a book like this without the input of scores of other people, those who have directly contributed and those who have – through their unending friendship and support – helped in less tangible but still crucial ways.

Special thanks go to Mike Ascherman, Johnny Edward, Michael Freeland (Chainmale), David Hamilton, Ross Hamilton, Simon Herbert, and Troy Hess for their help with on specific sections of the book: Simon provided valuable information for the Music and Politics chapter; Troy, David, Michael and Johnny gave generously of their time for the chapters on their careers and Ross has helped and supported this project from its earliest days.

Thanks to Jonno Andrews & Dyl Martinez, Steve & Jayne Boyd and family, Graham Clayton, Clayton D Conatzer, Jeffery Dalton, John Deane, Larry Flick, Barret Hansen (Dr Demento), Andy Lockley & Phil Peters, Sean McGhee, Lesley Milligan (proofreader par excellence), Paul 'Nasher' Nashman, Andy Partridge, Darren Peace and family, Phil Prosser and family, Joe Pineapples, Bob Purse, Alan Stonebridge, Alan Toye & Lindsey Skinner and family, Mitchell Winn, Windbag, Dave & Jo Woodward and family...and apologies to anyone I've missed out.

This book is dedicated to Niall, Henry, Felix, Nell and Ruby...

...and to the late Frederick Sidney and Margaret Joan Bullock.

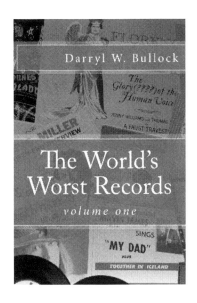

*If you enjoyed this book then
you'll probably like*

The World's Worst Records: Volume One

Featured on national radio in America, and a Top 10 hit of its own (in Amazon's Music Reference chart) *The World's Worst Records Volume One* is a must-have book for anyone interested in rock and pop music.

The World's Worst Records tells the extraordinary but true stories behind some of the most appalling audio crimes ever committed. Extensively researched, and featuring music by major stars, 'outsider' artists and almost forgotten singers and songwriters, people have been singing the book's praises: "Amazing, well-written and well-researched.'; "I love it! He's got a great writing style. I couldn't put it down," says US radio host Larry Flick. "I enjoyed it," says Andy Partridge, leader of legendary British rock band XTC. "It shocked me how many I knew."

Read about how Elvis Presley came to record a rock 'n' roll version of the nursery rhyme Old Macdonald; discover the truth behind actor Peter Wyngarde's one attempt at pop immortality; meet the beautifully bonkers Florence Foster Jenkins – possibly the most deluded singer in history; fid out which Paul McCartney record is most hated world over. Puzzle over why 60's flower-power icon Donovan would record a song about the toilet habits of astronauts.

An affectionate look at some of the worst recordings ever made, with over 250 pages and illustrated throughout, *The World's Worst Records Volume One* is available worldwide from Amazon. Electronic versions are also available through Amazon and Google Books.

www.worldsworstrecords.co.uk

64625710R00146

Made in the USA
Middletown, DE
16 February 2018